Peace Education: A Gender Perspective

Peace Education: A Gender Perspective

Loknath Mishra

KALPAZ

 The work was evaluated by Prof. Naresh Dadhich, Director, IDS, Jaipur on behalf of the ICSSR.

ISBN: 978-93-5128-133-7

Price: ₹ 990

First Published, 2016

Published by

Kalpaz Publications
C-30, Satyawati Nagar,
Delhi – 110052
E-mail: kalpaz@hotmail.com
Ph.: 9212142040

Cataloging in Publication Data—DK
Courtesy: D.K. Agencies (P) Ltd. <docinfo@dkagencies.com>

Peace education : a gender perspective.
pages cm
Includes bibliographical references.

1. Peace—Study and teaching. 2. Sex discrimination in education. 3. Women and peace. 4. Equality.

JZ5534.P43 2015 DDC 327.17207 23

Contents

	Preface	7
1.	Peace Education: A Gender Prespective	9
2.	Towards Gender Equity	15
3.	Gender Based Violence	23
4.	Different Forms of Gender Based Violence	30
5.	The Link between Gender Abuse and Women's Involvement in Illegal Activities	38
6.	Gender Equity in Education	42
7.	Gender Based Violence (GBV): Types, Levels, Causes and its Measures	54
8.	Education as A Means to Eradicate Gender Based Violence	67
9.	Psychological Perceptions of Gender Based Violence	76
10.	Child Trafficking: International Law and Relative Indian Scenario	85
11.	Gender Equality and Empowerment of Women with Special Reference to National Policy and Constitutional Provision	92
12.	Health Implications of Gender-Based Violence: A Global Overview	101
13.	The Different Faces of Gender Equality	112
14.	Gender Sensitisation through Text Books	117
15.	Women as Agents of Peace	124
16.	Gender Development and Complexities	136
17.	Gender Equity in Education for Promoting Peace	148
18.	Peace Education: An Approach to Eradicate Gender Violence	155
19.	Schooling and Skill Development: Enroute to Gender Equality and Inclusive Development	161
20.	Role of TransGender in Violence of Trilokpuri Area: A Case Study	177

21.	Gender Equality: Meeting the Needs of Peace, Development and Education	181
22.	Role of Peace, Gender –Equality and Women Empowerment in twenty-first Century	191
23.	Mental Health of Women Experienced Domestic Violence	197
24.	Importance of Woman Education for Promoting Peace Culture	205
25.	Education for Social Harmony: A Case Study on Peace Building among the Scheduled Tribes of Birbhum District, West Bengal	216
26.	Promoting Peace: A Case Study	228
27.	Psychological Perceptions of Gender Based Violence	238
28.	The Diffrent Faces of Gender Equality	247
29.	Schooling and Skill Development: Enroute to Gender Equality and Inclusive Development	252
30.	Role of Gender in Problems and Educational Aspirations of the Out of School Slum Children	268
31.	Gender Equality: A Developmental Strategy	277
32.	Gender Equity in Education	300
	Index	307

Preface

The humble piece of work has witnessed the light of the goddess MAA MANGALA.I bow my head to her mercy

Most approaches to peace building have either ignored or marginalized issues of gender and Women. Women consistently remain a minority of participants in peace building projects; they receive less attention than men in peace building policies; and gender analysis rarely informs peace building strategies. This is despite the many United Nations and European Commission resolutions which, for more than a decade, have criticized such marginalization and called for gender issues and women's needs to be given more serious attention in all policies relating to conflict and peace.

I am extremely beholden to my wife Mrs .Reeta Mishra and all the family members who have been a pillar of strength of my work. The editor is highly indebted to Prof.Mohammad Miyan Vice Chancellor ,Maulana Azad National Urdu University , Hydrabad ,Mr Amit Goel chairman vivek college of Education , his research guide Prof. Santanu Kumar Swain Faculty of Education BHU ,Varanasi ,Prof C.B Sharma Chairman NIOS. New Delhi , Prof K .C Kapoor Ex-vice-chancellor of Rajeev Gandhi Central University , Arunachal Pradesh .Er Deepak Mital secretary vivek college of Education , D.K Agarwal treasurer of our college Dr.O.P Gupta Director Administration vivek college Bijnor , for providing the guidance for developing the book.

I look forward to suggestions from all the readers for further improving the subject content as well as presentation of the book.

1

Peace Education: A Gender Prespective

Dr Lokanath Mishra

Principal, Vivek College of Education, Bijnor

Abstract

Gender is a term used in contrast to sex, to draw attention to the social roles and interactions between women and men, rather than to their biological differences. Peace Education would enable the girl child to address structural and cultural violence. She can actively participate in seeking effective and sustainable ways of resolving the situation and thus enhance all-rounded peace. It is essential to ensure windows of opportunity to promote more gender-equitable educational systems. This paper highlights about the role of gender in resolving conflicts and developing sustainable peace in the society.

Key words: Gender, Peace Education, Development

Overview

Gender relations are social relations, which include the ways in which men and women relate to each other beyond personal interaction. They include the ways in which the social categories of male and female interact in every sphere of social activity, such as those which determine access to resources, power and participation in cultural and religious activities. Gender also denotes the social meanings of male and female, and what different societies regard as normal and appropriate behaviour, attitudes and attributes for women and men. Although the details vary from society to society, and change over time; gender relations always include a strong element of inequality between women and men and are strongly influenced by ideology.

There are 'grey' areas about what is and is not biologically determined that are still subject to debate, not least amongst feminists. Some contend that women tend to be less pre-disposed to aggressive and violent behaviour because of certain biological characteristics. These include lower testosterone levels than men, and women's brain structure and development is different from men's. These and other characteristics make most women less likely to behave in challenging and competitive situations as most men can do. No scientific study argues that all forms of different behaviour patterns and roles in society can be explained by biological factors alone.

According to Kabonesa (2005), gender is an important concept in peace as it deals with social constructions that lead to differentiated treatment of males and females in terms of allocation of goods and services, productive resources and benefits accruing from resources-thus bringing, about differential impacts of development to men and women. "It is important to address gender differences during reconstruction and conflict resolution to avoid continued tension and achieve a fair and just process of development" (Kabonesa, 2005, p.19). Involving women and gender expertise in peace building process is clearly an essential step to re-establish political, legal, cultural and socio-economic structures. Women are particularly affected by gender specific forms of violence and tend to contribute considerably to conflict transformation and reconciliation on the ground, yet they are largely excluded from high level negotiations and the decision making processes leading to peace.

What is Peace Education?

Before going to define peace education we have to define peace first. Peace teaches love, non-violence, compassion and reverence for the environment and all of life. The processes of peace education include empowering people with the skills of conflict resolution and with the knowledge to help create a more safe and sustainable world. Peace education involves care, compassion and concern for oneself, for others and for the earth. A number of strategies to achieve peace exist, including peace through strength, pacifism, peace with justice and institution building, peace through sustainability, and peace education. These are not mutually exclusive, but in some cases complement each other. Peace education is more effective when it is adapted according to the social and cultural context and the needs of a society. It is enriched by the society's cultural and spiritual values along with universal human values.

Defining of Peace Education

Peace education is a holistic, participatory process that includes teaching for, and about, human rights, non-violent responses to conflict, social and economic justice, gender equality, environmental sustainability, disarmament and human security. The methodology of peace education encourages reflection, critical thinking, co-operation and responsible action. It promotes multiculturalism and is based on values of dignity, equality and respect. Peace education is intended to prepare students for democratic participation in schools and society.

In the words of Fran Schmidt and Alice Friedman (1998), peace education is holistic, and embraces the physical, emotional, intellectual and social growth of children within a framework deeply rooted in traditional human values. It is based on a philosophy that teaches love, compassion, trust, fairness, co-operation and reverence for the human family and all life on our beautiful planet. Peace education is skill building. It empowers children to join in creative and non-destructive ways to settle conflicts and to live in harmony with themselves and others. Peace building is the most desired task for every human being. It is a challenge to the human family in the present world scenario.

According to Betty Reardon, peace education is the transmission of knowledge and understanding the obstacles to, and possibilities of achieving and maintaining peace, training in skills for interpreting the knowledge and development of reflective and participatory capacities in applying the knowledge to overcoming problems and achieving possibilities.

According to Gandhi, there is no way to peace. Peace is the way. Peace education is defined as the pedagogical efforts to create a better world by teaching love, non-violence, compassion and reverence for all life.

Gender and Peace Education

Peace education encompasses a holistic perspective and includes human rights education, education for global citisenship, environmental education, conflict education, intercultural awareness and gender awareness education in—-formal, non-formal and informal sectors.

Both men and women have the potential for peacemaking and the responsibility to build and keep peace. The women, however, seem more creative and effective in waging peace. It is the women's emotional strength to transcend pain and suffering, and their predisposition to peace that provides them with greater potentials for peacemaking.

As peace educators, we advocate this holistic perspective as a comprehensive framework for the study of positive peace, arguing that the realisation of human rights is the most practical means to the achievement of positive peace. We also consider that a holistic human rights perspective is integral to a truly inclusive gender perspective that in the mode of holism includes the whole spectrum of sexualities, heterosexual, transsexual, bisexual and homosexual, all gender identities.

Now-a-days this practice has not got the required legal support as a result many Indian women still undergo all forms of abuse. Most police stations have male staff and when women report physical abuse by their partners, they are told to go and settle it with elders back home.

The wrong notion behind this is that a domestic private affair should not be brought out into the public domain as it would create public embarrassment for the male folk.

'Dowry payments encourage the perception that female children are a burden, causing other forms of discrimination, including increasingly limited inheritance rights for women and physical abuse'. Women's enhanced peace education would enable them to be more aware of their rights and be able to defend them but most importantly to be able to take better care of their health concerns. Studies have shown that a woman's education beyond primary school is a reliable route to economic empowerment and long-term change in the status quo, as well as a determinant of a family's health and nutrition. Education beyond ten or more years of school is also a reliable predictor of lower fertility, improved infant survival, reduced maternal mortality and enhanced levels of infant and child development and educational attainment.

Elshtain (1993) writes, "What women have had to contend with all these years is not simply or only the fact that men have been in a position of greater power over women. Men fear the sexual and reproductive power of women. This is reflected in the lengths to which they have gone to protect themselves by projecting that fear outward into social forms, by embedding the need to defend themselves against women in institutions and activities including Political. Men define themselves by that which is 'not-woman; therefore not vulnerable'". By using such petty excuses, like women's vulnerability, men continuously keep out women from getting opportunities that would enable them reach their full potential.

Education would enable more women to penetrate into the public domain thereby creating a level playing field, but without it, women will always be a mockery, kept out by petty excuses.

It is essential to ensure that windows of opportunity to promote more gender-equitable educational systems are pursued. This includes an analysis of the different needs and roles of not only boys and girls, but also of male and female teachers. Conflict, particularly disrupts the education of girls, due to issues including the dangers in travelling to and attending schools, over-supply of male teachers, lack of sanitary facilities, early marriage and pregnancy, lack of money for girls' school fees, as well as domestic needs as families struggle for survival. Girls and boys may also face security risks at schools, such as forced recruitment. A conflict-prone setting also presents opportunities for boys and girls, and for gender equality in education. There is an opportunity to transform curricula and educational systems in favour of gender equality. School protects girls against abuse such as sexual violence during conflicts, and equips adolescent girls for the roles and responsibilities they are required to take on during and after conflict, through literacy and numeracy skills.

This helps us to have a general picture of how pertinent gender looks as far as peace as concern. More areas should be added on depending on the context and particularities of each society.

Supporting Women's Organisations

Targeting women's organisations for support, especially those that have wide participation and/or where the leadership has strong connections to poor sections of society, a clear vision about what they want to achieve; and those which are built on an acknowledgment of the divisions between women and seek to build bridges between communities of women is the need of the hour. Supporting organisations which promote the issues about gender relations and cultural change (including violence, women's rights, and children's rights) should be encouraged.

Promoting Women in Institutions

- Involving women in identifying key areas for institutional reform (especially in the areas of security and law enforcement).
- Training and education for women to enable them to become viable candidates for leadership and decision-making positions in a wide range of institutions (including government bureaucracies).
- Training for women to develop and promote methods of institutional reform and to act as trainers themselves (especially in methods of consultation, institutional mediation and conflict resolution for use within organisations).

In reference to Mahatma Gandhi's statement on peace "being the way"; it is important to encourage women's education within the Indian system as a consistent strategy towards being one of the 'ways' to attain peace. In looking at the importance of education and most specifically with regard to combating aspects of structural and cultural violence, women's education is a first step towards doing small things in a big way that will eventually make a difference and influence positive progress within society.

The access to peace education should surpass primary and secondary education and go further to ensuring equal access to career development, training, scholarships and fellowships. This is due to the fact that Peace Education is not narrowed down to the four walls of a classroom but is a holistic approach that encompasses life skills, knowledge, capacities, aptitudes and ethical values thus preparing one to fully participate in all spheres within the society. Special assistance is given to the girl child so that the enrolment and retention rates of the girl child will be increased. Women also need to be represented at the decision and policy making level within the education sphere. In this way, from their own experiences, they can be able to enhance the designing of policies that would meet the girl child's needs to the fullest.

References

- Astri Suhrke with Kristian Berg Harpviken, Are Knudsen, Arve Ofstad, and Arne Strand, (2009) "Peacebuilding: Lessons for Afghanistan", CMI Report, http://www.cmi.no/public/2002/Reports/R2002-9.html
- Mishra. L (2010) Encylopaedia of Peace Education, APH Publication, New Delhi
- Lisa Schirch (2004) West African Network for Peace building and Conflict Transformation Program at Eastern Mennonite University http://www.womenpeacemakersprogram.org/women's_Peacebuilding_Manual_Chapters_1-4.pdf
- "Peace Inextricably Linked with Equality between Women and Men says Security Council, in an International Women's Day Statement," Security Council press release http://www.un.org/womenwatch/news/articles/chowdhuryiwd00.html

2

Towards Gender Equity

Dr Jaya Mukerji
Assistant Professor, Department of Education
Allahabad Degree College, Allahabad

Abstract

Gender inequality is created by human beings in society. In this paper some of the causes leading to gender disparity, in addition to women's entry into organisations and their career aspirations, where they find themselves in two contexts – social familial context and work context have been highlighted. Women face the push and pulls of these two contexts. Though women empowerment is so much talked of in today's world, but, if women are not able to balance between these two contexts, then the question of women being truly empowered does not hold true. The paper deals with the problems that women face while balancing their personal and professional roles. Women are not able to choose between the structures which are supportive and which are not. They feel embarrassed to state what could be done and what needs to be done. They suffer from feelings of insecurity and get entangled in dependant/ exploitative relationships. Men and women find it difficult to build healthy, interdependent, collegiate and functional relationships. Women are often ruled by society's normative and prescriptive rules which restrict them from making healthy choices. They are often overburdened and make compromises. Single women have their own dilemmas. All these problems can be resolved to a certain extent if women and men are sensitive to each other's pathos and clearly state them, realistically assess strengths and weaknesses, and be able to design more integrative processes. Certain attempts towards bringing about gender equity, such as, research in Women Studies, gender equality through social protection programmes, role of non-governmental organisations and information and communications technology in fighting inequalities have also been mentioned.

Keywords: Structures of inequality, gender disparity, balancing personal and professional roles.

The unequal status of women in society and the causes of disparity between men and women are not destined by nature but created by human beings in society. The patriarchal attitudes to women in the institution of the family are carried over to other institutions of society, including education and employment. Analysis attribute this phenomenon to socio-psychological causes, lack of motivation often due to lack of social support and nature of perception of women's role, personality characteristics, attitudes, acceptance of traditional roles, reinforced by society which is inherently patriarchal, inbuilt "power structure" in the institutions and gender bias.

In India, the overall scenario indicates under representation of women in governance and decision-making positions in all areas of public life. Even after several decades following independence, women continue to struggle for basic rights such as minimum wages, equal wages and property rights, in spite of several protective legislations. Women's access to resources such as land, credit, skill training and education in particular, is relatively poor, while they still carry the burden of a "double shift" at home cooking, cleaning, and caring for the young and the old, adversely affecting their abilities to contribute effectively in the labour market. As per an article, titled, *India ranks 135 on human development index: UNDP* on page 8 of Northern India Patrika, July 25, 2014: "India ranked 135 out of 187 countries on the human development index in UNDP's annual report 2014. Human development index is a composite statistics of life expectancy, education and income indices to measure the well-being of a country. On the gender inequality index, India ranked 127 out of 152 countries and on the gender development index, it ranked 132 of 148 countries, the report said...." Also, the report said that South Asia has the largest number of multi dimensionally poor people and that women suffer more than men.

An Overview of the Structures of Inequality Leading to Gender Disparity

1. Patriarchy

Patriarchy is a social system in which males are the primary authority figures central to social organisation; occupy roles of political leadership, moral authority and control of property, and fathers hold authority over women and children. It implies the institutions of male rule and privilege and entails female subordination. Historically, the term patriarchy was used to refer to autocratic rule by the male head of a family. However in modern times, it more generally refers to social systems in which power is primarily held by adult men. Anthropological evidence suggests that most prehistoric hunter-gatherer societies were relatively egalitarian, and that patriarchal social structures did not develop until many years after the end of the Pleistocene era, following social and technological innovations such as agriculture and domestication. Warlike, patriarchal structures were adopted in order to secure food sources and the virtues of men and women clearly marked out. Men should know how to administer the state and in the process benefit his friend and harm his enemies and also be careful not to suffer harm himself. Women should know how to order her house and obey her husband. In fact the sole role of women was reproduction.

This shows that patriarchy has kept the women at the lower rung of the social order.

2. Familial System Linked to Socio-political System Outside

The existing familial system gets closely linked to the socio-political system outside. The preservation and solidarity of the present discriminatory family structure becomes the guarantor for the status-quo with no change to socio-political and economic system. The discriminations, atrocities, injustices against women get perpetrated from the family to society and vice versa, thus making the personal to be political for the females.

3. Apprehensions about Achieving Success at the Cost of Destroying Family Peace

The unequal and hierarchical power based relations between men and women within family often has its impact on the women's professional life and activities outside. It is often seen that many women, for one reason or other voluntarily give up various opportunities to move upwards or demonstrate their potentials. This is not merely because of their concern for children and fear of unsettlement or due to their diffidence about their own capacity, but also due to the patriarchal reason that any movement upwards bringing success in one's career would ultimately lead to destroying stability and balance at home. Many skilled women take up jobs that are part time or have flexible timings or those that can be carried out from their own homes without neglecting their families.

4. Division between Public and Private Occupations

The family is considered to be falling within the private realm and therefore the work done within the household amounts to the private occupation of women. In the agricultural families much of the work of the women is closely linked to the household occupation of the family like weeding, cattle care, dairying etc., even if the women do not themselves earn through these activities. Women also perform household chores and reproductive functions, which do not fetch income and go unrecognised.

Women also engage themselves in other informal ways of earning income, like cottage industries. These are actually economically productive activities of the country and thereby an aspect of the public sphere. The private and public spheres are therefore closely intertwined. Also, sometimes the specific parts of products of bigger factories are produced at home by women. This shows that women contribute to national production and income. The separation between public and private spheres has been done in a way to devalue the work done by women and restrict them indoors and stop them from being free and productive members of society as men. In a country like India with more than sixty per cent of women living in rural agricultural families and nearly sixty per cent of women working as marginal workers in the urban sites, there can be no such private public distinction for women, either in work or even in the male female division of responsibilities. (Capacity Building of Women Managers in Higher Education, Manual I. p. 20).

5. Biological Factors

Biology determines gender status and women's status in society. Women are held to be weak, soft and vulnerable. Generally, restrictions have been imposed in most families on women's free movement for fear of being raped and abused, for fear of mixing up with "wrong" persons. The differences between men and women by way of values, mode of behaviour, life patterns and the supposed vulnerability of women, their need for protection and their inferiority by way of physical strength and potentialities are made out by the needs of the family, society and state. These are denoted by gender, gender roles and gender differences, and brought about by socialisation, historical traditions, customary norms and state machineries. Gender is a social act and a political tool, rather than a natural institution like sex. This gender can be altered, socially engineered and politically reconstructed while sex cannot be. Gender also implies that the relationship between women and men can be changed from a patriarchal to a just and equal relationship. Women in informal, unorganised and household sectors, the self employed, the piece rate workers, those who perform para agricultural tasks should be called "workers", thereby emphasing the role of women in the economy and recognising their contribution to national production. This adds to their worth, self-dignity and self-confidence.

Also there is another aspect to this gender disparity where one finds women pursuing their different career aspirations not being able to balance their personal and professional roles. Therefore, they are not able to discover their own identities or uniqueness of their existence. The problems faced by women entering into different types of occupational roles are as follows:

I. Women have developed social stereotypes about themselves as well as men. Women being physically weaker than men have throughout the ages appeared to have accepted male domination, giving men a sense of precedence and superiority. It was enunciated that a woman when young has to be sheltered by her father, later by her brother or husband or son, implicitly meaning that she was not empowered to act on her own. This led to the generation of an environment where women were made to feel unsafe and over the years they have often meekly submitted to male demands. Even when they perform their professional roles, they are not able to judge between structures and systems which are supportive and which are not. This inability on their part restricts them from seeing the support which is available.

Also, women are not able to state their convictions as well as their vision and perspective of formal systems clearly. They feel embarrassed to state what could be done and what needs to be done. Sexual openness and experimentation is on an increase due to increasing number of women being out in the world of men and demands of surrender are made due to designation, power, authority, insecurity and compulsiveness. Also, women face exploitation from other women higher authority in the same organisation.

II. Women often have fears of insecurity and they suffer from feelings of acceptance/rejection and thus get entangled in dependant and exploitative relationships and this stops them from asserting and acquiring a professional orientation. For instance, the mother-in-law might force her to do a certain amount of housework before leaving for her job. Such type of pressures may restrict her in putting a whole-hearted effort to rise in her career.

III. It is difficult for both women and men to build healthy, interdependent collegiate and functional relationships, to recognise each other's capabilities. Research findings suggest that women in significant positions have a vision and clarity of mission, are capable and competent, are autonomous, can exercise authority, can take significant responsibilities and aspire for positions appropriate to the tasks they are doing. Data of women managers in some organisations have suggested that most women find it easier to relate with their male superiors, colleagues and subordinates. The superiors find women sincere, dedicated and hardworking, and the subordinates respect women in the managerial cadre as they are not only professionally educated and qualified but also provide leadership roles which they can and do respect. However, for male colleagues the interface with women is somewhat distorted, as they very often start comparing themselves with their female counterparts. Men feel that women are given more consideration in the workplace so that they may attend to other duties at home; however as the same does not apply to men in the same organisation who have working wives, the former tend to feel hostile towards their female colleagues.

IV. Though women can accept uprooting and mobility quite well (moving from their parental home to that of the in-laws, husbands or their personal homes) they often feel guilty when they cannot make healthy choices on their own. Women are often ruled by the society's normative and prescriptive dos and don'ts, shoulds and should-nots, musts and must-nots. These often become compulsive and absolute. Then they feel like prisoners of people or the social system and get resentful.

V. In organisational settings women take total responsibility and are unable to delegate authority or share their work, do not know how to receive and accept support. This is sometimes the case at home too. This makes them feel overburdened and they tend to behave like martyrs.

VI. Women often make choices on the basis of economic necessity or as an escape from a boring life. They reject the positive choices based on their aspirations, competence, capabilities and work orientation. Women find it difficult to make a realistic positive appraisal of their strengths and their contribution and end up doing jobs which are not according to their inclinations. This process leads women to make many compromises.

VII. Single women encounter dilemmas associated with single status in the social context. They are far more vulnerable in terms of relationships be it social or occupational. Social stereotypes and perceptions generate stigma and women either become defensive or over protective of themselves. They do not trust and very often live with inner loneliness and isolation.

In order to bring about a qualitative change in the life space of both men and women, thereby working towards gender equity, certain points emerge.

- Women should not only clearly state and share their pathos but be sensitive to the pathos of men as well.
- Women-men relationships in social settings revolve around affiliated relationships but in organisations, around tasks. The difference between the two and the clarity of boundaries needs to be sensed by both. Both women and men are equally caught in socially affiliated dynamics. It is important that both discover each other's strengths and limitations and realistically assess each other's unique resources so as to build a strong foundation for working relationships.
- Every woman has the potential to be competent, capable, assertive, creative and dynamic, in essence to be a professional. The spirit of pursuing new horizons is forever awakened, and it is this spirit of women that needs to be fostered.
- Maturity to work with others without competing, feeling threatened or wanting to be the centre of the stage. In effect she must be able to work in groups——as a team as well as individually. The twentieth century organisations have had largely male models of work structure. Women's contribution would be to confront organisations for designing integrative processes where both men and women can

work together.

Educational process should raise and create social awareness and values like equity and social justice. Research in Women Studies should be encouraged. Research on women brings about tremendous new insights into women's status, work, contribution and conditions that could feed into public policies and programmes, which, in turn, lead to further support for research. There are many issues which need deep thinking. For instance:

1. Concepts of equality, dignity and gender justice; constitutional provisions; women's rights;
2. Effectiveness and impact of instruments of change like literacy and education, skill development and vocational education/training and income generation and employment.
3. Recognition of the importance of women's health, food and nutrition; re-socialisation on women's role and needs; questioning of male dominance and preference for male child.
4. Access to legal rights and property rights.
5. Review of the whole notion of marriage, post-marital location, sharing household chores and tolerance and encouragement of the women's autonomy, equal dignity and partnership in decision making.
6. Efforts directed to removal of violence (domestic and public); abuse (mental and sexual).
7. Consequences of judicial directives against sexual harassment at work place.
8. Effect of international conferences, conventions and networks.

Also, addressing gender inequality through social protection programmes designed to increase equity can prove to be an effective way in reducing gender inequality. Non-Governmental Organisations can help to build networks among women to create financial self help groups, introduce ideas about micro finance, allowing women to participate in management activities. Local NGOs can help in implementing projects that export the skills of women abroad to generate significant income.

Another opportunity to tackle gender inequality is presented by modern information and communications technology. Women becoming familiar with these digital tools can raise their voices against longstanding inequalities in the workplace and in their homes; also they become more aware and vocal about political and social issues. However, this often has a negative impact when women become victim of online harassment and getting cyber crime cells to chase, a case becomes an even bigger ordeal. (The Times of India, p. 9, July 22, 2014).

To conclude, women need to be empowered but this does not mean giving them more power. It only means giving them their due, to create an awareness and demand for education. Empowerment should be viewed as a process in which all voices are encouraged to be heard for the ultimate goal of securing mutually beneficial solutions. It is necessary to use the best talents of men and women in workplaces by creating a gender friendly atmosphere and recognising that quality and excellence should be the criteria for appointment to leadership positions, equally of both, men and women. Also women have to be proactive and come forward and work together to bring about change in their own immediate environment and question their socio-cultural beliefs, their own need to hold on to structured normative prescriptions, and realistically assess their strengths and limitations. Women are subject to inequality not only in the public sphere but also within the private sphere such as within the home and their intimate relationships. Tackling the continuum of inequality in both the public and private spheres is therefore essential to address the root causes of gender inequality. When we recognise our shared humanity then compassion becomes real and where there is compassion there is a relationship between equals – not a relationship between healer and wounded, thereby focussing on gender equality.

References

- Aggarwal, J.C. *Recent Developments and Trends in Education.* 3rd Ed. 2009, Delhi: Shipra Publications.
- Dutta, P.K. "Career Opportunities for Women". *Employment News*, May 12-18, 2007.
- Kaushik, Susheela. *Capacity Building of Women Managers in Higher Education*, Women's Studies Perspectives (2008). Manual I. New Delhi: University Grants Commission.
- Mashelkar, R.A. "Challenges before India". *Employment News*, November 11-17, 2000.
- *India ranks 135 on human development index: UNDP* on page 8 of Northern India Patrika, July 25, 2014.
- Pandey, R.S. *Development of Educational System in India*. 3rd Ed. 2008, Agra: Agrawal Publications.
- Pandey, R.S. *Documents of Modern Education in India*. 2nd Ed. 2006, Meerut: Surya Publication.
- Parikh, J. Indira. *Capacity Building of Women Managers in Higher Education*, Manual IV (2009). Foundation for Liberal and Management Education. *The Times of India*, p. 9, July 22, 2014.

3

Gender-Based Violence

Ruchi Dhyani

Research Scholar Punjabi University, Patiala

Abstract

Violence is not acceptable in any form in any civilised society. But it is the fact gender based Violence is prevailing all over the world and is an abuse of human rights. Victims of gender based violence are both men and women, but mainly women are the prime target. Gender based violence may be in the form of Physical, sexual and psychological violence occurring in the family, communities and occurring in public or private life. Gender based violence can be described as 'cradle to grave'. Now it is a time to raise a voice against gender based violence and it can be possible only when we give equality and respect for each and every woman of the world. Without women, we can't imagine the existence of men. A woman always in a top position than men from the start as they are their creator, even then they don't receive equality and freedom for their basic human rights and has to struggle for ending the discrimination.

Keywords: *Gender, Violence, Women.*

Introduction

"Around the globe, violence against women is an epidemic. Violence robs women and girls of their full potential and causes untold human suffering. Violence against women impedes economic development, threatens peace and prosperity, and inhibits full participation in civic life. For every woman who has been beaten in her own home, for the millions of women who have been raped as a weapon of war, for every girl who has been attacked on her way to school, for all of the children–girls and boys–who have witnessed this brutality, we must do better".

———— Vice President Joe Biden,

Statement on the Anniversary of the International Day for the Elimination of Violence against Women, November 24, 2010.

Gender base violence is not a new concept; it is prevailing from the beginning of every civilised society having its roots in the concept of inequality. Gender is used to distinguish the role of male and female in society. Today we become modern and advanced but still we don't give respect and equality right to women. Anyone can become the victim of gender based violence, but mostly women become its victim. Violence against women is too common and widespread throughout the world. Women are not even safe in their own houses. They become the victim of any kind of violence in their homes, workplaces. The World Human Rights Conference in Vienna, first recognised gender-based violence as a human rights violation in 1993. *United Nations declaration*, 1993, defined *violence against women* as "any act of gender-based violence that results in, or is likely to result in, physical, sexual or psychological harm or suffering to a woman, including threats of such acts, coercion or arbitrary deprivations of liberty, whether occurring in public or private life". Gender-based violence refers to violence perpetrated between people of the opposite sex. It is an established fact that women and girls are usually the victims of gender-based violence because of the unequal power relations between the sexes; however, men and boys are also victims of violence. Because Gender–based violence usually manifests itself as violence against women and girls, it is important to refer to the United Nations definition of violence against women, which, states;

- "Physical, sexual and psychological violence occurring in the family, including battering, sexual abuse of female children in the home, dowry related violence, marital rape, female genital mutilation and other traditional practices harmful to women, non–spousal violence and violence related to exploitation;
- Physical, sexual and psychological violence occurring within the community, including rape, sexual abuse, sexual harassment and intimidation at work, in education institutions and elsewhere, trafficking in women and forced prostitution;
- Physical, sexual and psychological violence perpetrated or condoned by the state wherever it occurs".
- Gender–Based violence occurs at three levels and these are the individual, the community and the national or state level. These three levels are mutually reinforcing. Violence can be physical, psychological, sexual, economic, social or cultural.
- Women always become the victim of violence because they don't raise voice against the culprits. Women are treated as they just born to bear all kinds of violence without complaining. Women become the victims of violence throughout their life cycle. There are many forms of violence against women which they face from pre-birth, infancy, childhood, adolescence, reproductive age and even in elderly age.

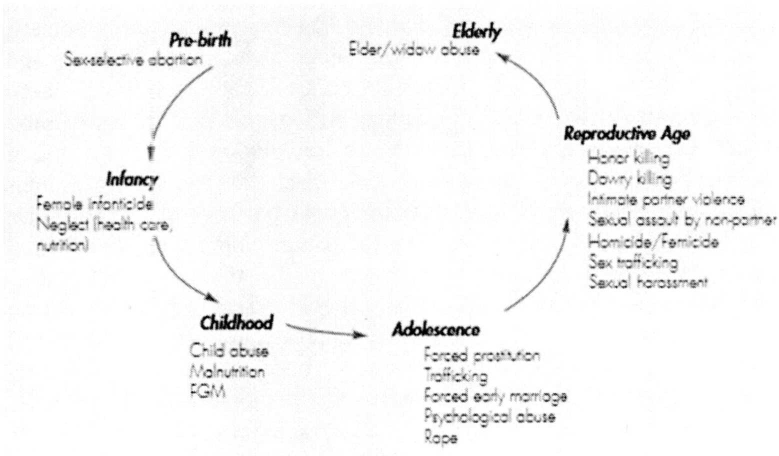

According to the 2006 UNICEF study, "State of the World's Children," in India, 7, 000 girls a day is aborted just because they are female. Different forms of violences are used for giving suffering to women like: Domestic violence 'is prevalent and a largely accepted part of family life in India' (Kumar et al. 2002). Statistics on domestic violence in India suggest that 45 per cent of women are slapped, kicked or beaten by their husbands (Ministry of Women and Child Development). According to the Crime against Women Report by the National Crimes Records Bureau (hereafter NCRB), in 2007,——20,737 women reported being raped, 75,930 women reported being tortured and 38,734 women reported being molested. Crimes against Women Report 2007 states that 8093 women were reported killed over Dowry Death. In addition, there were 5623 complaints lodged for the breach of the Dowry Prohibition Act, 1961 in 2007. According to a 2013 global review of available data, 35 per cent of women worldwide have experienced either physical and/or sexual intimate partner violence or non-partner sexual violence. However, some national violence studies show that up to 70 per cent of women have experienced physical and/or sexual violence in their lifetime from an intimate partner. Female genital mutilation (FGM) is another form of violence which is practiced by ethnic groups in 27 countries in sub-Saharan and north-east Africa, in Yemen and Iraqi Kurdistan, and to a lesser extent elsewhere in Asia and within immigrant communities around the world. FGM is defined by the World Health Organisation (WHO) as 'all procedures that involve partial or total removal of the external female genitalia, or other injury to the female genital organs for non-medical reasons. 'Approximately 140 million girls and women in the world have suffered female genital mutilation/cutting. In a survey done by the National Commission for

Women of 1200 women, nearly 50 per cent complained of gender discrimination and physical and mental harassment at work. While 40 per cent of the women said they "usually ignored" such provocation, 3.54 per cent said they reported these to their supervisors, 7.8 per cent of their colleagues and 1.24 per cent to the police. About 10 per cent said that they protested against such behaviour while 9 per cent said they warned the offenders. At least 20.17 per cent of the respondents said that no investigation was done on their complaints while 1.5 per cent said police harassed them again instead of making the inquiry. Trafficking in persons is an increasing problem that involves both sexual exploitation and labour exploitation of its victims. Trafficking affects all regions and the majority of countries in the world. Both men and women may be victims of trafficking, but the primary victims worldwide are women and girls, the majority of whom are trafficked for the purpose of sexual exploitation. Traffickers primarily target women because they are disproportionately affected by poverty and discrimination, factors that impede their access to employment, educational opportunities and other resources. Acid violence seems to be almost unique to South Asia, with most incidents occurring in Bangladesh, India and Pakistan. The New York Times (Dec, 26, 2001) reports that kerosene as well as acid has fast become the weapons of choice for attacks on wives in India.

Gender Based Violence (GBV) is predominantly a crime against women and represents a violence of women's human rights. The cyclic nature of GBV can be described as 'cradle to grave'. Three major factors responsible for gender based violence in worldwide and so common prevailing in each and every corner of society.

- Direct or personal violence means a direct assault on a person or group, whether physical, verbal or psychological, for example a man hits a woman.
- Structural violence is meant violence that is embedded in the very structures or institutions of our societies. Most obvious examples of this include poverty, starvation and exploitation. Further examples include gender discrimination and other forms of sexism, as well as racism and xenophobia, along with homophobia. Excessively high maternal and infant mortality rates are forms of structural violence because they are easily avoidable, and affect only specific sectors of the population, i.e., the most marginalised.
- Cultural violence is meant violence that is perpetuated through our cultures and ways of thinking and being that is used to justify direct or structural violence, for example, some men argue that a husband is fully entitled to rape his wife, or force her to have sex against her will. A further example of this would be "victim blaming" in the case of rape.

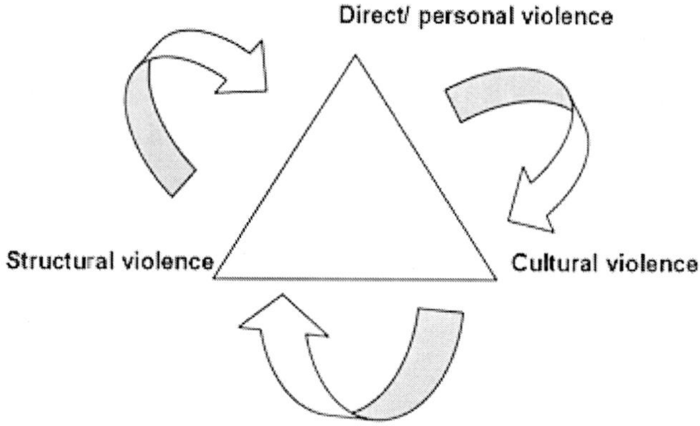

Fig. Three corner triangle

On the basis of this three corner triangle the major reason for gender based violence are

a. Economic inequality;
b. Existing patterns of using physical violence to resolve conflicts;
c. Male authority and control over decision-making (and excluding women from this process);
d. Restrictions on women's ability to leave the family setting.

Effects of Gender-based Violence

Gender based violence having a long lasting impact on the victims and it takes lifelong time to recover from such events. Victims always feel everyone is talking about them and never become normal and enjoying normal life. It's really difficult and time taking process to lead a normal life. Gender based violence is so common in society and anyone can become its target. Gender based violence have fatal, non-fatal and psycho social consequences on the survivor.

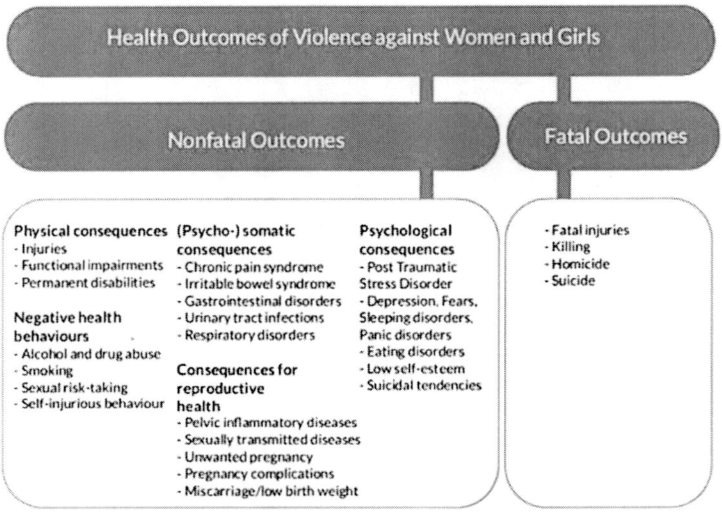

How to Stop Gender-based Violence

The United States recognises that for people to achieve their full potential, their lives must be free from violence. The strategy incorporates the following overarching priorities to ending gender-based violence:

- Prevention: of gender-based violence from occurring in the first place, and from recurring, by working with local grassroots organisations, civil society, and key stakeholders in the community, including men and boys;
- Protection: from gender-based violence by identifying and providing services to survivors once the violence occurs; and
- Accountability: to ensure that perpetrators are prosecuted and to end impunity by strengthening legal and judicial systems.

The most important step that everyone has to take to end the gender based violence is to break their silence against the crime and raise their voice for justice and this can be possible by creating awareness among the common masses and make them aware about the laws and regulation which are framed for the violence. Education also plays an important role in stopping gender based violence. Through education one becomes independent and knows about his rights and duties and knows how to take decisions and protect and secure oneself and other too. We have to increase the participation of males too, and educate them from the start of their life to respect and treat women equal and try to eliminate gender based discrimination. Government has to make stricter rules for the effective implementation of law machinery.

Conclusion

Gender based violence is spread all over the world and anyone can be the target, but mainly women and girls are becoming the victim of gender based violence. The grass root problem of gender based violence is the gender based discrimination. Women and girls always treated as inferior to men that's why they don't get their respectable place in society and become as an easy target for violence. Any kind of violence is not welcomed in any civilised society and women have to break their silence and raise voice against gender based violence. Men have to understand women are equally important and valuable in life and they must be treated equally.

References

- Bott, S.,A.Morrison, and M. Ellsberg. 2005. Preventing and Responding to Gender-based Violence in Middle and Low-income Countries: A Global Review and Analysis. World Bank Policy Research Working Paper 3618. Washington, DC: World Bank.
- http://preventgbvafrica.org/wpcontent/uploads/2013/11/ whenrightsarewronged.bm_.pdf
- http://www.health-genderviolence.org/guidance-for-health-care-professionals-in-strengthening-health-system-responses-to-gender-based-vi-4
- http://www.path.org/publications/files/GBV_rvaw_complete.pdf
- http://www.state.gov/documents/organisation/196468.pdf
- Kumar Satish, C., S. D. Gupta and G. Abraham (2002), Masculinity and Violence against Women in Marriage: An Exploratory Study in Rajasthan', (Ed.) Men, Masculinity and Domestic Violence in India: Summary Report of Four Studies. Washington, DC.
- Shri-Vedpathak Madhukar Ranchandra (2012) Gender Based Violence in India and Human Rights, 2 (12), Review of research, 1-11.
- World Health Organisation, 2012, "Female Genital Mutilation: Fact Sheet No. 241", Geneva.
- World Health Organisation, Global and Regional Estimates of Violence against Women, http://apps.who.int/iris/bitstream/10665/85239/1/ 9789241564625_eng.pdf, p2. For individual country information, see the full compilation of data in UN Women, 2012, Violence against Women Prevalence Data: Surveys by Country.

4

Different Forms of Gender-Based Violence

Palwinder Kaur

Research Scholar Punjabi University, Patiala

Abstract

Gender Violence is defined as "any act involving use of force or coercion with intent of perpetuating promoting hierarchical gender relations". Violence against women has been clearly defined as a form of discrimination in numerous documents. It is partly a result of gender relations that assumes men to be superior to women. Given the subordinate status of women, much of gender violence is considered normal and enjoys social sanction. Violence includes physical aggression, sexual abuse, and psychological violence. In extreme, but not unknown cases, death is the result. These expressions of violence take place in a man-woman relationship within the family, state and society., the problem of violence against women is a result of a long standing power imbalance between men and women. This is not a present problem rather it has its deep roots inserted since few decades. The government and voluntary organisations are making efforts towards ending violence against women which will be impossible if a common man is not supportive. This paper is an overview about domestic violence.

Keywords: Women, Violence, Gender

Introduction

Domestic violence, also known as domestic abuse, spousal abuse, battering, family violence, and Intimate Partner Violence (IPV), is defined as a pattern of abusive behaviours by one partner against another in an intimate relationship such as marriage, dating, family, or cohabitation. The World Human Rights Conference in Vienna, first recognised gender-based violence as a human rights violation in 1993. United Nations declaration, 1993, defined violence against women as "an act of gender-based violence that results in, or is likely to result in, physical, sexual or psychological harm or suffering to a woman, including threats of such acts, coercion or arbitrary deprivations of liberty, whether occurring in public or private life". (Saravanan, 2000)

According to the Merriam-Webster dictionary definition, domestic violence is: "the inflicting of physical injury by one family or household member on another; also-a repeated/habitual pattern of such behaviour.

Victims of Domestic Violence and the Manifestations

On children: They are targeted by parents on their education like putting pressure for getting highmarks, giving punishments like depriving food if not studying well, locking them up in a room, beating them, emotional torture like pushing their dreams to them, comparing with their friends etc., These children, failing to take the pressure, feel demotivated and consequently fall in depression. The other set of children start revolting and indulge in violent activities. In the lower strata of society the child is bonded for labour, parents don't send them to school, every child is converted into an income giver, depriving them of their childhood freedom and fun. These children remain illiterate, and join the below poverty line population. Few others, who flee from home, tend to indulge in illegal activities, and may later become criminals too.

Gender bias: Parents pay special attention to boys at home and dictate girls to carry out all domestic chores in favour of the males in the house. This leads the girl child to withdraw herself from the world, they may fall in depression or try to run away from home in dream of a better future ignorant of the fact that the outside world is waiting to swallow them with its evil mouth.

On women: In case of married woman, the in-laws and husband invariably do the domestic Violence in one form or another. The woman put up with the violence due to various reasons. Either she experiences the torture without making much noise about it, or she seeks extreme measures like suicide not able to put up with the violence. There are instances where she is killed by the in-laws/husband but the story is manipulated at the boy's end, and the truth never comes to the light. In case of working woman, though they are economically secure, they are unable to enjoy it as she and her finances are ruled by the man of the family. She has to keep proving her both in family and in her workplace. This theory holds good in women from all sects of the society. She faces emotional, financial, and at times physical injury too. There is another important domestic violence prevalent in married women as not producing baby in the first or second year of marriage. In any childless couple, the blame is given to the woman only and not to her partner. Yet another agony awaits if the woman delivers a child with disability. Without scientifically approaching the issue, the woman is blamed, and the husband deserts her too. The so called marriage institution does not ask the people concerned. Invariably, the single mother without support has to rear the child much against odds and struggles. If a woman falls terminally ill after the marriage, she is sent to her mother's place permanently. This is the biggest violence against women. Whereas, if a man loses his hand/leg in accident after marriage, the same woman has to serve him for life time. This is the basis of gender discrimination where women are taken for granted.

Type of Violence against Women

1. **Drug Related Violence**: An alcoholic beats his wife and children. There are incidences where under the influence of alcohol a father raped his own daughter. Alcoholism increases violence and consequently family interruption takes place.
2. **Rape and Custodial Rape**: In most of the cases the victim is branded as a woman of loose morals. Child and adolescents rape are on the rise, about 58 per cent are below 16 years. In recent years girl children in the age group of 6.12 years have been more victimised. Custodial rape is extremely heinous since the offenders are supposed to be guardians of the law. Witnesses refuse to testify against offenders or men in power, which makes it impossible for the victim to get justice.
3. **Harassment at Work Place and Eve Teasing** : Whether out of choice or out of compulsion, most of the women who are involved in the work place in all vital sectors of country' economy may fall in the unorganised sectors. They are ill-paid but don't leave the job due to increasing unemployment. This need for survival drives to as rape situations. Harassment at work place is real and pervasive. Example: Jokes with sexual undertone, obscene behaviour with sexual overtures and direct sexual harassment. It affects seriously women's psychological and physical well-being. Lack of action against the guilty persons has had an adverse effect on those women who have the courage to report and again it gives them further harassment, trauma and re-victimisation. Eveteasing is crime committed in crowed areas in the cities such as public transport, public parks, place of worship and tourists spots etc., which may be considered as legal problem as well as socio-psychological problem. It hampers the freedom of women and restricts her free movement.
4. **Dowry Related Violence:** The practice of demanding dowry has spread so much that death by burning is often seen as a punishment for the innocent young girls who are unable to satisfy the greed of their in-laws.
5. **Domestic Violence**: Subordination of women has led to violence. Incidence of domestic violence crosses all the barriers of class, income, race, culture and religion and is a highly under reported crime. Domestic violence is one of the greatest obstacles to gender equality and securing for women their fundamental rights to equal protection under the law and the right to life and liberty.

Forms of Domestic Violence

Domestic violence, so defined, has many forms, including physical aggression or assault (hitting, kicking, biting, shoving, restraining, slapping, throwing objects), or threats thereof; sexual abuse emotional abuse; controlling or domineering; intimidation; stalking; passive/covert abuse (e.g., neglect); and economic deprivation Alcohol consumption and mental illness can be co-morbid with abuse, and present additional challenges in eliminating domestic violence.

Violence committed by family members within the family is the most serious of all types of violence. Family violence refers to physical, psychological abuse of women by husband or his relatives. This is of course violation of trust and abuse of power in relationship where a woman should have the right of absolute safety.

Rape and Sexual Abuse is another brutal form of violence. It is commonly believed that women if married are safe in oursociety. But if the monster prevails in her family itself it would be rather very difficult for her to escape. Rape or sexual abuse can be committed by the relatives, family friends on helpless women. Demanding giving and accepting Dowry is illegal in India. The practice, however, still prevails in many sections of the society. The issue of dowry is probably the most common sources of domestic violence in India, where the husband along with his parents and relative tortures his wife for money. Incidents of murder or attempted murder for dowry-related reasons are regular items in the country's daily papers. Women are also victim of Mental or Psychological Torture. Using abusive words by family members in front of others causes mental illness among women because it is generally accepted that women are soft then men in this aspect.

Torture during Pregnancy is one of the in humane tortures ever. Women need special care and attention and nutritious food during pregnancy. Tortures during pregnancy can put the unborn baby and the mother in danger. It may increase the chance of miscarriage, infection, pre mature birth and sometimes death of the baby. Denials of facilities are nothing but a stress for the women to survive to deliver the baby. (Karlekar, 1998)

Forced Prostitution or other kinds of commercial exploitation by male husband or parents is another kind of violence against women reported worldwide. Women are tricked or forced by their husbands and relatives for money for prostitution. According to Heise's research the following factors are responsible for increasing the domestic violence in present society.

Cultural:

i. Gender-specific socialisation

ii. Cultural definitions of appropriate sex roles

iii. Expectations of roles within relationships
iv. Belief in the inherent superiority of males
v. Values that give men proprietary rights over women and girls
vi. Notion of the family as the private sphere and under male control
vii. Customs of marriage (bride price/dowry)
viii. Acceptability of violence as a means to resolve conflict

Economic:

i. Women's economic dependence on men
ii. Limited access to cash and credit
iii. Discriminatory laws regarding inheritance, property rights
iv. Communal lands, and maintenance after divorce or widowhood
v. Limited access to employment in formal and informal sectors
vi. Limited access to education and training for women

Legal:

i. Lesser legal status of women either by written law and/or by practice
ii. Laws regarding divorce, child custody, maintenance and inheritance
iii. Legal definitions of rape and domestic abuse
iv. Low levels of legal literacy among women
v. Insensitive treatment of women and girls by police and udiciary

Political:

i. Under-representation of women in power, politics, the media and in the legal and medical professions
ii. Domestic violence not taken seriously
iii. Notions of family being private and beyond control of the state
iv. Risk of challenge to status quo/religious laws
v. Limited organisation of women as a political force
vi. Limited participation of women in organised political system.

(Ellsberg and Gottmoellar, 1999).

Cause and Effects: Lack of education and awareness are the most common reasons for violence against women. Children who are subjected to abuse are likely to behave similarly as adults. Socio-economic status, substance and alcohol abuse also leads to violence against women in India.

Awareness:

1. These situations should change. Awareness among the neighbourhood is a must. As a responsible citisen, we must keep our eyes/ears open to help people who are in distress or who are in realm of such domestic violence. Any righteousness war can be rageded against this issue.
2. Teach the girl children from the beginning about their rights and equality from the childhood.
3. Take the help of any agency/Government for the domestic violence victims
4. Media and TV should conduct programmes regarding this biggest social issue. Also the serials produced with lots of negative characters should be banned by the government. Seek out support. You don't have to suffer alone. Inform people close to you (family friends, and neighbours) about your situation so they are prepared to react to suspected violence.
5. Try to start an individual savings account as an economic safety net. Have statements sent to a trusted relative or friend.
6. Talk to your children about what they should do if a violent incident occurs.
7. Teach children the address of your house, relevant emergency phone numbers, and the name of their grandparents in case of an emergency.
8. Call for police, medical attention, get legal help and counseling for yourself and your children. Use good judgment of relationship structure in the household and/or the community you live in before confiding in your in-laws or his friends for help.

Remedies for Domestic Violence

What exactly do we want?

A very important question in wake of domestic violence remedies is that what exactly we are looking for in the process of minimising their occurrences. Is it so that we want to gather more information about such cases for just expressing our concern over this issue with more accuracy, having facts and figures at hand? Or instead of just raising our voices, we want to clean up the mess with shear force and determination?

Role of Non-Governmental Organisations (NGOs)

The role of non-governmental organisations in controlling the domestic violence and curbing its worse consequences is crucial. NGOs continue to spread awareness amongst people regarding the legal rights they have in hand for fighting against the atrocities they are subjected to. They are encouraging more and more people to report any case of domestic violence so that proper action may be taken against the culprits.

Police and Health Care

Police plays a major role in tackling the domestic violence cases. They need to be sensitised to treat domestic violence cases as seriously as any other crime. Special training to handle domestic violence cases should be imparted to police force. They should be provided with information regarding support network of judiciary, government agencies/departments. Gender training should be made mandatory in the trainings of the police officers. There should be a separate wing of police dealing with women's issues, attached to all police stations and should be excluded from any other duty. Authorities should take steps to recognise Domestic Violence as a public health issue. A crisis support cell needs to be established in all major Government and Private Hospitals with a trained medical social worker to provide appropriate services. Training programmes must be organised for health professionals in order to develop their skills to provide basic support for abused people.

Documentation on the prevalence and the health consequences of domestic violence should be undertaken by the concerned government departments, health care institutions, NGOs and counseling centers. A nodal agency should also be set up for the annual consolidation of the documented work and publish the same for wider publicity among the masses for increasing Awareness. (Ahuja, 1987)

Conclusion

It is clear that violence against women is endemic in India. The reason is women in the country are highly vulnerable because of poor quality of life indicated by rampant poverty, lack of education, high under five mortality, poor health status, high fertility rate and high maternal mortality rate. Also contributing to the violence against women is societal mindset about women that has not changed much. Violence is perpetrated on women both inside and outside her home. The government and voluntary organisations are making efforts towards ending orminimising violence against women. The efforts of the government are in the shape of enacting relevant legislations, issuing orders and launching various women welfare schemes. But their implementation remains tardy, as the lower level government functionaries are not gender sensitive. On the other hand the voluntary organisations are taking both preventive as well as reactionary measures. But efforts of the voluntary organisations suffer from paucity of funds and infrastructure. Education of the girl child is the first step towards a better society with fewer incidents of violence. Campaigns aimed at men and boys to increase awareness and change attitudes about gender inequality are also effective tools. As individuals and responsible citisens, we need to spread awareness and report any act of violence against women around us.

Suggestions: (i) Special women police stations staffed with multi disciplinary female teams equipped to respond to the different needs of victim, have been set up in several countries, are an attempt to make police stations accessible for women. (ii) The judiciary must become more gender sensitive. (iii) Curriculum that teaches non-violence, human rights and gender issues should be included in elementary and secondary school, universities, colleges and other training institutes. Teaching about women contributors in history class, promoting girl participants in sports are some important steps in promoting gender equality. (iv). The judiciary must strongly reinforce the message that violence against women is a serious crime and the abuser will be held accountable (v) The police must be well positioned to provide assistance to victims. (vi) NGO's like women organisations which work in partnership with government must be promoted because they provide education and awareness programmes. The range of their services must be strengthened. (vii) Strategies must be formed at pre-complaint and complaint level.

Reference

- Ahuja, Ram (1987), Crime against Women, Rawat Publications, Jaipur
- http://www.youthkiawaaz.com/2010/02/domestic-violence-in-india-causesconsequences-and-remedies-2/
- Karlekar M (1998), Domestic Violence, Economic and Political Weekly, 33(27), 1741-1751
- Sheela Saravanan (2000), Violence against Women in India, Institute of Social Studies Trust, 1-7, 53-64.
- Heise, L., Ellsberg, M and Gottemoeller, M. (1999).*Ending Violence against Women.* Population Reports, Series L, No. 11. Baltimore, John Hopkins University School of Public Health, Population Information Program, December.

5

The Link between Gender Abuse and Women's Involvement in Illegal Activities

Rashmee Yadav, Jaya Singh, Sneh Lata Singh

Dr Mithilesh Verma Dr Neelma Kunwar (HOD)

Research Scholar, Department of Home Science

(Extension Education &Communication Management)

C. S. Azad Univ. of Agri. & Tech. Kanpur-208002

Abstract

In this study attempts to explain what happens to women who constitute a very vulnerable sub-group of the population when they experience violence. Being socially marginalised and in conflict with the law because of one's illegal activity leave women in potentially deadly situations. The conceptualisation developed here is an attempt to explain how the violence that the women in this sub-sample experience is unique because of: (a) the context that is occurs within; (b) the range of perpetrators; and (c) how the abuse for them is linked with illegal activity and arrest. It is, therefore, both an explanation of vulnerability to and consequence of abuse, as well as an explanation of a particular pathway to crime. The following discussion of recommendations emerges from this conceptualisation. It has been organised by category to facilitate dissemination of the findings and to encourage their serious consideration by various audiences and stakeholders in the field of violence against women. The understanding of violence against women can be broadened and deepened by focusing on the link between gender abuse and women's involvement in illegal activity – two of the most compelling problems facing contemporary criminologists. The groups of women who are most marginalised in society are vulnerable to both problems. A comprehensive response through public policy and programming can make a difference in reducing both violence against women and their growing involvement in criminal activity.

Keywords: Gender abuse, Involvement, Illegal Activities (Criminal Activities)

Introduction

The United Nations Declaration on the Elimination of Violence against Women defines violence against women as "any act of gender-based violence that results in, or is likely to result in, physical, sexual or psychological harm or suffering to women, including threats of such acts, coercion or arbitrary deprivation of liberty, whether occurring in public or in private life". This definition refers to the gender based roots of violence, recognising that "violence against women is one of the crucial social mechanisms by which women are forced into a subordinate position compared with men". It broadens the definition of violence by including both the physical and psychological harm done towards women and it includes acts in both private and public life. The declaration defines violence against women as encompassing, but not limited to; violence occurring in three areas—in the family, within the general community and violence perpetrated or condoned by the state.

Methodology

To complete the above objectives the research methodology employed and the study was conducted in Fatehgarh Jail (Farrukhabad) district during 2011-12, one jail was selected in this study. Thousand respondents were selected on the basis of dependent and independent variables namely age, caste, education, family income, occupation etc., were used. The collected data were subjected to statistical analysis for which statistical tools, percentage, weighted mean and correlation coefficient were used.

Result Discussion

Type of Family

Table 1. Distribution of Respondents according to Family Type

Family type	Frequency	Per cent
Nuclear	74	74.0
Joint	26	26.0
Total	**100**	**100.0**

Table 1; reveals that distribution of women respondents according to family type, majority of the respondents have nuclear family (74.0 per cent) whereas 26.0 per cent have joint family system. Now-a-days joint family system converted into nuclear system due to men and women equally engaged in work and generate the income.

Causes of Abetment of Suicide

Table 2; Distribution of Respondents according to the Causes of Abetment of Suicide

Causes of Abetment of Suicide	Yes	No	Mean score	Rank
Violence	22 (22.0)	78 (78.0)	1.22	I
Extra-marital affairs	19 (19.0)	81 (81.0)	1.19	II
Frustration	12 (12.0)	88 (88.0)	1.12	V
Loneliness	19 (19.)	81 (81.0)	1.19	II
Economic condition	14 (14.0)	86 (86.0)	1.14	IV

(Figures in parentheses denotes the percentage of respective value)

Table 2 shows that 22.0 per cent of respondents are involved in causes of violence given I rank with means score value of 1.22 followed by 19.0 per cent respondents are involved in causes of extra-marital affairs, loneliness hold II rank with mean score value of 1.19. While 14.0 per cent respondents were involved in economic condition hold IV rank with mean score value of 1.14 and only 12.0 per cent respondents were involved in frustration hold V rank with mean score value of 1.12.

Conclusion

"Violence against women is a manifestation of historically unequal power relations between men and women, which have led to domination over and discrimination against women by men and to the prevention of the full advancement of women…."

Suggestion

- Agencies that work with incarcerated women or women otherwise in conflict with the law must include attention to the various forms of violence, the women in this study reported. Re-entry and pre-release services, crime prevention and harm reduction programmes and probationary counseling must pay serious attention to the ways that violence influences women's choices and decisions.

- To ignore violence against women who are arrested, detained, sentenced and ultimately released back to their neighbourhoods seriously limits programmes effectiveness and may contribute to the revolving door between correctional facilities and some communities in this country.
- A third recommendation for direct service programmes is to develop interventions that are not only culturally specific, but to offer approaches that look specifically at the community context within which women live.

References

- Raj, A. and Silverman, J. (2002). Violence against immigrant women. *Violence Against Women,* 8 : 367-398.
- Jordan, Carol E. (2011). The university of Kentucky Center for Research on Violence against women. Science Inspired by Women's Stories. *Violence Against Women,* 17(9) : 1137-1158.
- Karlsson, Minn Salminen (2005). Turning women from criminals into victims discussions on abortion in the Catholic Church of Sweden. *European Journal of "Women's Studies,* 12(2) : 187-200.
- Chernoff, Nina W. and Simon, Rita J. (2011). Women and crime the world over. *Journal of Gender Issues,* 28.

6

Gender Equity in Education

Anup Kumar

Ph.D. Research Scholar, Himgiri Zee University Dehradun, Uttarakhand

Dr Anoj Raj

Associate Professor & Head Himgiri Zee University, Dehradun

Abstract

Gender equity in education refers to boys and girls experiencing the same advantages or disadvantages in attending school. Boys and girls should receive equal treatment and should not be discriminated on the basis of gender. Education is considered as one the most effective instrument for achieving gender equity and sustainable development. The key for the future of any country and any educational institution is the capability to develop, retain and attract the best talent. Boys and girls are equally talented and must be treated equally particularly in Education. The present study is seriously focusing on the equal participation of girls and boys in various aspects of society particularly in educational system. Gender is the most pervasive form of inequality, as it operates across all classes, castes and communities. According to the census of India, (2011) there are 914 girls for every 1000 boys in the 0-6 age group in India. In rural areas it is 919 girls for every 1000 boys, whereas 902 girls for every 1000 boys in urban areas. This ratio should be above 950. Female literacy rate in India is lower than the male literacy rate. Many families, especially in rural areas believe that having a male child is better than having a baby girl. So the male child gets all the benefits. Today, the female literacy levels according to the Literacy Rate 2011 census are 65.46 per cent where the male literacy rate is over 80 per cent. The numbers of girls' children who do not get education especially in the rural areas are still high. Gender-based discrimination in education is both a cause and a consequence of deep-rooted disparities in society. Poverty, geographical isolation, ethnic background, disability; traditional attitudes about their status and role all undermine the ability of women and girls to exercise their rights. Hopefully Education will be a gateway to achieve Gender equity.

Keywords: Education, Gender, Equity, Inequity, Girls Education, Literacy, Enrolment.

Introduction

Ancient Education System in India is also to be understood as being ultimately the outcome of the Indian theory of knowledge as part of the corresponding scheme of life and values. The system takes full account of the fact that Life includes Death and this forms the eternal truth. This gives a particular angle of vision, a sense of perspective and proportion in which the material and the moral, the physical and spiritual, the perishable and permanent interests and values of life are clearly defined and strictly differentiated. Education must aid in this self-fulfillment, and not in the acquisition of mere objective knowledge. According to the ancient Indian theory of education, the training of the mind and the process of thinking, are essential for the acquisition of knowledge.

"Education is unearthing the absolute humanity, manipulating every individual's intense openings, bonding between individual and society, interconnecting amidst people and nature, diminishing inequality between the literate and illiterate, harmonising one's inner self with what is functional, expanding and cultivating knowledge-based imagination and beauty consciousness, prosperity, and totality in life through application of knowledge". —— Rabindranath Tagore.

"Education, in its broadest sense, is the means of social continuity of life." Dewey opines having men and women in to consideration.

Girls' education is essential to the achievement of quality learning relevant to the twenty first century, including girls' transition to and performance in secondary school and beyond. Adolescent girls that attend school delay marriage and childbearing are less vulnerable to disease and acquire information and skills that lead to increased earning power. "A woman's education must be planned in relation to man" ——Rousseau

It has rightly been said "Educate a man and you educate an individual Educate a woman and you educate a family".

In general meaning we can accept that education deals with formation of habits of human beings, if so we need an education seriously focusing on promoting the equal participation of women and men in making decisions; reducing enrollment gap between women's and men's access; giving equality in learning process, educational outcomes and external results; and providing equal benefits for both sexes.

———Elmas Sahin, 2010

The present study is seriously focusing on the equal participation of girls and boys in various aspects of society particularly in educational system.

Problem Entitled

"Gender Equity in Education"

Review of Releated Litereture

- Madhumita, Bandyopadhyay and Ramya, Subrahmania (2008) provide an account of gender equity in schooling in India, with a particular emphasis on educational access. It aims to highlight educational access issues affecting both girls and boys in India and the types of initiatives needed to secure meaningful and sustainable access for all. Female enrolment has increased rapidly since the 1990s; there is still a substantial gap in upper primary and secondary schooling. Increased female enrolment is, however, compromised by persistently high rates of drop-out and poor attendance of girls relative to boys. Girls also constitute a large proportion of out-of-school children. Gender inequalities interlock with other forms of social inequality, notably caste, ethnicity and religion, with girls from Scheduled Castes, Scheduled Tribes and Muslim minorities particularly, constituting the population of out-of-school and drop-out children. There are also considerable inter-state variations in gender parity. While the greatest surges in female enrolment have been achieved in the most educationally disadvantaged states such as Bihar and Rajasthan, these states still have a long way to go to catch up with the better performing states of Kerala, Tamil Nadu and Himachal Pradesh.
- Elmas Sahin (2010) focuses on how and why education is the key to gender equality, importance of gender equity in education system in order to create a better environment for girls under traditional pressures. It will also query whether a philosophy of education offering the same opportunities to young women and men, teaching the same things at the same time, in the same place, with the same methods, and under the same system or is necessary or not. Gender equity in education runs to failure for millions of girls and women under the heavy weight of circumstances throughout the world and needs supporters to take more active roles as early as possible in breaking down the traditional resistance against the education of girls.
- Times of India (2014) points out, Gender equality in India is worst in the world. When India's Human Development Index is adjusted for gender inequality, it becomes south Asia's worst performing country after Afghanistan. New numbers in the UNDP's Human Development Report 2013 show Pakistan, Nepal and Bangladesh, which are poorer than India and have lower HDIs, all do comparatively better than

India when it comes to gender equality. The new UNDP report ranks India 136th out of 186 countries, five ranks below post-war Iraq, on the HDI. The HDI is a composite indicator composed of three equally weighted measures for education, health and income.

Objective of the Study

- To study the gender equity in Education.
- To study some serious concerns in Indian educational system.
- To study girls education.

Methodology

The present study is an attempt to discuss the gender equity in Education. Secondary data has been taken in to consideration. It is a data study and descriptive in nature. Some books, Journals and e-contents related to gender equity and professional development programmes were studied to find out some serious concern in gender equity in education. Content collected from various resources reflects the objectives of the study.

Gender Equity in Education

Gender equity can be defined as boys and girls are mostly not separated into different schools and class rooms. Boys and girls have very similar levels of educational attainment and achievement. Gender equity in education refers to boys and girls experiencing the same advantages or disadvantages in attending school, the same approaches in terms of teaching methods, gender neutral curricula, and academic orientation, all of which aim to ensure equal learning achievement and subsequent life opportunities (UNESCO, 2003).

Limited participation of one gender group in educational planning and management may also lead to decisions that fail to promote the participation, retention, and learning acquisition of female (or male) students in the school system. Furthermore, even where gender balance in management positions is achieved, biases in favour of one gender group (due to cultural norms or practices) may persist. The issue of gender inequality in education is not restricted to girls' and boys' access, participation, or achievement, but also involves the question of gender-balanced roles and participation in decision-making, planning and management in the sector. Despite the feminissation of the teaching profession in many countries, fundamental inequalities remain within leadership positions (Hungi, 2010) particularly in planning and management of education systems. For example, research conducted by (**Smulders, 1998**) highlights aspects of organisational culture in education institutions and how gender bias generated from management practices are often incompatible with female responsibilities at the household level.

Gender-based discrimination in education is both a cause and a consequence of deep-rooted disparities in society. Poverty, geographical isolation, ethnic background, disability, traditional attitudes about their status and role all undermine the ability of women and girls to exercise their rights. Harmful practices such as early marriage and pregnancy, gender-based violence, and discriminatory education laws, policies, contents and practices still prevent millions of girls' form enrolling, completing and benefitting from education.

Gender must therefore be integrated at all levels of education, from early childhood to higher education, in formal and non-formal settings and from planning infrastructure to training teachers. When gender equity in formal or informal education is attached importance, the vital issues such as gaps, divisions and conflicts between sexes in society are reduced. Despite progress in recent years, girls continue to suffer severe disadvantage and exclusion in education systems throughout their lives. An estimated 31 million girls of primary school age and 34 million girls of lower secondary school age were not enrolled in school in 2011. Sub-Saharan Africa has the lowest proportion of countries with gender parity: only two out of 35 countries. Furthermore, many countries will still not have reached gender parity. On current trends, it is projected that 70 per cent of countries will have achieved parity in primary education, and 56 per cent of countries will have achieved parity in lower secondary education.

Education is widely recognised as the gateway to economic security and opportunity-particularly for girls and women.

Girls' education is both an intrinsic right and a critical lever to reaching other development objectives. Providing girls with an education helps break the cycle of poverty. An educated women are less likely to marry early and against their will; less likely to die in childbirth; more likely to have healthy babies; and are more likely to send their children to school. When all children have access to a quality education rooted in human rights and gender equality, it creates a ripple effect of opportunity that influences generations to come. (UNICEF, 2014)

Gender equality is achieved when women and men enjoy the same rights and opportunities across all sectors of society, including economic participation and decision-making, and when the different behaviours, aspirations and needs of women and men are equally valued and favoured. Muslim countries worldwide have problems with gender equality. They dominate the bottom 10 countries in the Global Gender Gap Report, and none of the 10 most successful countries offering equal opportunities for men and women is Muslim. Girls lag behind boys in school attendance, making up 54 per cent of the out-of-school child population in the Arab states, a figure that has not changed since 2000. Of the 10 countries that fare the worst for child school attendance rates, seven are Muslim. These are Nigeria, Pakistan, Ethiopia, Cote d'Ivoire, Burkina Faso, Niger and Yemen—-countries that are often considered hot spots for acts of violence against women and schoolgirls. (Straits Times, 2014)

Gender inequalities, and its social causes, impact India's sex ratio, women's health over their lifetimes, their educational attainment, and economic conditions. Gender inequality in India is a multifaceted issue that concerns men and women alike. Some argue that some gender equality measures, place men at a disadvantage. However, when India's population is examined as a whole, women are at a disadvantage in several important ways.

Gender is the most pervasive form of inequality, as it operates across all classes, castes and communities. Yet, while gender equality has been a key objective of education policy in India for over three decades, it has lacked critical edge in implementation. In real terms, the dropout rates of girls, especially from the marginalised sections of society and the rural areas continues to be grim–9 out of every 10 girls ever enrolled in school do not complete schooling. (NCERT 2006). The 2011 Census in India revealed that there are 914 girls for every 1000 boys in the 0-6 age group in India. In rural areas it is 919 girls for every 1000 boys whereas 902 girls for every 1000 boys in urban areas, highlighting the imbalance in child-sex ratios. Ideally, this ratio should be above 950. This imbalance is a result of the practice of gender biased sex selection—-a manifestation of deep seated patriarchal mindsets leading to the preference for sons over daughters; aided by technological misuse. Some of the consequences of an imbalanced child sex ratio are an increase in violence against women and girls, trafficking for marriage and restrictions on mobility and choices of young girls. Another manifestation of patriarchy and discrimination is the high prevalence of child marriage, with almost one in two girls married before the age of 18 i.e., 43 per cent of women aged 20-24. Child marriage has a tremendous impact on the health, education and well-being of a girl. By 2015, India is expected to achieve the target on gender parity in education; however, the targets on women's economic empowerment and representation in National Parliament will not be met. In shaping the post 2015 development agenda, the attention of the world is focused on India and the role of the Government in promoting gender equality and women's empowerment focused on women's security, voice and empowerment. (U.N. India). It is essential to create continuing education opportunities which link literacy and education to self-development and skill based training, leading to greater bargaining power and self-esteem——-particularly for girls. Such programmes will act as a bridge between the children and adults, creating a positive environment for education and an instrument for social change. The foremost factor limiting female education is poverty. Economics plays a key role when it comes to coping with direct costs such as tuition fees, cost of textbooks, uniforms, transportation and other expenses. Wherever, especially in families with many children, these costs exceed the income of the family, girls are the first to be denied schooling. (Gaeta Sharma 2010) correctly points out that in the rural areas the girl child is made to perform household and agricultural chores. This is one of the many factors limiting girls' education.

Cleaning the house, preparing the food, looking after their siblings, the elderly and the sick, grazing the cattle and collecting firewood are some of the key tasks they have to perform.

Education can play an important role in redefining gender norms in India. Around the world, there have been numerous excellent examples of education changing people's way of viewing the world and leading to new forms of behaviour. Female education has long been acknowledged to have strong correlations with other dimensions of human and social development. Education has the power to transform people's lives. Promoting equality and encouraging diversity is core business for education.

Gender parity in educational attainment has been achieved by most of the countries, but further action is needed in many developing countries like India, to improve enrolment and retention of girls in primary education. Furthermore, women remain severely under-represented in key, growth-enhancing fields of education such as science, technology and engineering. Suddhasil Siddhanta (2004) says that the gender gap in education is not only significant but also have definite spatial pattern. Such pattern highlights a sad picture of entitlement failure for females, a phenomenon that provokes a deep question about the significance or depth of our development activity.

Society needs to understand that educating a female is as important and crucial as educating a male. There is no difference between man and woman when it comes to education. Each individual should encourage men to support women in this regard.

Data Analysis

Table No-1. Child Sex Ratio (0-6 yrs) in India

India/States/Union Territory#	Total	Rural	Urban
India	914	919	902
Jammu & Kashmir	859	860	854
Himachal Pradesh	906	909	878
Punjab	846	843	851
Chandigarh #	867	862	867
Uttarakhand	886	894	864
Haryana	830	831	829
NCT of Delhi #	866	809	868
Rajasthan	883	886	869
Uttar Pradesh	899	904	879
Bihar	933	935	906

Sikkim	944	952	917
Arunachal Pradesh	960	964	944
Nagaland	944	932	979
Manipur	934	929	945
Mizoram	971	966	978
Tripura	953	955	945
Meghalaya	970	972	957
Assam	957	957	955
West Bengal	950	952	943
Jharkhand	943	952	904
Orissa	934	939	909
Chhattisgarh	964	972	932
Madhya Pradesh	912	917	895
Gujarat	886	906	852
Daman & Diu #	909	925	903
Dadra & Nagar Haveli #	924	961	878
Maharashtra	883	880	888
Andhra pradesh	943	942	946
Karnataka	943	945	941
Goa	920	924	917
Lakshadweep #	908	888	915
Kerala	959	960	958
Tamil nadu	946	937	957
Puducherry #	965	957	969
A & N Islands #	966	975	947
Source: Census of India, 201			

Table-1 revealed that there are 914 girls for every 1000 boys in the 0-6 age group in India. In rural areas it is 919 girls for every 1000 boys, whereas 902 girls for every 1000 boys in urban areas. This ratio should be above 950.

Table No-2. Literacy Rates in India

State	*Litreracy*	*Male*	*Female*	*%change*
India	74.04	82.14	65.45	8.66
Kerala	94	96.11	100.76	3.14
Lakshadwep	91.85	95.56	82.69	5.19
Mizoram	91.33	93.35	86.72	2.53
Goa	88.7	92.65	82.16	6.69
Tripura	87.22	91.53	78.98	14.03
Daman and due	87.1	91.54	46.35	8.92
Andaman	86.63	90.27	71.08	5.33
Delhi	86.21	90.94	68.85	4.54
Chandigarah	86.05	89.99	64.81	4.11
Pudcherry	85.82	91.26	84.05	4.61
Himachal	82.8	89.53	73.51	6.32
Maharashtra	82.34	88.38	69.87	5.46
Sikkim	81.42	86.55	66.39	12.61
Tamil Nadu	80.09	86.77	73.14	6.64
Nagaland	79.55	82.75	70.01	12.96
Manipur	79.21	86.06	71.73	8.68
Uttarakhand	78.82	87.4	67.06	7.2
Gujrat	78.03	85.75	63.31	8.89
West Bengal	76.26	81.69	66.57	7.62
Dadara and Nagar Haweli	76.24	85.17	47.67	18.61
Punjab	75.84	80.44	62.52	6.19
Harayana	75.55	84.06	56.91	7.64
Karnatka	75.36	82.47	66.01	8.72
Meghalya	74.43	75.95	71.80	11.87
Orrisa	72.87	81.59	62.46	9.79
Assam	72.19	77.85	63	8.94
Chattisgarah	70.28	80.27	59.58	5.62
Madhaya Paradesh	69.32	78.73	54.49	5.58
Uttar Padesh	67.68	77.28	51.36	11.41
Jammu and Kashmir	67.16	76.75	49.12	11.64
Andhra Pradesh	67.02	74.88	58.68	6.55
Jharkhand	66.41	76.84	52.04	12.85
Rajasthan	66.11	79.19	47.76	5.7
Arunachal Pradesh	65.38	72.55	53.52	11.04
Bihar	61.8	71.2	46.4	14.8

Source: *Census of India, 2011*

Table-2 clearly highlights, female literacy rate in India; it is lower than the male literacy rate. Female literacy levels are 65.46 per cent where the male literacy rate is over 80 per cent. Here are some facts about different states literacy rate, Kerala is the only state in India to have 100 per cent literacy rate. It is followed by Goa, Tripura, Mizoram, Himachal Pradesh, and Maharashtra, Sikkim. The lowest literacy rate in India is seen in the state of Bihar.

Table No-3. Percentage of Boys and Girls Enrolment in Primary Classes Classes 1st to Vth

States	Boys	Girls
Andhra Pradesh (AP)	51.5	48.5
Arunachal Pradesh	51.04	48.96
Assam (AS)	50.34	49.66
Bihar (BR)	50.53	49.97
Chhattisgarh (CG)	51.03	48,97
Goa (GA)	52.02	47.98
Gujarat (GJ)	53.35	46.65
Haryana (HR)	54.29	45.71
Himachal Pradesh (HP)	52.41	47.59
Jammu and Kashmir (JK)	52.34	47.66
Jharkhand (JH)	51.01	48.99
Karnataka (KA)	51.62	48.38
Kerala (KL)	51.23	48.77
Madhya Pradesh (MP)	52.26	47.74
Maharashtra (MH)	52.95	47.05
Manipur (MN)	50.13	49.87
Meghalaya (ML)	49.92	50.08
Mizoram (MZ)	51.7	48.3
Nagaland (NL)	50.91	49.09
Odisha(OR)	51.71	48.29
Punjab (PB)	54.85	45.15
Rajasthan (RJ)	53.41	53.41
Sikkim (SK)	52.26	52.26
Tamil Nadu (TN)	51.35	48.65
Tripura (TR)	50.98	48.02
Uttar Pradesh (UP)	51.41	48.59
Uttarakhand (UK)	52.7	47.3
West Bengal (WB)	50.82	50.8

Source: *DISE Data 20013-14*

Table-3 indicates the enrolment of boys and girls in all over India. Boys' enrolment is almost more then 50 per cent.Whereas girls' enrolment is under 50 per cent. Girls enrolment in primary classes is not satisfactory. Punjab is the lowest in girls' enrolment which is 45.15 per cent followed by Haryana by 45.71 per cent. Rajasthan is the highest in girls' enrolment.

Findings of the Study

- It was revealed from the study that there are 914 girls for every 1000 boys in the 0-6 age group in India. In rural areas it is 919 girls for every 1000 boys, whereas 902 girls for every 1000 boys in urban areas. This ratio should be above 950.
- Study highlights, female literacy rate in India; it is lower than the male literacy rate. Female literacy levels are 65.46 per cent where the male literacy rate is over 80 per cent. Here are some facts about different states literacy rate, Kerala is the only state in India to have 100 per cent literacy rate. It is followed by Goa, Tripura, Mizoram, Himachal Pradesh, and Maharashtra, Sikkim. The lowest literacy rate in India is seen in the state of Bihar.
- The enrolment of boys and girls in all over India. Boys' enrolment is almost more then 50 per cent. Whereas girls' enrolment is under 50 per cent. Girls enrolment in primary classes is not satisfactory. Punjab is the lowest in girls' enrolment which is 45.15 per cent followed by Haryana by 45.71 per cent. It shows the gender inequity in enrolment.

Conclusion

Girls' education is essential to the achievement of quality in learning which is very relevant to the twenty-first century. Gender is the most pervasive form of inequality, as it operates across all classes, castes and communities. Literacy is the main foundation for social and economic growth. There are 914 girls for every 1000 boys in the 0-6 age group in India. In rural areas, it is 919 girls for every 1000 boys, whereas 902 girls for every 1000 boys in urban areas. This ratio should be above 950. Female literacy rate in India is lower than the male literacy rate. Many families, especially in rural areas believe that having a male child is better than having a baby girl. So the male child gets all the benefits. Today, the female literacy levels according to the Literacy Rate 2011 census are 65.46 per cent where the male literacy rate is over 80 per cent. The numbers of girls' children who do not get education especially in the rural areas are still high. Gender-based discrimination in education is both a cause and a consequence of deep-rooted disparities in society. Poverty, geographical isolation, ethnic background, disability; traditional attitudes about their status and role all undermine the ability of women and girls to exercise their rights. Harmful practices such as early marriage and pregnancy, gender-based violence, and discriminatory education laws, policies, contents and practices still prevent millions of girls' form enrolling, completing and benefitting from education. Yet, while gender equity has been a key objective of education policy in India for over three decades, but there is a need to serious implementation. Only Education can become a gateway of Gender Equity.

References

- Bandyopadhyay, M., & Subrahmanian, R. (2008). *Gender Equity in Education:A Review of Trends and Factors.* National University of Educational Planning and Administration.
- Hungi, N. (2011). *Is there gender equity in school managerial positions?* Paris: UNESCO.
- NCERT. (2006). *Gender Issues in Education* (1st Edition ed.). New Delhi.
- Smulders, A. (1998). *Creating space for women Gender-linked factors in managing staff in higher education institutions.* Paris : UNESCO.
- Siddhanta, S., & D. N. (2004). Disaggregated Pattern of Gender Gap in Education in Indian Population: A Fresh Exploration.
- Sharma, G. (2010). Gender inequality in education and employment. New Delhi.
- Sahin, E. (2010). Gender Equity in Education.Çag University (Ed.)., (pp. 216-220).

Websites

- http://www.ncert.nic.in/rightside/links/pdf/focus_group/gender_issues_in_education.pdf
- http://www.in.one.un.org/task-teams/gender-equality-and-empowerment
- http://timesofindia.indiatimes.com/india/Gender-equality-in-India-among-worst-in-world-UN/articleshow/18982029.cms
- http://unesdoc.unesco.org/images/0011/001119/111905eo.pdf
- http://www.unicef.org/education/bege_70640.html
- http://www.straitstimes.com/the-big-story/asia-report/pakistan/story/education-gender-equity-20141014
- censusindia.gov.in/vital_statistics/Vital_Rates/Vital_rates.aspx http://www.dise.in/

7

Gender Based Violence (GBV): Types, Levels, Causes and its Measures

Ms Ishrat Naaz
Research Scholar, PhD, Jamia Millia Islamia

Abstract

Gender-based violence occurs in all societies of the world, within the home or in the wider community and it affects women and girls disproportionately. Violence against women has been clearly defined as a form of discrimination in numerous documents. The World Human Rights Conference in Vienna, first recognised gender-based violence as a human rights violation in 1993. In the same year, United Nations declaration, 1993, defined violence against women as "any act of gender-based violence that results in, or is likely to result in, physical, sexual or psychological harm or suffering to a woman, including threats of such acts, coercion or arbitrary deprivations of liberty, whether occurring in public or private life". This paper attempts to discuss the concept and different levels/stages of gender based violence that occur globally. Usually gender based violence happens in three contexts—-the family, the community and the state and at each point key social institutions fulfil critical and interactive functions in defining legitimating and maintaining the violence. The paper also tries to discuss different types of gender-based violence like ***Pre-natal sex selection, child and forced marriage, honour killing, dowry deaths, domestic abuse,*** rape, commercial sexual exploitation, domestic violence, and female genital mutilation. The chapter also explores the different causes of gender-based violence especially on the females which are deeply rooted in the way society like cultural beliefs, power relations, economic power imbalances, and the masculine idea of male dominance. In the end the chapter attempts to explore different measures to combat Gender based Violence.

Keywords: *Causes, Gender Based Violence, Levels, Measures and Types*

Introduction

Gender Based Violence (GBV) is a phenomenon of epidemic proportions prevalent in many families, communities, societies and cultures across the globe. Many women and girls, and to a lesser degree men and boys, either directly experience or face the consequences of some form of gender based violence in their lifetime. Around the world, as many as one in every three women has been beaten, coerced into sex, or abused in some other way, most often by someone she knows, including by her husband or another male family member; one woman in four has been abused during pregnancy.

"Violence against women both violates and impairs or nullifies the enjoyment by women of their human rights and fundamental freedoms... In all societies, to a greater or lesser degree, women and girls are subjected to physical, sexual and psychological abuse that cuts across lines of income, class and culture". ——Beijing Declaration and Platform for Action, paragraph 112.

Gender-based violence both reflects and reinforces inequities between men and women and compromises the health, dignity, security and autonomy of its victims. It encompasses a wide range of human rights violations, including sexual abuse of children, rape, domestic violence, sexual assault and harassment, trafficking of women and girls and several harmful traditional practices. Any one of these abuses can leave deep psychological scars, damage the health of women and girls in general, including their reproductive and sexual health, and in some instances, results in death.

Violence against women has been called "the most pervasive yet least recognised human rights abuse in the world". Accordingly, the Vienna Human Rights Conference and the Fourth World Conference on Women gave priority to this issue, which jeopardises women's lives, bodies, psychological integrity and freedom. Violence may have profound effects – direct and indirect – on a woman's reproductive health, including:

- Unwanted pregnancies and restricted access to family planning information and contraceptives.
- Unsafe abortion or injuries sustained during a legal abortion after an unwanted pregnancy.
- Complications from frequent, high-risk pregnancies and lack of follow-up care.
- Sexually transmitted infections, including HIV.
- Persistent gynaecological problems.
- Psychological problems.

Studies from India suggest a relatively high prevalence of GBV and estimates vary widely, from 18 per cent to 70 per cent of women, reflecting in part a wide variety of methodologies to document such violence. Although the issue has been highlighted in India with the Protection of Women from

Domestic Violence Act in 2005, GBV remains under-reported.

Concept of Gender-Based Violence

Women are vulnerable to violence at all stages of life. They are threatened by female infanticide, incest, child prostitution, rape, partner violence, psychological abuse, sexual harassment and harmful traditional practices such as forced marriage. In 1993, the UN Declaration on the Elimination of Violence against Women offered the first official definition of gender based violence,

Article 1: Any act of gender-based violence that results in, or is likely to result in, physical, sexual or psychological harm or suffering to women, including threats of such acts, coercion or arbitrary deprivations of liberty, whether occurring in public or in private life (Population Reference Bureau, 2001 pg. 3).

Article 2: Article 2 of the Declaration states that the definition should encompass, but not be limited to, acts of physical, sexual, and psychological violence in the family, community, or perpetrated or condoned by the State, wherever it occurs. These acts include: spousal battering; sexual abuse, including of female children; dowry-related violence; rape, including marital rape; female genital mutilation/cutting and other traditional practices harmful to women; non-spousal violence; sexual violence related to exploitation; sexual harassment and intimidation at work, in school and elsewhere; trafficking in women; forced prostitution and arbitrary deprivation of liberty whether occurring in public or private life.

The 1995 Beijing Platform for Action expanded on this definition, specifying that it includes: violations of the rights of women in situations of armed conflict, including systematic rape, sexual slavery and forced pregnancy; forced sterilisation, forced abortion, coerced or forced use of contraceptives; prenatal sex selection and female infanticide. It further recognised the particular vulnerabilities of women belonging to minorities: the elderly and the displaced; indigenous, refugee and migrant communities; women living in impoverished rural or remote areas, or in detention.

Levels/Stages of Gender-Based Violence

Radhika Coomaraswamy (1992) points out that women are vulnerable to various forms of violent treatment for several reasons, all based on gender.

1) Because of being female, a woman is subject to rape, female circumcision/genital mutilation, female infanticide and sex related crimes. This reason relates to society's construction of female sexuality and its role in social hierarchy.

2) Because of her relationship to a man, a woman is vulnerable to domestic violence, dowry murder, *sati.* This reason relates to society's

concept of a woman as a property and dependent of the male protector, father, husband, son, etc.

3) Because of the social group to which she belongs, in times of war, riots. Or ethnic, caste, or class violence, a woman may be raped and brutalised as a means of humiliating the community to which she belongs. This also relates to male perception of female sexuality and women as the property of men.

Combining these types of abuse with the concept of hierarchical gender relations, a useful way to view gender violence is by identifying where the violence towards women occurs. Essentially, violence happens in three contexts:

1. The family/Home;
2. The community; and
3. The state.

At each point key social institutions fulfil critical and interactive functions in defining legitimating and maintaining the violence.

Violence within the Home/Family

Domestic violence is the most prevalent form of gender-based violence. It typically occurs when a man beats his female partner. Psychological abuse always accompanies physical abuse and majority of women abused by their partners are abused many times. Physical, sexual and psychological violence against women within a couple and in the family consists of sexual abuse, female genital mutilation and other traditional practices harmful to women and girls, marital rape, dowry-related violence, incest, non-spousal violence like a son's violence against his mother and violence related to exploitation and deprivation of freedom. Population Reference Bureau, (2000) reported Murray and Richard's findings of 1986 that in the United States, more than a million and half women are beaten by their partners each year. It also reported that in the 1995 Egypt Demographic and Health survey, 35 per cent of women were reported being beaten by their husbands during marriage. In spite of these available data on gender-based violence, there is no accurate information on gender-based violence in some countries. A culture of silence surrounds cases of violence against women in most countries, making it difficult to get a true picture of its extent. Some of the reasons why it is difficult to get an accurate account are that most of the gender-based violence occurs in the private sphere – within families, inside homes, and out of sight.

Violence against Women within the General Community

Physical, sexual and psychological violence occurring within the general community include rape, sexual assault, sexual harassment and intimidation in school or work, forced treatments and abusive medication, the exploitation and commercialisation of women's bodies which is related to increased poverty that is mainly a result of unbridled economic liberalism. These types of violence occurring within the general community also include contraception imposed on women by constraints or force, forced sterilisation or abortions, selective abortion of female foetuses and female infanticide (World March of Women, 2000).

Violence against Women Perpetrated by the State

Physical, sexual and psychological violence are too often perpetrated or tolerated by states that priorities custom or tradition over the respect of fundamental freedom. In some countries, the rise of religious fundamentalism is extremely disturbing as regards women's right to their economic autonomy and their freedom of choice. The social exclusion of women is so great that it constitutes a new form of apartheid. Women are considered second class beings, of lesser value, deprived of their fundamental rights. Violence against women is also exercised as a weapon of war in situations of armed conflict. It has many forms including murder, rape, sexual slavery, hostage taking and forced pregnancy (World March of Women, 2000). Coomaraswamy cited in Salami (2000), identified some additional violations of human rights and fundamental freedoms such as the trafficking in women and girls for sex trade, forced prostitution, rape, sexual abuse and sex tourism that have become the focus of internationally organised crimes.

Types of Gender-Base Violence

Despite numerous treaties, declarations and interventions from rights groups and NGOs, violence against women is still widespread and often goes unreported. One of the most common types of violence against women is performed by a husband or male partner, not an unknown assailant.

Few of the gender based violence have been discussed below.

Pre-natal Sex Selection

A moving report titled *Gender Violence in India* by Prajnya shows that violence against women is on the rise in India. The report finds that pre-natal sex selection practices have resulted in at least 10 million missing girls, since ultrasounds and other sex selection tests became available two decades ago-a striking example of modern technology facilitating age old prejudices.

Child and Forced Marriage

According to this report, South Asia has the highest rate of marriages involving girls under the age of eighteen. Girls and women are often forced into marriage for a variety of reasons. Some include bringing families together for business reasons. Others involve family honour.

Commercial Sexual Exploitation

In some developing countries of the world, most girls are made to prostitute under the guise of sex tourism. Sex tourism according to UNICEF Document happens when rich men travel during the holidays from the advanced countries of the world to places like Brazil, the Dominican Republic, and Thailand etc., to have sexual dealings with children of 13 or 15 years. According to Salami (2000), the Nepal Carpet Factories are common sites of sexual exploration by employers as well as recruitment centers for Indian Brothels. More than 50 per cent of the workers in the factories of Indian Brothels according to Salami are children. These types of violence against women do a lot of physical and psychological damage to the victims. They are exposed to series of health risks including respiratory diseases, sexually transmitted infections, unwanted pregnancies and drug addiction.

Rape

Forcing anyone into sexual intercourse against her will is rape. It is a violent, terrifying and humiliating assault. Rape is a pervasive form of gender-based violence. It has long symbolised in a man's ability to have his way with a woman. Most rapists are known by those they attack and they are often the victim's father, partner, neighbour or some other household figure. Rape is considered a crime against a person. In some societies, like India, the rape of a girl is thought to bring shame on her family. The family may consider marrying the girls to her rapist as the only way to recover her honour. In some cases, the girl is condemned to prostitution (Feming, 1999). Rape happens to all ages, educational levels, religions, sexual orientations and physical descriptions. Rape is an act of power, anger and dominance over another. In India, Madhya Pradesh has reported the highest number of rape cases (3,010) accounting for 14.5 per cent of total such cases reported in the country. Nearly 9.5 per cent (1,972) of the total victims of rape were girls under 15 years of age, while 15.2 per cent (3,152) were teenage girls (15-18 years). Nearly two-third was women in the age-group 18-30 years. Rapists were known to the victims in as many as 19,188 (92.5 per cent) cases in 2007. Neighbours figured as the most common of perpetrators: in 36 per cent of the cases a neighbour was involved. In politically unsettled lands, wartime rape and other forms of gender-based violence remain a constant threat. In these places, rape has been used as an instrument of war to humiliate the enemy.

Honour Killing

Honour killings or crime is committed in India (particularly in Haryana, Uttar Pradesh and Tamil Nadu) in order to salvage the "honour" of a clan, community or family that has somehow been "violated". Usually the violation occurs through the actions of a woman in the community choosing a husband, lover or boyfriend, against her family's wishes. Breach of caste rules also lead to violence.

Dowry Deaths

Dowry deaths occur when a woman is either murdered or driven to suicide because the family that she has married into demands a higher dowry (or money given by a woman's family to her husband and in-laws). Since 2006, there has been an increase of 6.2 per cent in dowry deaths in India. Nearly 25.7 per cent of total such cases reported in the country were reported from Uttar Pradesh (2,076) and Bihar followed next with 14.5 per cent (1,172).

Domestic Abuse

Indian women are equally vulnerable to domestic violence. A total of 75,930 cases were reported in the country in 2007 with an increase of 20.3 per cent over 2006 and 35.8 per cent over the average of the previous 5 years (2002-2006).

Female Genital Cutting or Female Genital Mutilation

Female Genital Cutting (FGC) is a traditional practice that involves cutting or altering the female genitalia as a rite of passage or for other socio-cultural reasons (Mohammed, Ali and Yinger; 1999). Female Genital Cutting according to Population Reference Bureau, (2000) is practiced in 28 African countries and in about 20 Middle Eastern and Asian nations. Mugenzi (1998) commented that FGC is an act of controlling women sexually. World Health Organisation (WHO) (1999), claimed that more than 130 million girls worldwide have undergone female genital cutting also known as female genital mutilation. According to Brady (2001), many women who undergo female genital cutting have serious health consequences which include shock, pain, infections, injury of the adjacent tissue and organs, urinary retention and tetanus. Long-term effects may include cysts and abscesses, urinary incontinence, psychological and sexual problems and difficulty during childbirth. Obstructed labour may occur if a woman is infibulated. All of these damage a girl's lifetime health.

Causes of Gender-Based Violence

The causes of gender-based violence are many and varied depending on the types of violence. Traditional attitudes towards women around the world help perpetuate the violence. Stereotypical roles in which women are seen as subordinate to men constrain a woman's ability to exercise choices that would enable her end the abuse.

Njenga (1999) who was the chairman of the Psychiatric Association in Kenya discussed with women in Kenya on reasons for the rise in gender-based violence. He opined that the causes are quite diverse. One of the causes is the space people live in. The more crowded people are, Njenga commented, the more domestic violence there is likely to be. Njenga (1999) concluded that poverty, which also determines where and how a person lives, is one of the contributing factors. Financial insecurity is another cause of gender-based violence. Njenga (1999:6) commented that if a man cannot establish his authority intellectually or economically, he would tend to do so physically. Another cause is the image created by the society which portrays a man to be viewed as being strong, educated, creative and clever while a woman is the opposite of all these traits. The way parents bring up their children, which create disparity between boys and girls, also is a source of gender-based violence in later life. When a boy grows up, knowing that he is not supposed to wash his own clothes, cook or help in the house, if he grows up and gets married to a woman who comes from a home where duties are equally shared between girls and boys, this can create tension that might lead to violence.

Another reason could be the perpetrator's belief that the victim deserves the violence because of his/her gender or is asking for it because s/he did not conform to social norms. For example, in India (2009), activists of a group that calls itself the *Sri Ram Sena,* entered a pub in Mangalore and beat up women there because they were drinking alcohol. The 'crime' committed by the women was that they were going against 'traditional Indian values' and the punishment they 'deserved' was the beating. Typically, the perpetrators of such acts believe they are teaching a lesson to the victim(s) and putting them in their place even though what the perpetrators are doing is against the law. This position of righteousness often comes from a deep-rooted anxiety to ensure that power equations are maintained in society — the dominant group continues to remain dominant and the oppressed continue to remain oppressed. In the view of the perpetrators, they are not doing anything wrong because the oppressed are 'naturally' inferior to them.

Sometimes, gender-based violence is used to 'teach a lesson' or 'dishonour' an entire community. Such acts are commonly committed during conflict situations like riots or wars. It is intended as a form of psychological warfare wherein the enemy believes in shaming the opposite camp by performing such acts. The idea is to 'emasculate' the men of the opposite camp because they failed to 'protect their women'. These notions are built on gender stereotyping — men must be protectors and women must be virtuous. For instance, there have been several cases in India in which upper caste men have raped Dalit women to 'degrade' the entire community and 'put them in their place'.

Saran (1999:19) gave another cause, which she regarded as a myth; she opined that a woman's dress and behaviour can cause rape. This myth according to her places the blame for rape on a woman and views men as unable to control themselves. She concluded that if a woman is known as a party animal or a tease and wears provocative clothing, she is asking for attention, flattery, or just trying to fit in. She is not asking to be raped.

Bitangaro (1999:9) had summarised the causes of violence against women as being deeply rooted in the way society is set up-cultural beliefs, power relations, economic power imbalances, and the masculine idea of male dominance.

Measures to Combat Gender Based Violence

It is vital that specific measures be taken to uphold the human rights of women and to address the gender-based violence to which they are subjected. The seriousness of the different forms of gender-based violence, given the magnitude of this violence and its consequences for individuals and society, makes it imperative that urgent initiatives be taken to support and protect victims, and to ensure that women are able to assert and exercise their rights as human beings and that society has instruments at its disposal to punish aggressors. It is equally vital that preventive strategies be designed and implemented at the political, legislative, legal and educational levels; the positive effects of such strategies will become evident over the medium and long term.

Effective measures to deal with this problem cannot be adopted without taking into account the dominant cultural model and the processes of symbolic reproduction that confer legitimacy on gender-based violence. Because the roots of the problem are structural, it is essential to implement public policies which will modify the mechanisms that lead to the perpetuation and propagation of gender-based violence and will engender an environment that is conducive to equality between men and women and respect for the dignity of human beings.

The origins of gender-based violence can be traced to a variety of socio-cultural factors, namely: hierarchical relationship between women and men; the differentiated socialisation of boys and girls; the political, economic and legal discrimination faced by women; the use of violent means to resolve interpersonal conflicts; and unequal symbolisations and valuations of women's and men's bodies and sexuality. As a consequence, it is vital to promote women's access to decision-making processes and to the exercise of power in its different dimensions, since strengthening their participation in these processes will surely contribute to the elimination of the violence women face and to an egalitarian distribution of the rights and responsibilities of all citisens, whether male or female.

The State should foster a national and regional discussion on the effects of discrimination against women, the violation of their rights as human beings and, in particular, the consequences for society of gender-based violence. Sensitisation to this issue and the creation of a greater awareness of it should be accompanied by the establishment of institutional mechanisms which provide for participation in the discussion, along with the governmental sector, of representatives of civil society and organisations that have developed agendas for action and have delved into the issue, as well as the entire spectrum of women's groups and sectors, whose participation should be channelled through the organisations they have formed. This discussion should encompass an analysis of the ideological and cultural aspects which result in continued violation of human rights, so as to contribute to a collective recognition of the unacceptability of violence, within both the family and the wider community, and to the creation of a social climate which rejects acts of violence.

Since formal education plays a vital role in handing down values and attitudes, a major effort should be made to ensure that boys and girls undergo the same type of socialisation in order to put an end to the perpetuation of violence from one generation to the next. The educational system should modify textbooks which foster rigid social and sexual roles and contribute to the existence of asymmetrical and hierarchical relationships within the family and society. School curricula should include topics related to human rights and, in the context of education for peace, students should be exposed to alternative methods of resolving personal and group conflicts which are based on negotiation and mediation instead of aggression and violence. In addition, teachers need to be trained so that they are able to detect incidents and situations of gender-based violence in the families of their students.

Governments must provide support to academic institutions in the form of scholarships and grants so that studies can be conducted on the incidence and prevalence of gender-based violence and research can be done on the ideological and cultural aspects which give rise to and perpetuate the phenomenon.

In view of the important role played by the media in the perpetuation of prevailing standards and values and the contribution they could make to raising the public's awareness and promoting changes in human relationships, the media should address the phenomenon of gender-based violence with the aim of acting as mechanisms of identification and education, by informing people about the magnitude of the problem, the forms it can take and the rights protecting women. In order to the media play a positive role in preventing and eliminating gender-based violence, Governments must promote communications policies which make it possible to denounce acts of discrimination against the female population and to co-ordinate public awareness campaigns that portray any act of aggression against women or violation of human rights as unacceptable and as a crime.

With regard to laws and regulations, it is essential to eliminate all forms of discrimination enshrined in different countries' civil, criminal and labour laws, as well as those manifested in legal practices and procedures. To this end, judges, lawyers, police officers and public-sector officials in general should, irrespective of their sex, be trained to recognisesexism and discrimination as part of the performance of their duties, to facilitate the reporting of crimes and to provide protection and assistance to victims.

Government bodies responsible for improving the status of women must work together and coordinate their activities with other institutions, including ministries, local governments and non-governmental organisations; they should also contribute to the creation of social support networks for the victims of gender-based violence, since the whole of society is responsible for eliminating such violence, and community participation is vital if the impunity of aggressors is to end. There is a strong connection between gender-based violence against women and a lack of equity in the economic, socio-cultural and political spheres; as a consequence, initiatives in this field must be of an integrated nature, should include complementary income-generation, housing and vocational training programmes for women, and should be accompanied by the adoption of policy measures concerning health, recreation and social and political participation.

Conclusion

Gender Based Violence (GBV) is a global public health concern that has only recently received significant research and policy attention. It is one of the most common forms of violence globally and includes physical, sexual, emotional, and economic violence. Studies from India suggest a relatively high prevalence of GBV and estimates vary widely, from 18 per cent to 70 per cent of women, reflecting in part a wide variety of methodologies to document such violence. Although the issue has been highlighted in India with the Protection of Women from Domestic Violence Act in 2005, GBV remains under-reported.

The World Health Organisation (WHO) estimates that at least one in every five of the world's female population has been physically or sexually abused at some time (Population Reference Bureau, 2001). Gender-based violence arises from the patriarchal system which since time immemorial has exerted control over women's lives (World March of Women, 2000). Gender-based violence affects both the physical and psychological integrity of women. However, subtle the violence may be in form, it has no less devastating effect. Gender-based violence can affect the female psychologically, cognitively and inter-personally.

The seriousness of the different forms of gender-based violence, given the magnitude of this violence and its consequences for individuals and society, makes it imperative that urgent initiatives be taken to support and protect victims, and to ensure that women are able to assert and exercise their rights as human beings and that society has instruments at its disposal to punish aggressors. It is equally vital that preventive strategies be designed and implemented at the political, legislative, legal and educational levels; the positive effects of such strategies will become evident over the medium and long term.

References

- Alder, Christine (1992), "Violence, gender and social change", *International Social Science Journal*, No. 132, Southampton, England, Blackwell Publishers/United Nations Educational, Scientific and Cultural Organisation (UNESCO).
- Bitangora, B. (1999). "Rape, the Silent Cancer among Female Refugees". In: Conveying Concerns; *Women Report on Gender-based Violence*. Washington: Population Reference Bureau, (2000) MEASURE Communication.
- Feming, A. (1999). "Rape-Are you at Risk?" in Conveying Concerns: *Women Report on Gender-based Violence*. Washington. Population Reference Bureau, (2000).
- Heise, L; Ellisoberg and Gottemoeller, R. (1999). "Ending Violence against Women" Population Reports Series (ii). Baltimore: John Hopkins University.
- Meziecbi, K. A. (1994). "Contemporary issues in social studies Education". In: *Social studies in Schools* (eds.) Joof, G.W. and Amadi, H.C. Onitsha: Outrite Publishers.
- Mohammed, A., Ali, N. and Yinger, N. (1999). "Female Genital Mutilation: Programmes to Date" What Works and What Doesn't. Geneva, World Health Organisation Press.
- Mugenzi, Joan (1998). "Killing Women's Sexuality" In: Conveying Concerns: *Women Report on Gender-based violence*. Washington. Population Reference Bureau, (2000) MEASURE communication.
- Njenga, F. (1999). "If your Husband is Abusive, Leave Him!" In: *Conveying Concerns: Women Report on Gender-based Violence*. Washington. Population Reference Bureau, (2000) MEASURE communication.
- Population Reference Bureau (2000). Washington Measure Communication. Gender violence in India
- Prajnya Report (2010). Gender Violence in India
- Salami, I.I. (2000). "The Girl-Child: Work and Health Hazards". *Journal of Women in Academics (I)*. Gender-based Violence and the Challenges for Social Studies Education.
- Saran, S. (1999). "Rape Are you at Risk?" In: Conveying Concerns: Women Report on Gender-based Violence. Washington. Population Reference Bureau, (2000) MEASURE communication.
- Vlachovd, M. Biason, L. (2005). *Women in an Insecure World: Violence against Women Facts, Figures and Analysis.* Geneva Centre for the

Democratic Control of Armed Forces (DCAF).

- The World March of Women Advocacy: Guide to Women's World Demands (2000).
- World Health Organisation (WHO). "Female Genital Mutilation: Programmes to Date. What works and What Doesn't". Geneva: World Health Organisation Press.
- "Women's Vision" (1998). "A Fight against the Knife". In Conveying Concerns: Women Report on Gender-base Violence. Washington. Population Reference Bureau, (2000) MEASURE communication.
- World Bank (1993), *World Development Report, 1993. Investing in Health*, New York, Oxford University Press.

8

Education as A Means to Eradicate Gender Based Violence

Shaheen Parveen

Research Scholar, Department of Education

H.N.B. Garhwal Central University Srinagar (Garhwal), Uttarakhand

"No human development goal can be achieved as long as women and girls continue to suffer from violence or live in fear of it"

— **Dr Babatunde Osotimehin**

God has created man and woman both are the same and have the right to enjoy the same opportunity woman have served as nurturers and care giver in society. They have been subjected to different forms of abuse.

Gender Based Violence (GBV)

Violence against woman is a persistent and universal problem occurring in every culture and social group. GBV is particularly disbursing phenomenon which exists in all regions of the world. The term refers to any harmful act that is perpetrated against one person's will and that is based on socially prescribed (Gender) differences between male and female, around the world, at least one in every three women has been beaten, coerced into sex or abused in her lifetime most often by someone she knows, including a member of her own family, an employer or a co-worker. It includes acts that inflict physical, mental or sexual harm or suffering, threats of such act, coercion and other deprivations of liberty, whether occurring in professional or in private life.

GBV is predominantly a crime against women and represent a violation of human rights. The cyclic nature of GBV can be described as "cradle to grave". GBV is violence against women based on women's subordinate status in society and it happens because of their gender. In most cultures traditional beliefs, norms and social institutions legitimised and therefore perpetuate violence against women. It is violence involving men and women in which the female is usually the victim and which is derived from unequal power relationship between men and women. Violence is directed specifically against a woman because she is a woman or affects women disproportionately. Social acceptance of male superiority, domination and control by women, and the reinforcement of such by the family, school, policy makers and religious institutions contribute to the prevalence of GBV worldwide. GBV includes physical, sexual, psychological and domestic violence.

Forms of Gender Based Violence

Violence can be classified into four categories-—Physical, Sexual, Psychological and Emotional. Violence against women is not limited to discrimination, physical abuse and emotional abuse but can take various other forms as well some of them are:

Violence and Gender Discrimination Act at Birth, Infancy and Early Childhood

These types of GBV includes collective sex abortion of female fetuses, neglect of girls which results in malnutrition, female infanticide which is common in isolated and rural parts of south and east Asia, immunisation coverage is better for male children and often the female children receive partial or no immunisation at all.

Examples of gender-based violence throughout the life of a woman include:

- Pre-birth: Sex-selective abortion.
- Infancy: Female infanticide, physical abuse, neglect, poor nutrition, and lack of immunisation and medical care.
- Girlhood: Child marriage, female genital mutilation (FGM), trafficking, child prostitution, sexual abuse, poor nutrition, lack of immunisations and medical care, and minimal or lack of educational opportunities.
- Adolescence: Forced marriages, date rape, FGM, limited or lack of social interaction, acid throwing, dowry deaths, sexual harassment at school and workplace, mass rape during war and civil unrest, lack of safe motherhood facilities, forced prostitution, and trafficking. Other types of violence include economic and social discrimination.
- Young and middle-aged women: Intimate partner abuse, marital rape, dowry abuse, psychological and sexual abuse of women at the workplace, rape, widow abuse, and lack of access to health care including access to safe motherhood facilities.
- Elderly women: Physical and mental abuse of elderly women and widows including rape and neglect.

Acid Attacks

It is a harmful practice against women. In an acid attack acid is thrown, usually by a man on to the face of a girl or woman with the intent of disfiguring her. The reason of this most heinous crime may be vary but the most common reason for this act is rejected marriage proposal by the victim.

Dowry Deaths

Unfortunately the practice of dowry abuse, which is a violation of human rights against woman, has been increasing in south Asian countries especially in India. A woman is subjected to ill treatment by her husband and in-laws when the dowry she has brought is considered insufficient. She may be abused verbally, physically or be subjected to humiliation.

Child Marriage and Forced Marriage

In many parts of Asia, Africa and Middle East there is a tradition of marrying young girls before they attain puberty forcefully. The impact of this trauma can be subtle prolong and often hard to access to counseling services. The practice of child marriage is a violation of the human rights of girls who are deprived of their dignity and self respect.

Practice of Sati and Devdasi

Sati and Devdasi are special forms of cultural violence against women. In the practice of sati, the widow was burned on the funeral pyre along with her dead husband. Devdasi tradition is prevalent in south India which means 'servant of god'. Devdasies are adolescent girls who are lured into prostitution in the name of religion. These young girls may suffer from depression, or traumatic stress syndromes and injury as a result of physical violence.

Honour Killing

Globally hundreds or even thousands of young girls and woman are murdered each year by their families in the name of family honour. Honour killings are perpetrated for a wide range of offenses. Marital Infidelity, premarital sex, flirting, inappropriate attire can be perceived as impugning the family honour

Sexual Violence

WHO defines sexual violence as: any sexual act, attempt to obtain act, unwanted sexual comments or advances or acts to traffic, otherwise directed, against a person's sexuality using coercion, by any person regardless of their relationship to the victim, in any setting, including but not limited to home and work. The following are forms of sexual violence: Marital rape, date rape, rape by strangers, sexual harassment, which includes demanding sex in return of favour, forced abortion, forced virginity inspections forced prostitution and trafficking of women and children for sexual exploitation".

Globalisation and New Forms of Gender Violence

In the absence of any safety net, globalisation has enhanced control over sexuality, fertility and labour of women migrants. Innocent rural girls as well as educated adolescent girls are inducted into the workforce. Cross country migration of girls and women for domestic work, industrial and professional services such as nursing, secretarial practice, telemarketing and business process outsourcing has increased.

Trade in the organs of destitute women and children from poor Asian communities have gained demonic proportions. Soft porn as well as hard-core pornography and cyber sexual violence are used for humiliation and intimidation of women and girls. Cyber stalking is also on the rise. Policy intervention is needed to deal with online sexual violence. An increasing number of women from cities are also reporting harassment through spam, cyber porn and SMS messages.

Smut parties for executives of multi-national and indigenous houses have become routine affairs, and governments do not take action in spite of *prima-facie* evidence provided by the media (Shyam 2002).

The Sites of Gender Based Violence

Family

Family is one of the primary sites of gender violence it prepares its members for social life, forms gender stereotypes and perceptions of division of labour between sexes. Family is the arena where physical abuses (spousal battering, sexual assault, sexual abuse) and psychological abuse occur. Domestic violence also takes place in family.

Community/Society

Society as a group sharing common social cultural, religious or ethnic belonging, it perpetuates existing family structure and power inequalities in family and society. It justifies the behaviour of male abuses aimed at establishing control over in the family and supports harmful traditional practices such battering and corporal punishment.

Work place can also be a site of violence. Either in governmental service or in a business company, women are vulnerable to sexual aggression (harassment intimidation) and commercialised violence (trafficking for sexual exploitation).

State

State legitimises power inequalities in family and society and perpetuates gender-based violence through enactment of discriminatory laws and policies or through the discriminatory application of the law. State is responsible for tolerance of gender violence on an official level (i.e., in the family and in the community).

Information and Communication Technologies (ICTS)

GBV is performed not only in the real world but the virtual world of ICT is also a place where this type of violence is dominant. Genderit.org identifies three distinct categories of ICTs or information and communication technologies:

- Information technology that uses computers;
- Telecommunications technology including telephones, facsimiles and satellite broadcast of radio and television; and
- Networking technologies including the Internet and mobile phones.

In other words, ICTs are all or any forms of "technology and tools that people use to share, distribute, and gather information to communicate with one another, one on one, or in groups".

There are several points of intersection between gender violence and ICTs. While both men and women are equally vulnerable to several forms of fraud and identity theft, young women, children and those who are gay or lesbian are also vulnerable to violence of other kinds. In some cases, this violence can and has spilled over to the 'offline' world. For instance, harassment online or via mobile phones is often an additional dimension of sexual harassment at the workplace. Relationships that are forged online through dating sites are as susceptible to violence as any others. Increasingly, women face abuse and harassment online from strangers and casual acquaintances as well as former partner.

When does this Violence Occur?

Domestic, sexual and gender-based violence are global health, human rights and developmental problems. These problems have profound, immediate and long term consequences involving physical, psychological and social effects. Despite the various forms of domestic and sexual violence worldwide, there is one clear pattern in the occurrence. A growing body of international research examines the extent and patterns of gender-based violence across a range of countries. This work indicates that these forms of violence and abuse are universal, occurring in all countries of the world. It also reveals that, generally, the perpetrators are well known to their victims. A ten-country study on women's health and domestic violence sheds light where few data were previously available (WHO, 2005). The study finds that, depending on the country, between 15 per cent and 71 per cent of women reported physical or sexual violence by a husband or partner and that significant numbers of women experience more than one form of abuse. In fact women most often describe patterns of abusive behaviour and repeat victimisation in these relationships. The most common patterns are women experiencing physical abuse only, or physical abuse and sexual abuse, and both patterns are accompanied by the controlling behaviour of their intimate partner.

The studies that are available consistently indicate that domestic and sexual violence are experienced by both women and men (see Coker et al, 2002;

Schafer et al, 1998 for the international context). To date the emphasis, particularly in large-scale research, has been on men's violence towards women. This inclination has severely limited the extent to which issues relating to domestic and sexual violence are addressed for both women and men. Gradually, however, prevalence studies are beginning to cover the extent of domestic and sexual violence among both men and women.

In India, the problem of gender-based violence is getting worse. National Crime Record Bureau statistics show crimes against women increased by 7.1 per cent nationwide since 2010. There has been a rise in the number of incidents of rape recorded too. In 2011, 24,206 incidents were recorded, a rise of nine per cent from the previous year. More than half of the victims are between 18 and 30 years of age. Figures indicate that 10.6 per cent of total victims of rape were girls under 14 years of age, while 19 per cent were teens between the ages of 14 and 18. Alarmingly in almost 94.2 per cent of cases offenders were known to the victims and those involved included family members, relatives, and neighbours. Under the IPC (Indian Penal Code) crimes against women include rape, kidnapping and abduction, homicide for dowry, torture, molestation, sexual harassment, and the importation of girls. A total of 2,28,650 incidents of crimes against women were reported in the country during 2011. The north eastern city of Tripura recorded the highest rate of crimes against women at 37 per cent, compared to the national crime rate of 18.9 per cent. Kidnapping and abductions are up by 19 per cent and trafficking rose by 122 per cent in the same period. Crimes that include the Indian term "eve-teasing" or harassment and heckling and sexual innuendoes against women in public places including streets, public transport, cinema halls, along with the rape of minors and women in tribal and villages often go unreported and unrecorded. According to records, Madhya Pradesh, a state with a large population of tribes, has recorded 3406 rape cases, the highest number of incidents in the country in 2011. India's profile as an emerging modern nation has taken a beating by the recent rape case, as widespread gender-based violence has been exposed.

How extensive is the problem and what are the barriers to its resolution?

Some states fail to criminalise and/or to punish marital rape and so-called honour killings. Laws that prevent a woman from owning property or travelling without a male guardian make women vulnerable to control by abusive spouses in the home, and failure of the state to provide safe alternative housing. Failure of police to protect a woman suffering violence for women and their children, leave women trapped in dangerous situations. Economic systems that perpetrate the increasing feminisation of poverty contribute to the exploitation of women and girls through prostitution, slavery and trafficking. Women are often victims of violence at the hands of the state itself, when in detention, during armed conflict and during periods of social instability. At the same time, the state may be the most important enabler for eradicating gender-based violence.

Security Council Resolution 1325 recognised women's role in making the world more secure. This is part of a broader re-conceptualisation of 'security' and security providers. Current threats have prompted are cognition that 'security' is not only the protection of states, but an indivisible need and value that all people have the right to enjoy. The task of the security sector is thus to create conditions that enable all people to satisfy their need for security and safety.

This concept of security goes beyond state centered military security and focuses on the ability or inability of state institutions to ensure the protection of all citisens. It enables the identification of vulnerable groups that bear the brunt of poverty, armed conflict, malfunctioning of the security sector and inefficient legal protection. It recognises the contribution of civil society to security. Within this framework, violence against women can be seen as a malfunctioning of the security sector: the failure to protect women, the failure to empower women, and the commission of violence against women.

Gender Based Violence and Education

Usually GBV Starts from family. Girls' Education is affected because of discrimination of Gender. They are prohibited from the opportunity to get education. Because of malnutrition their physical and mental health is affected which directly affects their education they could not get the education according to their ability. The practice of dowry abuse is another reason which affects opportunity to get higher Education to the girls because parents thought if their daughter is highly qualified then they have to give a huge amount of dowry to get a perfect groom for her. There are many forms of GBV like acid attack, rape, kidnapping and because of these people refuse to send their daughter to outside the house and schools. Government provides many provisions for women education but women could not get it because of GBV.

Education is the main factor by which GBV can be ended. Family is the informal means of education and a child learns in the family. If a girl is respected in family and there is no discrimination for her then she will be safe from GBV. In the family man will be taught to behave respectfully with girls. School is another agent to stop the GBV. In a co-ed school where boys and girls taught together and live together they automatically started to develop a feeling of respect and understanding. Education is a means by which women can fight with such kind of social injustice.

There are many issues to consider in developing appropriate responses to the problem of gender-based violence. It is important to understand that such violence is complex and must be viewed in an interdisciplinary sense, one that bridges societal implications and their impact on individuals.

Recognising the seriousness of sexual and dating violence is of critical importance because it signals an air of condemnation for such behaviour. Therefore, issues of violence must be addressed both as a problem affecting students and adults, and as a social issue to be discussed in the classroom.

Given adolescents' particular vulnerability to sexual and dating violence, educational programming must incorporate issues of sex-role stereotyping and gender expectations. Though violence prevention and conflict resolution programmes emphasise qualities of cooperation and communication, they do not necessarily have a "gendered" perspective. In fact, a recent survey of young adolescent violence prevention programmes reported that only four out of 51 programmes specifically listed prevention of teen dating violence and/or rape as a goal.

There are various ways to integrate sexual and dating violence issues in the curriculum, including incorporating such specific components as violence prevention, conflict resolution, gender equity, health education, and peer leadership programmes. In addition, there already exist several curricula that specifically address sexual and/or dating violence on youth. However, most of these approaches depend upon individual class presentations without ensuring other aspects of necessary institutionalised support.

In addition to curricula, programmes, and comprehensive support services, schools must take an unequivocal stand against sexist bias, harassment, and violence. A number of school and states are currently adopting sexual harassment policies. The incidence of sexual and dating violence has critical implications for education and therefore requires a broad and comprehensive approach. This work cannot be done in one arena alone because the issues themselves are so pervasive. The critical feature of creating diverse opportunities is to break the silence and to empower young people, because such violence undermines the foundations of respect and equity that ought to define human relationships.

References

- Acid Survivors Foundation. Acid attacks statistics http://www.acidsurvivors.org/statistics.html.
- Council of Europe's Equality Division, *Summary of the Plan of Action to Combat Violence against Women*. Logar, Rosa. 2000.
- International Center for Research on Women Violence against women must stop.2005 http://www.icrw.org/docs/2005_bries-mdg_violence.pdf.
- International Child Development Centre, *available at* http://www.eurochild.gla.ac.uk/Documents/monee/pdf/MONEE6/monee6.htm.

- Interactive Population Center. Violence against girls and women. http://www.unfpa.org/intercenter/violence/intro.htm.
- Male Violence against Women and Children in Families: A Brief Survey of the Situation in Europe, presentation for the Women's World Forum Against Violence, 23-25 November, Valencia, Spain.
- *National Violence against Women Survey*. Washington, DC: U.S. Department of Justice, *available at* http://hivinsite.ucsf.edu/topics/abuse/2098.40a8.html.
- Tjaden, P. and Thoennes, N. 1998. *Prevalence, Incidence, and Consequences of Violence against Women: Findings from* The Monee Project/UNICEF: 1999.
- United Nations Population Fund (UNFPA). 2000. *The State of the World Population 2000*. New York: UNFPA, *available at UNIFEM Trust Fund to Eliminate Violence against Women*, UNIFEM.
- WLF Facts and Figures, *Gender Violence, available at* http://www.learningpartnership.org/facts/gender.phtml.
- United Nations Children's Emergency Fund. Domestic violence against women and girls. June 2000. http://www.unicef-irc.org/publications/pdf/digest6e.pdf.
- *Women in Transition*, Regional Monitoring Report No 6. Florence, Italy: UNICEF Spindel C., Levy E., Connor M., 2000. *With an End in Sight: Strategies from* The Tribune Newsletter No. 46, 1991.

9

Psychological Perceptions of Gender Based Violence

Dr Sudarsan Raju Chandolu

Narekeli pramod kumar

Principal, College of Education, Andhra University Asst professor Mizoram University

Abstract

Gender based violence is a silent enemy in the global society, a never ending phenomenon. Gender-based violence includes psychological, sexual, and physical violence such as domestic violence; rape and sexual abuse of children by family members; forced pregnancy; sexual slavery; traditional practices harmful to women, such as dowry-related violence; burning or acid throwing, honour killings, female genital mutilation, dating violence in mid-adolescence, violence in operational conflict, emotional abuse, compulsion and abusive language. Forced marriages, trafficking of women and girls for prostitution, sexual harassment and threats are additional examples of violence against women. Gender-based-violence is not exclusively a woman's concern. It is both a cause and consequence of gender perceptions. The use of the term 'gender-based violence' provides a new context in which to examine and understand the never ending phenomenon of violence against women. It shifts the focus from women as victims to gender and the unequal power relationships between women and men created and maintained by gender stereotypes as the basic underlying cause of violence against women. Present paper focus on important contributions, psychological perspectives and approaches of gender based violence.

Keywords: *Gender, Violence, Women, Psychological, Society and Global*

Introduction

Gender-based violence, recently emerging as a persistent global issue, significantly contributes to preventable mortality and morbidity for women across diverse cultures. The term "gender-based-violence" refers to violence that targets individuals or groups on the basis of their gender. The United Nations Human Right Committee on the Elimination of Discrimination against women defines it as "Violence that is directed against women because she is a woman or that affects women disproportionately". This includes psychological, physical, sexual harm, suffering, and the threat of such acts, compulsion and other deprivation of freedom. Together with "sexual violence" and "violence against women", "gender-based-violence" is used interchangeably. This does not mean that all acts against a woman are gender based violence.

A new lexicon, prompted by the expansion of human rights analysis, describes particular threats including dowry deaths, honour murder, sati, and disproportional exposure to HIV/AIDS as well as globally generic threats including marital rape, abuse, battering and murder. Stress related syndromes, depression, chemical dependency, substance abuse, and suicide are consequences observed in the context of violence in women's lives. Emerging psychological, social, legal, medical, and educational strategies promote social change beginning with raising the status of women. The gravity and variability of gender based violence across cultures compel to promote the recognition, intervention and prevention of gender-based violence that are both locally specific and internationally instructive. The causes of gender-based violence were the attitudes to women, girls and children in general, which are linked to the social construction of female and male. Poverty and some cultural practices.

Gender-based violence is physical, psychological, or sexual violence perpetrated against an individual or group on the basis of gender or gender norms. The majority of victims of Gender-based violence are women, but many victims of Gender-based violence are male. Gay, bisexual, and transgendered individuals are often targeted due to their perceived failure to conform to societal gender norms (Stemple, 2009). Forms of Gender-based violence include, sexual abuse, sexual assault, rape, economic violence, intimate partner violence, violence arising from traditional practices such as dowries and female genital mutilation, honour killings, trafficking in human beings for purposes of sexual harassment and intimidation, forced prostitution, sexual exploitation, and bullying based on failure to conform to perceived gender roles.

Defining the Scope of the Problem

Gender-based violence occurs in every corner of the world. Its manifestations and prevalence rates vary, and robust statistics are scarce. For example, the UN Secretary General's report (2006) cites in-country studies estimating that from 10 to 70 per cent of women have experienced violence. Gender-based violence targeting gay, lesbian, transgendered and bisexual people is also endemic. Approximately 80 countries criminalise consensual homosexual acts and multiple countries fail to prosecute crimes against those who identify as gay, lesbian, or transgendered. Unable to cover each type of Gender-based violence comprehensively, we focus on the social psychological context of Gender-based violence and interventions that are informed by and seek to change this context. We connect social psychological perspectives and existing evidence regarding the impact of reduction and mitigation strategies in order to contribute to the broader conversation about reducing all forms of Gender-based violence.

Types of Gender-based-Violence

Types of gender-based violence are as follows:

- Physical Violence – beating, punching, kicking, biting, burning, killing, selling and trading in human beings for forced sexual activities, forced labour, slavery and removal of organs.
- Sexual Violence – robbing the dignity of woman that includes rape and marital rape, child sexual abuse, forced prostitution, sexual harassment, forced sodomy or anal rape and sexual exploitation.
- Verbal Violence – use of abusive and filthy language against a woman or her near and dear ones.
- Emotional Violence – leading to internal deprivation of love and affection, depriving her custody of children, concern, compassion and care.
- Psychological Violence – non-sexual verbal abuse that is insulting, degrading, demeaning; humiliating acts, denying basic expenses for family survival, isolating a person from family and friends, restricting movements, deprivation of liberty, deprivation of liberty and free movement.
- Intellectual Violence – denial of rights to take part in decision making and discussion for pressing issues.
- Harmful Traditional Practices – female genital mutilation, early marriage, forced marriage, honour killing and maiming, killing, withholding food for female children.
- Social Violence – discrimination or denial of opportunities and services, demeaning, disparaging and humiliating a woman or her parental relatives and friends.
- Financial Violence – depriving financial means and bare of daily life necessities, it also includes taking away, misuse and donating the assets which a woman possesses or earns.
- Other forms of Violence – denial of education, access to health facilities and treatment, reproductive rights, etc.

Psychological Perception of Gender based Violence around the World

Gender based violence is quite common in almost all the developing countries. The phenomenon of violence against women within the family in India is complex and extremely embedded. Gender-based violence is not just a 'women's issue', but an issue that concerns all men and not just individual perpetrators. Gender based violence is the most pervasive of all types of violence in the world is multidimensional, multisectoral, multidisciplinary and holistic. It provides a complete structure, which includes psychological factors, not enough concentration has been given to psychological perspectives. Psychologists around the world have made contributions in research, clinical assessment and intervention for prevention of gender-based violence.

Although each country has unique factors that determine the services and resources available to battered women and children's are exposed to domestic violence and abusive partners, it is the interaction among gender, religious beliefs, political structure, attitudes towards violence in general and violence towards women, such as civil conflicts and wars, state-sponsored violence and the migration between countries that ultimately determine women's vulnerability and safety.

Psychological Perspectives on the Elimination and Prevention of all forms of Violence

The Psychology Coalition at the United Nations (UN) is to advocate for UN agencies, Governments, civil society organisations, all other stakeholders, and the Special Rapporteur on Violence Against Women, to take into account important contributions that psychological perspectives and approaches can make to treating, eliminating and preventing violence against women and girls (VAWG) worldwide.

Since the 1993 Human Rights Conference in Vienna officially recognised violence against women as a human rights violation, increased awareness of the forms and levels of violence against women and girls, which include: rape in armed conflicts, domestic violence, genital mutilation or cutting, sexual exploitation in trafficking, and forced prostitution. However, in spite of Government commitments, United Nations policies, programmes and advocacy of civil society association, violence against women and girls continues to be a human rights abuse in all countries and across all sectors of society.

Significance of Psychological Perspectives Gender Based Violence:

- Implement the UN Secretary-General's Campaign "Unite to End Violence against Women and Girls" and publicise support for human rights and social justice for all.

- Provide human resources, policies, programmes, facilities, and services to promote the mental health and psychosocial recovery and well being for women and girls who have experienced physical, sexual or psychological violence, including services delivered by qualified psychologists themselves or other trained mental health providers.
- Establish programmes to promote the education of men and boys in human rights and to promote and mobilise males as partners in the elimination of violence against women and girls.
- Provide programmes to promote the psychosocial empowerment of women and girls who have suffered violence, so that they are less vulnerable to future instances of violence and better equipped to cope with violent situations if these should arise.
- Promote access to effective responses and practice by psychologists and mental health workers by facilitating communication at a global level through the use of technology, including cell phones and other devices.

Consequences of Gender Based Violence

The consequences of gender-based violence are many and they include poor health, depression and death in some situations. Violence also breeds violence so that children living and growing up in a violent home are likely to be violent and so the cycle of violence is sustained. Violence also really creates psychological and emotional problems for the survivors of it. While the violence may be an incident in the life of the perpetrator, it has life long consequences for the survivors.

Contributing Factors of Gender-Based Violence

Research has identified factors associated with Gender-based violence at the individual, situational, and societal levels. Various academic disciplines and practitioners weight each level differently in their theories and the design of interventions. For example, clinical psychologists and legal scholars have often focused on the individual level, specifically on the pathological personality traits of Gender-based violence perpetrators as a means to identify, counsel, or prosecute potential or previous perpetrators (Fischel, 2010). Sociological and feminist scholarly perspectives traditionally focus on situational and societal levels, such as gendered power asymmetries in a society or an organisation (Brownmiller, 1975; Tangri, Burt, & Johnson, 1982). A social psychological perspective on factors contributing to Gender-based violence focuses on the interaction between individual characteristics and the immediate situation in which Gender-based violence occurs (Anderson & Anderson, 2008).

The social psychological perspective posits that Gender-based violence occurs as a result of the interaction of individual, situational, and societal factors (Anderson & Carnagey, 2004; Malamuth, 2003). Within a given society, many individuals' exhibit personality traits or are exposed to norms that promote or condone Gender-based violence.

Cause and Effects

Societal and situational causes of gender-based violence:

From a social psychological perspective, societal factors will be most predictive of a GBV event when they are salient in the immediate situation. Such societal factors include power asymmetries, gender norms, roles, scripts, societal representations of women, and armed conflict or other crises, among others. These factors can become salient when physical or social arrangements create the expectation of such a factor (e.g., the asymmetrical representation of men at a meeting promotes the idea of male dominance at the organisation), when implicit rules that stem from these factors are violated (e.g., a man's behaviour that appears to violate a gendered norm causes him stress), or when they are raised in social interactions or media communications (e.g., representations of violence against women are primed by pornography playing on a nearby computer screen).

Individual Causes of Gender-based Violence:

Societal and situational factors alone cannot explain GBV; they likely combine with individual stressors and attributes to fuel GBV. We explore these interactions in this section, beginning with a discussion of the literature's shift from focusing on a pathological model of GBV perpetrators to a non-pathological model. We then focus on qualities deemed to be non-pathological predictors of GBV perpetration, such as low self esteem, impulsivity, and sexism, among others. Both the pathological and non-pathological literatures are plagued by the methodological problem that GBV prevalence is often measured through self-report or biased samples of convicted perpetrators of GBV (excluding those who evade conviction or treatment).

Effects of Gender-based violence:

Effects of gender based violence are categorised as physical, psychological, and socio-economic effects. The effects are:

- *Physical:* Sexual and Reproductive health problems, Injury, Chronic health problems, Disability and Death.
- *Psychological:* Effects can be both Dirct/Indirect. Anxiety, depression, fear, inability to concentrate, mistrust of others, loneliness, post-traumatic stress disorder, suicide, etc., are direct effects and indirect effects are psychosomatic illnesses, withdrawal, alcohol or drug use etc.
- *Socio-economic:* Rejection, ostracism and social stigma at community level; Reduced ability to participate in social and economic activities;

Acute fear of future violence, which extends beyond the individual survivors to other members in community; Damage to women's confidence resulting in fear of venturing into public spaces (this can often curtail women's education, which in turn can limit their income-generating opportunities); Increased vulnerability to other types of gender-based violence; Job loss due to absenteeism as a result of violence; Negative impact on women's income generating power.

Interventions

Though many interventions have been designed to combat and reduce GBV, we focus on programmes whose methodology is clearly described and which have been empirically evaluated. The set of inadequately detailed evaluations of interventions is large, leaving methodological and theoretical gaps. To compensate for the empirical shortcomings, we rely on psychological models of behaviour change to hypothesise potential mechanisms through which interventions may be effective.

Primary Interventions

- Educational interventions
- Preventing dating violence
- Interventions Outside of School for Adolescents and Young Adults
- Programs Directed towards Likely Targets of GBV
- Anti-trafficking interventions
- Rape and assault prevention interventions

Secondary Interventions

- Media campaigns targeting individuals suffering GBV
- Group interventions to change violent behaviour or reduce repeat violence
    - *Psycho educational model*
    - *Cognitive behavioural model*
    - *Gender-based cognitive behavioural approaches*
- Individual Interventions to Reduce Gender-Based Violence
- Legal Responses to Gender-Based Violence

Conclusion

The root cause of gender-based violence lied in unequal power relations between women and men. However, a variety of factors on the society level, community level, family level and the level of individual, often combine to raise the probability of violence occurring. The effects of gender-based violence are far-reaching and extend beyond the individual survivor, to the family and society as a whole. Potential social responses to gender-based violence are most effective when there is a common understanding of the nature and causes of gender-based violence and it is addressed from all angles, through the participation of multiple sector and entire communities.

Various theories of gender-based violence, and theories of how to reduce gender-based violence, place different weights on individual, situational, and societal factors that drive gender-based violence. By placing interventions in the context of social psychological theory and evidence, identify the driving factors of gender-based violence and the most useful ways to measure intervention outcomes. Psychological approach by targeting perceived social norms about domestic violence with media and makes available information to ameliorate or address violence. Gender-based violence reduction programmes are conscientiously develop a theory of the specific form of violence they aim to reduce and intervene by examining the individual, situational, and societal factors that support the most frequent instances of that violence. The vast literature regarding gender-based violence is demonstrative of many of the successes of prior decades of interventions and studies that increased understanding of gender-based violence and reduced its incidence and severity.

References

- American Psychological Association. (2007). Report of the AP A Task Force on the Sexualisation of Girls. Washington, DC.
- Krug E et al., eds. (2002). *World Report on Violence and Health.* Geneva, World Health Organisation.
- Manjoo, R. (March 2012). Statement of the Special Rapporteur on Violence against Women, Its Causes and Consequences to the Commission on the Status of Women.
- Pickup, F., Williams, S., Sweetman, C. *Ending Violence against Women: A Challenge for Development and Humanitarian Work*, Oxfam GB 2001.
- UNHCR (2003) "Sexual and Gender-Based Violence against refugees, returnees and internally displaced persons. May 2003.
- United Nations (2002). Women, Peace and Security, Study submitted by the Secretary-General pursuant to Security Council resolution 1325 (2000), United Nations, New York.
- Walker, Lenore E. (1999). Psychology and domestic violence around the world. American Psychologist, Vol 54(1), 21-29.
- Website: UN Millennium Goals: www.un.org/millenniumgoals/
- World Health Organisation (2012). Mental health and psychosocial

support for conflict-related sexual violence: principles and interventions. Access at: http://www.unicef.org/protection/files/Summary_EN_.pdf

- World Health Organisation. (November 2012). Violence Against Women: Intimate partner and sexual violence against women. Fact Sheet No. 239. http://www.who.int/mediacentre/
- World Health Organisation: www.who.int/gender/violence

10

Child Trafficking: International Law and Relative Indian Scenario

Avinash Singh

Santosh Kumar Sahu

MATS Law School, Raipur (Chhattisgarh)

Introduction

Child trafficking a moot subject of research is a social quandary that is extending its arms on the global level and is more particularly being a quandary for the developing and underdeveloped nations forms the core of the present chapter. The reason and the problems that trafficking procures if very stringently observed will clarify the issue and challenges that are lying ahead the government and society to handle. There are several general problems that need to be addressed and will be subsequently focused upon in the chapter but apart from reaching to solutions of the general problems the region or country specific problem resolution scheme is also being well scheduled in the chapter. Trafficking may be of many types depending upon the subject matters that are being part of the respective trafficking like human, animal, birds etc., but the present study limits its scope in and only child trafficking. Trafficking has a very wide interpretative potential that includes men, women and children being subject to trafficking and hence the author shrinks the scope of research area over the children only. Child trafficking is an issue that needs greater concern not because of the nature of harm but because of the nature of victim being affected in the present situation.

One of the definition of the trafficking in human being definitional of the words that speaks as: "The recruitment, transportation, transfer, harbouring or receipt of persons, by means of the threat or use of force or other forms of coercion, of abduction, of fraud, of deception, of the abuse of power or of a position of vulnerability or of the giving or receiving of payments or benefits to achieve the consent of a person having control over another person, for the purpose of exploitation. Exploitation shall include, at a minimum, the exploitation of the prostitution of others or other forms of sexual exploitation, forced labour or services, slavery or practices similar to slavery, servitude or the removal of organs." This definition is traceable in the Council of Europe Convention on Action against Trafficking in Human Beings that considered trafficking as human rights violation and hence made provisions to end the problem of trafficking vis-à-vis maintaining gender equality in the system.

Trafficking is something that gets a mixed response from the society and here it creates a quandary to resolute the problem of same. Trafficking is having an altered consequence of which eventual response is well accepted and handled among a stratum of society.

Present chapter tries to cover major issues and challenges that the society is facing in terms of child trafficking and hence the chapter outcomes with several suggestions that are indented to affect and successfully change the present scenario. Constitution being the guiding document for any law in country seeks more societal appreciation while implementing the same and therefore provisions and its due implementation should also be done in accordance with the constitutional scheme. Chapter also lies down a structure that will present the constitutional backing of rights of the children against trafficking and then will in same flow also spotlight upon those directives that will clear the obligatory situation of state to cope up with the problem of child trafficking. Present chapter more emphatically stresses to focus on Indian aspect of the trafficking that is the active problem before the country and the shelling of the problem in a global colour creates more problem as the consequence to take cross border measures will be highly questionable that may sometime captures negative eye on world community.

The heterogeneous look of the problem of child trafficking as mixed with sexual activities like prostitution and turned into a booming commercial industry have created further problems to tackle the situation and hence finding an inclusive solution to it. After discussing with such matters functioning in and out of Indian society, the author moves to the last analytical viewpoint over the international documents and provisions related thereto that will lead to the ultimate consequence mirroring the original aspect of child trafficking in the international arena. Trafficking is nonetheless a global phenomenon of which victim list is starched across the globe and hence international organisations are working with the mutual assistance of states to end the misery of trafficking but since the efforts are done globally, the problem generators or the perpetrators are also working in an inclusive manner and strategically evading from the traps that have been thrown periodically. These criminals or people involved in trafficking are supposed to get more stringent actions against them by the respective government but the likelihood of adverse is more opted in the present. Present situation is so vigorous to handle that one cannot predict the future of endeavours that are sequentially being implemented by the state governments and hence this chapter while continue to deal with international provisions with an overview and insight at several other aspects relating to the same problem. Government is coming with technologically advanced mechanism wherein the online portal and online reporting of missing child to police station for reporting and finding the missing child is one of the most innovative steps that is being implemented in present day but remains unproductive in absence of its dissemination among the common public. The chapter will vehemently argue in raising the concern among public to support for such cause so as to make the efforts howsoever small as effective one and also a societal support is needed for all other future endeavours since the public is the only perpetrator and suffer in this whole trafficking saga.

Child and Trafficking: A Constitutional Viewpoint

Constitution of India also known as "grund norm" has influenced the legal scheme of our country that could also be seen in while analysing the laws relating to the child trafficking in India. Child rights are one of the most precious rights that finding parallel place in the constitution with all others rights given to the citisens or non-citisens. Except from the all other general provisions, there are some additional protections that are endowed to the children placed in the sacrosanct part III of the constitution that details the Fundamental Rights to the citisens. Article 23 of the Indian Constitution that reads as "Prohibition of traffic in human beings and forced labour –

(1) Traffic in human beings and beggar and other similar forms of forced labour are prohibited and any contravention of this provision shall be an offence punishable in accordance with law.

(2) Nothing in this article shall prevent the State from imposing compulsory service for public purpose, and in imposing such service the State shall not make any discrimination on grounds of religion, race, caste or class or any of them is the only expressed fundamental right that tries to protect the rights of the children among other human beings and hence creating a right generating situation in the society that will be required to meet the need of weapon for fighting with the social evil of trafficking. Once the prohibition of trafficking and forced labour is a Fundamental Right of the citisen, the citisen gains power to enforce this right against the state and state will be obligated to take an action whenever such act criminalised by constitution takes place.

Apart from said provision enshrined in Article 23, there are other fundamental rights that serve the purpose to restrict the human trafficking as those cardinal among other fundamental rights have approached to its widest interpretation that is known as "right to life" enshrined in Article 21 of the constitution. Apex court on many occasions have deployed an humanitarian approach while interpreting rights under Article 21 and hence the child trafficking matter would be on limelight of inspection as it relates directly to the right of survival with other socio-economic rights that are mandated for peaceful existence of any society. In case of Kharak Singh *vs.* State of Uttar Pradesh court cleared the life doesn't mean mere animal existence but a dignified survival with the liberty in all aspects. Court took this view in accordance with an American celebrated decision came in case of Munn *vs.* Illinois where American Supreme Court while interpreting the term "life" have concluded with the following phrase that is still holding a significant relevance in present society worded as "Something more than mere animal existence. The inhibtion against its deprivation extends to all those limbs and faculties by which life is enjoyed. The provision equally prohibits the mutilation of the body by the amputation of an arm or leg, or the putting out of an eye, or the destruction of any other organ of the body through which the soul communicates with the outer world".

Also the fundamental Rights triangle being recognised in case of Maneka Gandhi *vs.* Union of India will also work in sync while resolving the problem of trafficking and holding its serious nature to resolve the said issue. State is more obligated with more force to eradicate the problem since it effects the significant constitutional principles of equality, freedom of life and liberty preserved in Article 14, Article 19 and Article 21 respectively. Although constitution of India also holds due protection to non-citisens as in Article 14, 21, 20, 25(1), 27 etc., that provide power to protect the alien persons when they were being trafficked in India that evidence the intention of constitution framers to protect all human beings irrespective of its place of birth and this shows the globalised view of protection of children marked in Constitution of India.

After analysis on the fundamental rights based approach, now we will scrutinise the structure that is out of Part III but still is given more importance while adhering any function in accordance with Indian constitution that is Part IV of Constitution of India enshrining Directive Principle of State Policies that are Social and Economic rights given to the citisens of India by way of directions provided therein for state that need to be followed while formulating policies of social welfare. Significance of Part IV can be traced from the one among most landmark judgment of Keshavananda Bharathi *vs.* Union of India wherein court has developed situation of harmonisation between Fundamental Rights and Directive Principles while interpreting any combating situation between fundamental rights and directive principles. Among other general provisions of directive principles Article 39(e) and (f) bears more importance that any other provisions for restricting child trafficking as Article 39(e) reads as: "The State shall, in particular, direct its policy towards securing that the health and strength of workers, men and women, and the tender age of children are not abused and that citisens are not forced by economic necessity to enter avocations unsuited to their age or strength" and Article 39(f) reads as "The State shall, in particular, direct its policy towards securing that children are given opportunities and facilities to develop in a healthy manner and in conditions of freedom and dignity and that childhood and youth are protected against exploitation and against moral and material abandonment". Both of the provisions of Article 39 clearly depicts the responsibility of state towards securing the safety of children as especially additionally endowed on state for facilitation of protective and development regime to the children.

Therefore, the constitutional scheme mixed with fundamental rights and directive principles clears the path for a stringent action of state to cope up with the issue of child trafficking and hence making its presence rescind from society.

Indian Scenario of Child Trafficking: Issues and Challenges

Millennium development goals among which the foremost goal is to eradicate poverty is scheduled to be opted by the government according to sub-group report on 11the Five Year Plan being published by Ministry of Women and Children. Millennium Development Goal Three also recognises that, trafficking is a major impediment for the development of women and child vis-à-vis adversely affects human rights.

Quantum of victims under Child Trafficking Protection Act is not bouncing very high comparing it with the victim rate of other laws but still this data may be erroneous as many children are sold or purchased for the trafficking purpose may have procured as by trafficking them from any other territory of country. Data are also highly mistaken as kidnapping that is highest reported victim rate counting 4464 victims in average between year 1999 to 2004 was separately kept spaced out with victims of child trafficking holding a small quantum of 72 victims in average between the same span of time i.e., between year 1999-2004. Even the Ministry of Home Affairs Government of India recognises that 90 per cent of total trafficking within the country that is afterwards used for sexual exploitation. It is astonishing to mention that kidnapping leads to more child trafficking than any other route but the data available in regard to child trafficking is relatively very low just because the non addition of the kidnapping that leads to child trafficking. This data will obliviously and most undesirably weaken the formulation of such laws and prove them ineffective to work in the Indian scenario to combat with the child trafficking. Immoral trafficking prevention Act is the guardian law for dealing with trafficking cases and hence with the insufficient data and erroneous compilation of set of data will more harm that gaining control over the trafficking. However, the sex ratio gap in states may also lead to minor cause of trafficking but this problem is again society generated that can be preserved by maintaining child sex ratio in states and hence can stop killing the female child in state. In this way the report shows the connection between female child killing and child trafficking that result as a matter of concern for the government.

Author derives an adhesive co-relation between child trafficking and smuggling as both of them involve transmission of objects on territorial basis wherein both of them are prohibited by law. Smuggling involves goods and other materials while trafficking particularly involves human body that comes into commercial exposure after reaching to its consequence. Child trafficking is the matter of greater concern because it possesses more harm to the victims as trafficking is more profitable than smuggling and hence a stringent view is adopted for the eradication of the same.

This problem raises another issue that may have most compelling reason for continuation of channel for the trafficking purpose. Children are being trafficked from state like Chhattisgarh, West Bengal, Odisha etc., through middleman and are deployed in various field of working wherein prostitution counts one of the major exploitation area. Several times it is observed that those who are indulged in trafficking are not using the forceful means but contradictory to it, the families of the children are willingly approving their child to get trafficked in lieu of monetary consideration. Probabilities are high that many times parents didn't know that the area of said employment of their children will be in the sex industry where the children are sexually exploited to earn money. This consensual manner of trafficking creates problem in tracking the offensive event of trafficking and hence making it more complex to stop the child trafficking as children are incapable to raise the concern against themselves being of minor age and intellect comparing with that of a major trafficked victim. Present situation of age gap can perfectly explain the reason to put higher concern over the issue of child trafficking than any other form of trafficking.

One of the challenge that came along the way of child trafficking is sometime itself the children stratum who in absence of basic necessities and in addict of ill habits organise groups undertaking illegal means to feed their addiction that may extend to diverse number of habits like alcohols, correction fluid, rubber cement, eraser marker, gasoline etc. Said challenge is an oxymoron in terms of present efforts wherein one side we are combating to deal and solve the issue of child trafficking and on other side children are themselves involved in encouraging these social evils. The main flourishing resource is both the society as well as the paralytic policies of government that have together played a crucial role in moving the children on path of inclusive disaster.

Conclusion

Thus the chapter concludes with the observation that there might be several factors that are working against the proper implementation of the laws made for tackling the child trafficking issues but still the abundance of laws do not come into way to restrict stretching the ambit of the governmental authorities that will work in sync with the society to eradicate the problem of child trafficking. Also there is need to differentiate between the in-house trafficking that may be one of the major problem and can be easily restricted by way of local government machinery unlike the cross-border trafficking that has comparatively higher complexities in its implementation.

One among the suggestion is that the society must stand against is the problem of child trafficking and due to higher perceptibility of health hazard and other reasons make the children the vulnerable for any such exploitation. There are several conflicts of interest between the prostitution by consent and hence it creates a problem to trace the differentiation between normal prostitution and prostitution involved trafficking but in case of children trafficking, it is very easy to recognise the exploitation as child is incapable to give consent. Child trafficking can also be restricted if children are provided with those essential amenities that are needed for sustaining a normal living condition that will lower the selling rate of children among poor families. There are laws against the people involved in trafficking, but still no express laws that especially prosecute the families that encourage and practice the child trafficking. There are laws that may attract penalty for parent and relatives indulged in trafficking but a new smooth framework will increase the deterrence among families and relative as it also counts a larger share in case of trafficking.

11

Gender Equality and Empowerment of Women with Special Reference to National Policy and Constitutional Provision

Dr Chitra Singh Tomar
Asso. Profeessor Dept of Education
S.N. Sen B.V.P.G.College
The Mall- Kanpur
Dr NishaAgrawal
Head/Asso. Profeessor Dept of Education
S.N. Sen B.V.P.G. College
The Mall- Kanpur

Abstract

Gender discrimination and women empowerment is a greatly discussed matter. Women's rights and issues have always been a subject of serious concern of academicians, intelligentia and policy makers. From post-oral society to contemporary information and global society, the role of women has changed drastically. The role of a typical housewife who catered to all the requirements of the households including the rearing and upbringing of children in various sub-roles of daughter, daughter-in-laws, wife, mother, aunt etc., has been played quite efficiently. With the process of industrialisation, modernisation and globalisation showing its deep impact on human society all over the world, the role and responsibilities of women has attained new definition and perspective.

The problem of gender discrimination needs to be addressed with several front such as economic, social, legal, educational and political. Women may be empowered by various activities such as calculating the amount of their labour and add it to the GDP, proper enactment of legislations, mobilisation of purposeful actions etc., to understand the danger of gender discrimination among all persons in the society, stopping the politician follow the divide and rule policy in the society on the basis of religion, caste and creed.

Hence, compulsory female education strengthening adult literacy programme holding seminars and debates at the grass root level are essential to empower the women. Enactment of equal remuneration act, more research work in women relevant curriculum which will make the girls self-reliant are quite important response through local management mechanism organising career campaigns in the college will certainly help in strengthening the women empowerment.

Last but not least a multifaceted approach covering the regional and local needs must be strengthened after all a concerted effort by all sections of society, the voluntary organisations and the government is must to empower the women. Developing skills and techniques on women setting up of micro enterprises for women will definitely help in increasing women empowerment.

Gender discrimination and women's development is a greatly discussed matter even though sensitisation regarding this subject is grossly ignored on the lower level. The gender and development approach through gender analysis seeks to understand the roles, responsibilities, resources and priorities of women and men within a specific context, examining the social, economical and environmental factors which influence their roles and decision making capacity. The gender discriminate belief is repeatedly recognised merely at the stage of the gender system's impact on women. The practice of male-female differentiation results in structural deprivation of the female of life.

Women empowerment is the buzzword now days. Over the past decade, gender equality and women's empowerment have been explicitly recognised as key note only of the health of nation. Women's rights and issues have always been a subject of serious concerns of academicians, intelligentias and policy makers.

The continuity of changes in socio-economic and psycho-cultural aspects of human living has influenced the role of women. With the process of Industrialisation, modernisation and globalisation showing its deep impact on human society, all over the world. The role and responsibilities of women has attained new definition and perspectives.

Gender inequality and structural reform has voiced about the likely ill effects of macro-economic reforms on the situation of women; liberalisation has been seen to lead to increased feminisation of poverty. While increased feminisations of the workforce appear to be a global phenomenon, it has been pointed out that the increase in place in low paying and unprotected jobs, leading to the rise in the casualisation of the female workforce.

There are at least three circumstances under which increasing women's power may reduce discrimination against girl children:

1. They may use their power altruistically to improve the well-being of all of their children regardless of gender.
2. Women who are better educated and spend more time outside of the home may become aware of gender inequality and subsequently have a growing sense of responsibility for remedying them in their households.
3. If women has same sex preferences and thus favour their own gender, they may lead to allocate increased resources under their control towards girls.

   Gender discrimination takes many forms as well as exists in most part of the world from Japan to Morrocco, From Uzebikistan to U.S.A. However, inequality is not one homogenous phenomenon, but a collection of desperate and interlinked problems. Looking through the laws of discrimination, here are some major areas of discriminations against women in India and the impact pertains to the manifestation of gender ideology in declining sex-ration, illiteracy, poor-health, over work unskilled, mistreatment and professional inequality. Ownership inequality etc., are the visible aspect of gender system.

Sex Ratio

The sex ratio in the country remain unfavourable to females, it was 972 at the beginning of the twentieth century and thereafter shows continuous decline. The famous economist Amartya Sen drew attention to this anamaly in an article in 1990 as "Over 100 million women are missing". Be calculated that is all the women who were born in India since independence in 1947 had been allowed to live the same way as men were, there would have been at least one hundred million more women in India, which have disappeared and they all have been died. They were either killed as infants at birth or died of neglect through malnourishment poor hygiene and disease all causes that were preventable.

Education

Education is widely recognised as the gateway to economic security and opportunity particularly for girls and women. So far as the gender equality is concerned, education is included among the millennium development goals and many developing country government none officially recognise this goal as a priority.

Women and girls receive far less education than man due to social norms and prevailing discrimination. India has the largest population of non-school going working girls. India's constitution guarantees free primary school education for both boys and girls up to age 14. This goal has been repeatedly reconfirmed, but primary education in India is not universal. The literacy rate for women is 39 per cent v/s men 64 per cent while the rate of literacy of women in four northern states is lower than the national average as in Bihar, U.P., M.P. and Rajasthan.

Professional Inequality

Gender discrimination is a big way of professional incompetency. In terms of employment as well as promotion in works and occupation women often faces greater handicap than men. (Amartya Sen 2001).

The employment situation in India as the studious available data suggests is the presence of discrimination against women at all levels. Labour Force participation Rates (LFPRs) are lower for women than men, disparity being particularly high in urban areas. The disparity is the source of some concerns, for high labour participation rate for women have been shown to raise nutrition level for their children. Lower mortality rate and raise sex ratios by combating traditional male biases. In terms of skill development women are impeded by their lack of mobility, low literacy level and prejudiced attitude towards women because there is a popular notion among employers who feel that the men gave a greater responsibility in supporting the family than the women and therefore a greater right to job.

Health

Girls and women below the age of 30 have higher death rates from illness than men in the same age group. Poor health status of Indian women is the major cause of deficient sex ratio.

Communicable diseases, maternal and parental conditions and malnutrition accounts for 68 per cent of death and disabilities among Indian girls and women. Higher rates of disease and mortality among women and girls are probably the results of a failure to give young girls and women medical care, food and social security compared to that given to boys and men.

Factor Resposible for Gender Discrimination

Inspite of various and widespread rights applied to all women without exception, many women are systematically desired their rights from the day they are born. Women discriminations begin at home only and has multiple causational factors as:

1. Traditional social practices and patriarchal codes and beliefs are responsible factors for discrimination against women. Gender discrimination throughout the lifecycle of the women derives essentially from cultural patterns, in particular the harmful effects of certain traditional or customary practices and all acts of extreme linked to race, sex, language or religion that perpetuate the lower status according to women in the family. Thus, the root by discrimination

against women lies in the religious and cultural practices in India.

2. Awareness or illiteracy is also a step towards this menace. The girls not attending schools are mostly discriminated due to their lack of awareness lack of self confidence, proper understanding and lack of vision.

3. Poverty is also a reason of gender discrimination which also enhances illiteracy. Economy plays a vital important role of obstacle when it comes of coping with direct tution fees, cost of textbooks, transportation uniforms and other expenses and while in families, the cost exceeds the income of the family—-girls are the first who are sacrificed or to be desired schooling.

4. Many societies still favour sons and view girls as an economic burden i.e., unwelcoming status of girl child which leads continuous declining sex ratio which is considered to be a major consational factor of victimisations of gender discrimination.

5. The dowry system is considered to be curse for girls while a way of earning as a boon for boys. Dowry seems to be a part of gift which can be refund by her husband. Girls are less likely to earn an income while boys will grow up to be wage earner and all these limited economic opportunities can be a part of their higher mortality rate in Indian societies.

6. Socio- economic causes are responsible for women's health. Women's disadvantaged social position, which is often related to the economic value placed on familiar roles helps perpetuate poor health, inadequate diet, early and frequent pregnancy and a continuous cycle of poverty, from infancy female in many part of the world received less and lower quality food and are treated less often when sick and then only at a more advanced stage of disease. In so many countries, women are less educated receive less information than men and have less control over decision making and family resources.

7. The inadequacy of law enforcement and lack of legal awareness hampers efforts to fight violence against women. Gender discrimination is exacerbated by social pressure notably the shame of denouncing certain acts that have been perpetuated against women; women's lack access of legal information aid or protection; lack of laws to effectively prohibit gender discrimination; failure to reform existing laws; inadequate efforts on the part of public authorities.

8. The socialisation process puts men and women on a different footing in social attitudes, beliefs and practices. Indian women have low level in both education and formal labour force participation. They have little autonomy. Living under the control of first their fathers, then their husbands and finally their sons, all of these factors exert a negative impact on health education and social upbringing of the

women.

9. Gender discrimination and women empowerment is a greatly discussed matter. Women's rights and issues have always been a subject of serious concern of academicians, intelligentia and policy makers. From postoral society to contemporary information and global society, the role of women has changed drastically. The role of a typical housewife, who caters to all the requirements of the households including the rearing and upbringing of children in various sub-roles of daughter, daughter-in-laws, wife, mother, aunt etc.

National Policies in the Backdrop of Constitutional Privileges for Empowerment of Women

India is a country of extreme diversities in language, religion caste and socio economic class. The constitution of India provides equality of all irrespective of gender, caste, religion, race and place of birth and is considered as the vehicle for social transformation to realise the goals of the independence movement which aimed at socio-economic emancipation of millions of Indians. India is also the first country to have given voting rights for women along with its independence.

'Gender' refers to the rules, norms, customs and practices by which biological differences between male and females are translated into socially constructed differences between men and women or boys and girls.

Although women constitutes nearly half the population, their population has begun to slide owing to the increasing practice of female infanticide, repeated child births, malnutrition due to poverty poor healthcare etc. Their population is begun to fall now with 927 women to 2000 males. Similarly, their literacy rate has not increased proportionately to that of males. It was 8.85 per cent (1951), 29.76 per cent (1981), 54.16 per cent (2001) which is lesser in comparison of males. In the same way women keep the same deteriorating shameful rate not in literacy but in other spheres as in education, job opportunities, social issues, gender justice and crime against them-—they are left out in all classes and castes.

Gender should be at the Centre of any development. The need of gender sensitivity which stands serious attempts to understand the lives of women from their own perspectives. There is a great need to access education, health and economic input and output of women to do this. It is necessary to acknowledge women's contribution to production and their ownership interrelated to the issues of:

Health:Nutrition and infectious diseases including sexually transmitted.

Education: Literacy rate, Job opportunity wastage & stagnation in studies.

Economy: adequate housing, income, job placement, sources of income etc. to be examined properly.

Indian women are the beneficiaries of various constitutional privileges as:

Article-14 Equality before Law for Women: The state share not deny to any person/Citisen equality before law or equal protection of the law before India.

Article-15(I) Prohibition of Discrimination on the Basis of Religion, Race, Sex, or Place of Birth: The state shall not discriminate against any citisen on ground of religion, race, sex and place of birth or any of them.

Article-16 (II):- No Citisen shall, on ground only of religion, race, caste decent place of birth, residence or any of them be ineligible for or discriminated against in respect of any employment or office under state.

Article 39 (9) & (D) 'A': All indicate towards securing equal opportunities for men and women while Article 42 stall shall make provision for securing human conditions for work and maternity relief.

Article 51(A): indicate towards the dignity of women.

Article 243 D(3) make provision for not less than one third of the local number of offices at each level to be seemed to women. While,

Article 243T (3): not less than 1/3 majority to be secured for women in open elections in municipality.

The Goal of national policies is to bring out advancement, development and empowerment of women. The policy will be widely disseminated so as to encourage active participation of all state holders for achieving its goals.

Thus, the problem of gender discrimination needs to be addressed with several fronts such as economic, social, legal, educational and political. Women may be empowered by various activated such as:

1. Calculating the amount of their labour and add it to the GDP
2. Proper enactment of the legislation
3. Mobalisation of purposeful actions
4. Understand the danger of gender discrimination among all persons in the society
5. Stopping the politician to follow the divide and rule policy in the society on the basis of religion, caste and creed.
6. Compulsory female education strengthening adult literacy programme holding seminar and debare at the grass root level are essential to empower the women.

7. Enactment of equal remuneration Act, more research work in women empowerment preparation of more relevant curriculum which will make the girls self reliant are quite important.
8. Empowering the communities with response through local management mechanism, organising career campaigns in the college for the girls will certainly help in strengthening the women empowerment.

Last but not the least a multifaceted approach covering the regional and local needs must be strengthen. The voluntary organisations and the government should act to empower the women. Developing skills and techniques of women, setting up of micro enterprises for women will definitely help in increasing women empowerment.

References

- Agnihotri's (1997), workforce participation, kinship and sex ratio variation in India, Gender, Technology and Developmnent.
- AIDS: India (2006), India, China look to Thailand as more women infected, available at womenone.org
- Bhan, Gautam (2001) India gender Profile, report No. 62, Institute of Development studies.
- Chatterjee, M (1990) Indian women, their Health and Productivity. World Bank discussion papers 109, Washington D.C.
- Crime in India (2003), National Crime Record Bureau, Government of India, New Delhi.
- Desponde S & Deshpande I (1999), Gender based discrimination in the urban labour market in : Tpapola, A. Sharma (eds) 'Gender and Employment in India, Vikas Publishing – New Delhi
- Gupta M. S. (2005) Emplowering women through legal and government based approaches in India, Bihar Economic Journal, Conference Volume.
- India (2004), A Reference Annual, Ministry of Information and Broadcasting Government of India, New Delhi
- Mudur Ganpati (1996) 'India's women get poor deal or Healthcare, World bank – New Delhi.
- Pandey, Vinita (2005), Empowering women in India 'Changing Horizons the Kalenjian Experiences' Journal of South Asia Women studies, Macrch 3, 10 (1).
- Pradhan, Rajeev (2011), 'The Future of Women's Right' Navyug Book International-New Delhi.

- Rathod P. B. (2009) 'Women and Development ABD Publishers – Jaipur.
- Sarkar, Sidharth (2010) "Gender, Poverty and Sustainable Livelihood" Arise Publishers & Distributors – New Delhi
- Sen Amartya (2001) 'Many faces of gender inequality. Frontline, 18:22 Victoria, A.Velk off and Arjun, Adlakha (1998), women's Health in India, women's of the women. International programme centre.
- Sarkar, Sidharth and Acheanpong, I. K. (2010), Gender work and Poverty. Arise Publishers & Distributors – New Delhi

12

Health Implications of Gender-Based Violence: A Global Overview

Dr Anita Sharma

Assistant Professor (Psychology)

Department of Psychology Himachal Pradesh University, Shimla

Email: anitahpu@gmail.com

Virender

Research scholar

Department of Psychology

Himachal Pradesh University, Shimla

Abstract

This chapter provides an overview of the extent and nature of gender-based violence and its health consequences, particularly on sexual and reproductive health. Violence against women is now well recognised as a public health problem and human rights violation of worldwide significance. It is an important risk factor for women's ill health, with far reaching consequences for both their physical and mental health. Gender based violence takes many forms and results in physical, sexual and psychological harm to the women throughout their lives. Gender based violence is often the manifestation of unequal power relation between men and women in society and the secondary status of the women because of which women have to suffer a range of health problems in silence. Violence against women is the most pervasive yet least recognised human rights violation in the world. It also is a profound health problem, sapping women's energy, compromising their physical health, and eroding their self-esteem. In addition to causing injury, violence increases women's long-term risk of a number of other health problems, including chronic pain, physical disability, drug and alcohol abuse and depression. Gender based violence is a phenomenon of epidemic proportions prevalent in many families, communities, societies and cultures across the globe. Many women and girls, and to a lesser degree men and boys, either directly experience or face the consequences of some form of gender based violence in their lifetime. Gender based violence manifests itself in multiple forms and involves a wide variety of perpetrators from intimate partners and family members, to strangers to institutional actors such as police, teachers and soldiers. Intimate partner violence is the most pervasive form of gender based violence experienced by women and girls. This chapter will aim at describing a few problems related to women's health which are directly linked to their experience as victims of gender based violence.

Keywords: *Gender-based violence, Health, Women*

Introduction

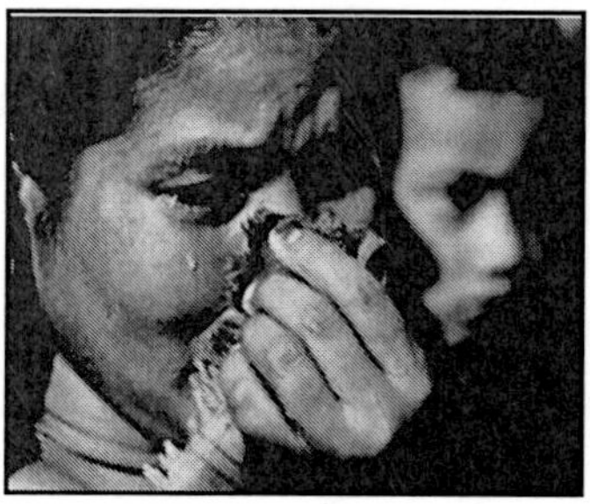

Gender-based Violence (GBV) is a global public health concern that has only recently received significant research and policy attention. It is one of the most common forms of violence globally and includes physical, sexual, emotional, and economic violence. Studies from India suggest a relatively high prevalence of GBV and estimates vary widely, from 18 per cent to 70 per cent of women, reflecting in part a wide variety of methodologies to document such violence. Although the issue has been highlighted in India with the Protection of Women from Domestic Violence Act in 2005, GBV remains under-reported (*Coast, Leone, & Malviya, 2013).*

Gender based violence (GBV) is any act or threat of harm inflicted on a person because of their gender. It is rooted in gender inequality therefore women are primarily affected. Gender based violence refers to an act that results in or is likely to result in physical, sexual and psychological harm or suffering, including threats of such acts, coercion or arbitrary deprivation of liberty, whether occurring in public or private life. It encompasses sexual violence, domestic violence, sex trafficking, harmful practices (such as female genital mutilation/cutting), forced/early marriage, forced prostitution, sexual harassment and sexual exploitation etc. Gender based violence is a phenomenon of epidemic proportions prevalent in many families, communities, societies and cultures across the globe. Many women and girls, and to a lesser degree men and boys, either directly experience or face the consequences of some form of gender based violence in their lifetime. Gender based violence manifests itself in multiple forms and involves a wide variety of perpetrators from intimate partners and family members to strangers to institutional actors such as police, teachers and soldiers. Intimate partner violence is the most pervasive form of gender based violence experienced by women and girls. Nearly one out of every three women globally has experienced psychological, physical or sexual partner violence during their lifetime. While gender based violence is a universal problem, it is a problem of extreme magnitude in less developed countries.

Gender-based violence is a product of social context and has been traditionally condoned and culturally sanctioned in India. This is reflected in women's attitudes towards violence: analyses of National Family Health Survey data (2005) in rural South India show that 96 per cent of women believe that Intimate Partner Violence (IPV) is acceptable in at least one circumstance. Given the social dimension of GBV and IPV, it is interesting to note that increased socio-economic status is associated with the lower likelihood of IPV in India, while lower dowry levels are associated with significantly higher subsequent risks of violence.

Violence against women of which domestic violence is a part, is almost a universal phenomenon that cuts across the regional, social, cultural, economic boundaries and threatens the health, well-being, rights and dignity of women in streets, in workplace, and at home. The risk factors vary from culture to culture, but the consequences are almost similar all over the globe (Gunilla & Claudia, 1979). The term gender based violence has been defined as "acts or threats of acts intended to hurt or make women suffer physically, sexually or psychologically, and which affect women because they are women or affect women disproportionally" (Klein, 2004). Gender based violence extends across women's life span which begins pre-birth with sex-selective abortion and battering during pregnancy; and continuing through infancy and childhood with differential access to food and medical care, and sexual abuse; during adolescence with dating violence, economically coerced sex, and forced prostitution; and in adulthood with violence from an intimate partner, marital rape, dowry abuse, homicide, and sexual harassment. The most common forms of violence against women are physical, sexual and emotional abuse by a woman's husband or intimate partner. Violence against women is one of the most widespread human rights violations as well as a public health problem in need of urgent attention. It clearly impacts people's ability to achieve the highest attainable standard of physical and mental health (Claudia & Heidi, 2009).

Data from the International Crime Victimisation survey, cited in the World Report on Violence and Health, reports that 1.9 per cent of women aged 16 and above in Mumbai report having been sexually assaulted in the last five years. In one six-state study, 40 per cent of women reported physical assault by a male partner. Recent estimates of lifetime partner violence among ever-married women are 39.7 per cent for all types of violence (emotional, physical or sexual). A study of 2,000 pregnant Indian women found that 30.7 per cent of women who had not wished to have sex had been forced to do so, while a separate survey of 397 women in rural South India reported that 34 per cent of women had been hit, forced to have sex by their husband, or both. A study in Uganda and Bangladesh reported that more than 80 per cent and 94 per cent of women surveyed respectively had experienced physical, sexual or psychological violence at some point in their marriage/intimate relationship.

Women experience gender-based violence in the family, in the workplace, in the street, in trafficking, and in warfare. Among these different contexts, intimate relationships are a primary location for the victimisation of women. Violence against women is now well recognised as a public health problem and human rights violation of world wide significance. It is an important risk factor for women's ill health, with far reaching consequences for both their physical and mental health. Gender based violence takes many forms and results in physical, sexual and psychological harm to the women throughout their lives. Gender based violence often the manifestation of unequal power relation between men and women in society and the secondary status of the women because of which women have to suffer a range of health problems in silence. Violence against women is "any act of gender-based violence that results in, or is likely to result in, physical, sexual, or psychological harm or suffering to women, including threats of such acts, coercion or arbitrary deprivation of liberty, whether occurring in public or in private life" (Krantz, Gunilla & Claudia, 1979).

What are the health implications of widespread GBV? Evidence from India reflects global patterns, and shows implications for murder, attempted suicide, mental ill-health, poorer health outcomes for women and children, and HIV risk. Reproductive tract infections (RTIs) also account for a large burden of disease in low-income settings because of their role in making HIV transmission more effective and because of their impact on reproductive and child health. Beyond health concerns, domestic violence has substantial social and economic costs that impact at the individual, household, community, and national levels. The financial costs of GBV range from direct costs (including health care, judicial, and social services) to indirect costs (including lost productivity from paid and unpaid work and foregone lifetime earnings from mortality due to GBV).

The consequences of gender-based violence include severe short-and long-term damage to women's health and significant risks for the health of their children (Bharati, 2014). The most immediate physical health consequences are the consequences of injuries such as acute and chronic pain, cuts, burns, bruises, broken teeth, broken bones, damages to eyes and ears. For women the risk of injury from physical assault seems to increase when the assailant is an intimate. Chronic stress-related problems include functional gastrointestinal disorder, appetite loss and viral infections such as cold and flu (Campbell, 2002). Violence during pregnancy poses a threat to health and at its extreme can result in death of the mother and her unborn child (Bacchus, Mezey & Bewley, 2004). The main health effect specific to abuse during pregnancy is the threat to health and risk of mother, fetus, or both from trauma. This can overlap of intimate partner violence and child abuse (Campbell, 2002). Gynecologic problems are the most consistent physical health difference between battered and non-battered women (Stephenson, Michael & Saifuddin, 2006). Female genital mutilation (FMG), a culturally supported form of gender-based violence is associated with a range of serious health problems, including infection, chronic pain, sexual dysfunction, and obstetric complications (Outlook, 2001).

From a worldwide review of violence against women, Heise, Ellsberg and Gottemoeller (1999) concluded that two of the most common forms of such violence are associated with intimate relationships and include physical abuse by an intimate male partner and sexual violence, such as rape and other forms of coerced sex. This review was based on almost 50 population based surveys from Africa, the Near East, Latin America and the Caribbean, Europe, and North America and indicated that between 10 per cent and 50 per cent of women report being physically or sexually harmed by an intimate male partner at some point in their lives.

Similar findings have been reported from Europe (Hagemann-White, 2001). They indicate that across many cultures intimate male partners (spouses, ex-spouses, partners, ex-partners) perpetrate a significant amount of violence against the women with whom they are or were involved in an intimate relationship. Reporting incidence figures, a French survey found that nine per cent of women had experienced violence in an intimate relationship in the previous 12 months (Jaspard et al., 2001). Lifetime prevalence figures tend to be significantly higher. Römkens (1997) found that 26.2 per cent of Dutch women had experienced physical violence in a heterosexual relationship at some point in their lives. Among Irish women who had lived in intimate relationships, 18 per cent had experienced sexual violence (Kelleher et al., 1995). In a Swiss survey, 20.7 per cent of women reported being abused by their intimate partner (Gillioz, de Puy, & Ducret, 1997). Surveys in Finland (Heiskanen & Piispa, 1998) and Sweden (Lundgren & Westerstrand, 2002) report even higher estimates, suggesting that physical and sexual violence is so closely woven into intimate relationships that they pose a significant risk to almost one out of two women who enter into them.

Statistics Canada (1993) reported that 25 per cent of women surveyed in Canada indicated that a current or former male partner had physically assaulted them since age 16. For the U.S. as well, Sharp and Campbell (1999) concluded that the most common form of violence women experience occurs in intimate relationships and is physical and sexual abuse by an intimate partner. The U.S. National Crime Victimisation Survey of 1992–1993 estimated that 29 per cent of all violence against women in the U.S. was perpetrated by a current or former intimate partner (Federal Bureau of Investigation, 1993). Research sponsored by the U.S. Department of Justice estimates that for each year between 1992 and 1996 about eight in 1,000 women (compared to one in 1,000 men) experienced violence by an intimate partner, male or female (Greenfield et al., 1998). The Bureau of Justice Statistics (1998) estimated that between 1976 and 1996, 44 per cent of female homicide victims were killed by a spouse, ex-spouse, or boyfriend (42.5 per cent by a relative, stranger, acquaintance, or friend, which included an exboyfriend).

The U.S. National Violence against Women Survey of 1995/1996 found that violence against women occurs primarily in intimate relationships, and that women are four times as likely to be victimised in the context of intimate relationships than are men (Tjaden & Thoennes, 2000). Prevalence estimates from the survey indicate that 64.0 per cent of the women experience other forms of coerced sex. This review was based on almost 50 population based surveys from Africa, the Near East, Latin America and the Caribbean, Europe, and North America and indicated that between 10 per cent and 50 per cent of women reported being physically or sexually harmed by an intimate male partner at some point in their lives.

The continuum of violence against women (Kelly, 1987) extends to casual dating relationships and sexual harassment. The U.S. National College Women Sexual Victimisation (NCWSV) study surveyed a random sample of 4,446 women who were enrolled in 2- or 4-year institutions of higher education during fall 1996. The study assessed the incidence of 12 types of sexual victimisation, including completed rape and attempted rape. About 3 per cent of the sample had experienced either a completed rape (1.7 per cent) or an attempted rape (1.1 per cent), a victimisation rate of 27.7 in 1,000 female students. Of the 123 rape victims in the sample, 22.8 per cent were victimised more than once. In about 20 per cent of the completed and attempted rape incidents, the victim was injured, citing most often either bruises, black-eyes, cuts, scratches, swelling, or chipped teeth (Fisher et al., 2000).

Health Implications

Sexual violence has profound impact on the mental, physical and reproductive health of the victim. The consequences of gender-based violence include severe short and long term damage to women's health, significant risks for the health of their children, and staggering societal expenditures in the medical, justice, and social service systems, and the workplace (Miller, et al., 1996). The most immediate physical health consequences are the consequences of injuries such as acute and chronic pain, cuts, burns, bruises, broken teeth, broken bones, muscular and skeletal injuries, and damage to eyes and ears (Grisso et al., 1991; Mullerman et al., 1996; Varvaro &Lasko, 1993). For women, the risk of injury from physical assault seems to increase when the assailant is an intimate. The U.S. National Violence against Women Survey found that 41.5 per cent of women reported being injured during their most recent assault by an intimate, compared to 19.9 per cent of men. In addition, 31.5 per cent of female rape victims reported being injured during their most recent rape, compared to 16.1 per cent of male rape victims, and 39.0 per cent of female physical assault victims were injured during their most recent assault, compared to 24.8 per cent of male assault victims.

Long-term physical health consequences seem to be related, at least in part, to the chronic stress generated by violence and abuse and include symptoms and illnesses affecting the neurological, cardiovascular, gastrointestinal, muscular, urinary, and reproductive systems (Martinez etal., in press), such as vaginal discharges, eating disorders, diarrhea or constipation, fainting or passing out, frequent or severe headaches, difficulty passing urine, problems with sleeping, shortness of breath (McCauleyet al., 1996), and neurological symptoms (Cascardi et al., 1992).

Acts of sexual violence have severe consequences for women's reproductive system causing nonspecific pelvic, genital, and breast pain; severe menstrual problems; urinary tract infections; pelvic inflammatory disease;vaginal and anal tearing; and sexually transmitted disease including HIV/AIDS (McFarlane et al., 1996; Plichta & Abraham,1996). While most of these findings pertain to the health impact of physical and sexual violence, psychological abuse alone can have devastating consequences, including depression, post-traumatic stress disorder (PTSD), anxiety, and an increase in physical health problems (Coker et al., 2000; Martinez et al., 2002; O'Leary, 1999).

Mental Health Implications

The physical side of abuse is easily seen, but the psychological wounds are hardly seen and these affect every single aspects of the life of the victim. The psychological impact of domestic violence affects women more than the physical injuries. Numerous researchers have documented that the "association between violence from one's spouse, low self-esteem, and suicidal tendencies is very strong, especially when compared to the women's pre-battering life phase" Fischbach & Herbert. 1997). Sometimes victims may take long time to recover from and may develop extreme symptoms years later in response to stressful incidents. Regular alcohol consumption by the husband, harassment by the in-laws, exposure to harsh physical discipline during childhood and witnessing father beating the mother during childhood were other factors that were strongly associated with increased risk of poor mental health (Kumar, Jeyaseelan, Ahuja, & Chandra, 2005). Physical and sexual violence negatively impacts women's mental health. Mental health consequences include depression, post-traumatic stress disorder (PTSD), anxiety, sleeping disorder, eating problems, suicidal tendencies, and increased use of alcohol and other drugs. PTSD is commonly conceptualised as an anxiety disorder occurring subsequent to a traumatic event which is perceived as highly threatening. There is some evidence that PTSD is directly associated with more suicidal attempts and this mediates the link between partner violence and suicidal attempts (Maria, Patricia, & Tarrier, 2009; Campbell & Lewandowski, 1997; Plichta, 1996). Women, who live with violent men, develop serious health problems as a consequence of the repeated violence and fear they experience. Stark & Flitcraft (1996) have identified this as "Battered Woman Syndrome", characterised by recurrent assaultive injuries, stress-related injuries, isolation, substance abuse and mental illness (Pamela & Emma, 1999).

Implications for Child Health

The acts of sexual violence have severe consequences for women's reproductive system causing nonspecific pelvic, genital and breast pain, severe menstrual problems, urinary tract infections, sexually transmitted diseases including HIV/AIDS. Evidence from health facilities suggests that abused women's reproductive health is compromised through much higher rates of gyneocological problems, HIV and sexually transmitted infections (STIs), miscarriages, abortions, low birth weight, and unwanted pregnancy (Kishor & Johnson 2006). Sexual violence also results in unplanned pregnancy. Sexual and physical violence against women during pregnancy affects their children's health through later entry into prenatal care, fetal distress, pre-term labours and births, low birth-weight infants, miscarriages, and still births (McFarlaneet al., 1996).

Loss of Healthy Years of Life

In its 1993 World Development Report, the World Bank tried to estimate the overall health burden of gender-based violence in terms of healthy years of life lost due to domestic violence and rape among women aged 15–44. The relative impact of gender-based violence on disability-adjusted life years depends on the overall burden of disease, which is lower in more industrialised than in less industrialised countries. In industrialised countries, nearly 20 per cent of healthy years lost are attributable to gender-based violence. Worldwide, the threat of gender-based violence to women's health is comparable to tuberculosis, HIV, cardiovascular disease, and cancer, and about three times as big as the effect of war (Heise et al., 1994).

Health Implications of Violence against Women

A recent study published by the WHO in 2013 systematically reviewed studies providing data on health effects of physical and sexual intimate partner violence and non-partner sexual violence against women. The review identified, among others, the following consequences of violence against women:

Globally, 38 per cent of all murders of women are reportedly committed by intimate partners.

- Out of all women who experienced physical and/or sexual violence by an intimate partner, 42 per cent experienced injuries, as a result.
- Compared to women who have not experienced partner violence, women survivors of such violence face a 16 per cent higher risk of having a low-birth weight baby, are more than twice as likely to have an induced abortion, and are more than twice as likely to experience depression.
- In some regions, women who experienced sexual intimate partner violence are 1,5 times more likely to acquire HIV and 1,6 times more likely to have syphilis, compared to women have not experienced such violence.
- Women who have experienced non-partner sexual violence are 2,3 times more likely to have alcohol use disorders and 2,6 more likely to have depression or anxiety, compared to women have not experienced such violence (WHO, 2013).

While health consequences of GBV are similar across low, middle and high-income countries, the nature or severity of the effects of such violence may vary according to context-specific factors, such as poverty; gender inequality; cultural or religious practices; access to health, legal and other support services; conflict or natural disaster; HIV prevalence; and legal and policy environments.

Conclusion

Millions of girls and women suffer from gender-based violence and its consequences because of their sex and unequal status in society. Violence against women is a serious violation of human rights. The women who have experienced physical, sexual and psychological violence suffer a range of health problems, often in silence. Hence, attention has been paid to the serious health consequences of the abused and the health needs of the abused women and girls. Necessary measures are warranted to combat such situations. Substantial legislative changes have recently taken place in India, but the low levels of reporting and sentencing in GBV cases mean that these laws remain 'paper tigers' (*Coast, Leone, & Malviya,2013).* Without the adequate collection and reporting of data on gender-based violence – whether through crime rates or health system data – the continued under-reporting of GBV will reinforce the lack of attention that it is afforded. Unless gender-based violence is counted, it will continue not to count.

References

- Bacchus, L., Mezey, G. & Bewley, S. (2004). Domestic violence: prevalence in pregnant women and associations with physical and psychological health. *European Journal of Obstetrics & Gynecology and Reproductive Biology*, 113, 6–11.

- Bharati S. (2014). Impact of violence on women's health. *International Journal of Interdisciplinary and Multidisciplinary Studies,* 1(3), 84-86.
- Campbell, J.C. (2002). Health consequences of intimate partner violence. *The Lancet*, 359 (13):1331-1336.
- Campbell, J. C., & Lewandowski, L. A. (1997). Mental and physical health effects of intimate partner violence on women and children. *Psychiatric Clinics of North America,* 20, 353–373.
- Cascardi, M., Langhinrichsen, J., & Vivian, D. (1992). Marital aggression: Impact, injury and health correlates for husbands and wives. *Archives of Internal Medicine,* 152, 357–363.
- Claudia, G. M. & Heidi, S. (2009). Protection of sexual and reproductive health rights: Addressing violence against women. *International Journal of Gynecology and Obstetrics,* 106:144–147.
- Coker, A. L., Smith, P. H., McKeown, R. E., & King, M. J. (2000). Frequency and correlates of intimate partner violence by type: Physical, sexual, and psychological battering. *American Journal of Public Health*, 90, 553–559.
- Fischbach. L. R. & Herbert, B. (1997). Domestic Violence and Mental Health: Correlates and conundrums within and across cultures. *Social Science Medicine,* 45(8):1161-1176.
- Fisher, B. S., Cullen, F. T., & Turner, M. G. (2000). *The sexual victimisation of college women.*
- Washington, DC: National Institute of Justice.
- Gillioz, L., de Puy, J., & Ducret, V. (1997). *Domination et violence envers la femme dans le.*
- *couple*. Lausanne, Switzerland: Editions Payot.
- Greenfield, L. A., Rand, M. R., Craven, D., Klaus, P. A., Perkins, C. A., Ringel, C., Warchol, G., Matson, C., & Fox, J. A. (1998). *Violence by intimates* (National Criminal Justice Publication No. 167237). Washington, DC: U.S. Department of Justice.
- Grisso, J. A., Wishner, A. R., Schwarz, D. F., Weene, B. A., Holmes, J. H., & Sutton, R. L. (1991). A population-based study of injuries in inner-city women. *American Journal of Epidemiology,* 143, 59–68.
- Gunilla K. &, Claudia, G.M. (1979). Violence against Women. *Journal of Epidemiology and Community Health,* 59(10): 818:821.
- Hagemann-White, C. (2001). European research on the prevalence of violence againstwomen. *Violence against Women,* 7, 732–759.
- Heise, L., Ellsberg, M., & Gottemoeller, M. (1999). *Ending violence*

against women. Population.

- Reports, Series L, No. 11. Baltimore: Johns Hopkins University School of Public Health.
- Heise, L. L., Pitanguy, J., & Germain, A. (1994). *Violence against women: The hidden health burden*. Washington, DC: World bank Discussion Papers, No. 255.
- Jaspard, M., Brown, E., Condon, S., Firdion, J. M., Fougeyrollas-Schwebel, D., Lhomond, B., Maillochan, F., & Schittz, M.-A. (2001). *National survey on violence against women inFrance (ENVEFF)*. Paris: Institute de démographie de l'Université de Paris I.
- Kelleher and Associates (with O'Connor, M.) (1995). *Making the links. Toward an integrated strategy for the elimination of violence against women in intimate relationships with men*. Dublin, Ireland: Women's Aid.
- Kelly, L. (1987). The continuum of sexual violence. In J. Hanmer & M. Maynard (Eds.), *Women, violence and social control* (pp. 46–60). London: Macmillan.
- Kishor, S. & Johnson, K. (2006). Reproductive health and domestic violence: Are poorest women uniquely disadvantaged?. *Demography*, 43(2):293-307.
- Klein, R. (2004). Sickening relationship: Gender-based violence, women's health, and the role of informal third parties. *Journal of Social and Personal Relationships*, 21(1):146-165.
- Kumar, S., Jeyaseelan, L., Ahuja, S. & Chandra, R. (2005). Domestic violence and its mental health correlates in Indian women, *The British Journal of Psychiatry*, 187: 62-67.
- Lundgren, E., & Westerstrand, J. (2002, September). *The omnipresence of violence in equal Sweden: The first prevalence* lopment (1993). *OECD Health Systems: Facts and trends 1960–1991*. Paris: Organisation for Economic Cooperation and Development.

13

The Different Faces of Gender Equality

Dr Anu Rahi

Thakurdwara, Moradabad

Introduction

During the early years, in this country women were not entitled to the same right and privileges as men, they were not allowed to vote and were usually required to surrender control of their property to their husband upon marriage, moreover their educational and occupational opportunities were severely limited. It was commonly believed that a woman's place was in the home; raising children and tending to domestic affairs.

The first efforts to achieve equality for women occurred in the 1800s. During the early part of that century, co-educational studies at the university level were offered for the first time. State laws were passed which allowed women to retain their property after marriage. Also, the first women's rights became active in the abolitionist movement during the civil war era. Some became well known public orators, an uncommon occupation for women at the time.

Women were long considered naturally weaker then men, squeamish, and unable to perform work requiring muscular or intellectual development. In most pre industrial societies, for example, domestic chores were relegated to women, leaving "heavier" labour such as hunting and plowing to men. This ignored the fact that caring for children and doing such tasks as milking cows and washing clothes also required heavy, sustained labour. But physiological tests now suggest that women have a greater tolerance for pain, and statistics reveal that women live longer and more resistant to many diseases. The resulting stereotype that "a woman's place is in the home". has largely determined the ways in which women have expressed themselves.

Despite their increased presence in the workforce, most women still have primary responsibility for house work and family care.

Difference between Gender Equality and Gender Equity

"Gender equality requires equal enjoyment by women and men of socially valued goods opportunities, resources and rewards".

In other worlds, gender equality refers to equal access to social goods, services and resources and equal opportunities in all spheres of life for both men and women. When there is gender inequality women are more likely to be disadvantaged and marginalised; but we should not ignore the negative impact that gender inequality can have on men as well. Therefore, gender equality is the concern of all and changes must be brought about for both men and women. However, this is not to say that men and women are equally affected by gender inequality. It remains true that women have the greater share of disadvantages. Another incidents of the work place that demonstrates the inequality in the treatment of men and women is sexual harassment.

Sexual Harassment

Sexual Harassment refers to "Unwanted sexual advances, wether touches, looks, pressures to have sex, or even jokes." (Hnslin & Nelson, 1996, p. 300). It can be of two forms.

The first one known as quid pro quo harassment occurs when the harassment is linked to the granting of a benefit; for example, a woman is pressured to have sex with her employer in order to get a promotion.

The second type refers to sexual harassment that is not linked to any privilege but results in unfriendly environment. Over the years as women come to realise that offensive behaviour of a sexual nature at the workplace need not to be accepted as a normal and invitable part of job. Anybody can be a victim of sexual harassment be it a men or woman.

Sexual harassment is not an issue to be taken lightly. It can have ruinous results on the victim's physical as well as mental health and it certainly adversely affects the productivity of the worker who stands as victim there is still the unfortunate tendency to consider male norms as a measure for women's position. Providing women and men with the same opportunities is the first step; but for true gender equality to be achieved there is a need for gender equity.

Gender Equity

"Gender equity is the process of being fair to women and men". (UNFPA) Gender equity implies fairness in the way women and men are treated. The different life experiences and needs of men and women are taken into consideration and compensation is made for women's historical and social disadvantages. Gender equity thus serves to level the Playing field and empower women. Therefore, we can say that fair dealing is essential to achieve true equality.

Position of Women In India

Where we worship goddess Luxmi, Durga, Gauri etc., there are most Indian communities prefer son and this is something that is widespread throughout the country. Cultural beliefs have made people to submit to the notion that having sons is one way to go to haven after death and guarantees financial security. Therefore, it is clear that these culture work to devalue the role of women in these societies, they strive to achieve equality with men, making gender equality in India an issue.

Gender discrimination continues to be an enormous problem within Indian society. Traditional patriarchal norms have relegated women to secondary status within the household and workplace. This strongly affects women's health, financial status, education and political involvement. Women are commonly married young, quickly become mothers, and are then burdened by stringent domestic and financial responsibilities. They are frequently malnourished since women typically are the last member of a household to eat and the last to receive medical attention. Only 54 per cent of Indian women are literats as compared to 75 per cent of men, women receive little schooling, and suffer from unfair and biased inheritance and divorce laws. These laws prevent women from accumulating substantial financial assets making it difficult for women to establish their own security and autonomy.

In 2009 the passing of the compulsory education Act was a historical moment for the children of India that clearly indicated the commitment of the state to providing educational opportunities for all children. The act reinforced faith in school education as being in the best interest of children as well as society. The Act makes available to the girl child in a very real sense all that is overdue to her.

Domestic Violence

Globally one out of every three women faces violence at the hands of their husbands, fathers, or brothers and uncles in their homes. Domestic violence can be described as when one adult in a relationship misuses power to control another through violence and other forms of abuse psychological violence includes verbal abuse.

Such violence may also include rape and sexual abuse; psychological violence includes verbal abuse. Harassment, confinement and deprivation of physical, financial and personal resources for some women emotional abuse may be more painful than physical attacks because they effectively undermine women's security and self-confidence.

Working women i.e., those who are in paid employment, face problems at the workplace just by virtue of their being women. Social attitude to the role of women lags much behind the law. The attitude which considers women fit for certain jobs and not others.

Problems at Workplace

Sexual harassment at the workplace is a universal problem even though the occurance of sexual harassment at the workplace is widespread in India and elsewhere. This is the first time it has been recognised as an infringement of the fundamental rights of a women under Article 19(1)(g) of the constitution of India "to practice any profession or to carry out any occupation, trade or business. In India, Articles 14, 15 and 21 of the Indian constitution provide safeguards against all forms of discrimination.

In any civilised society. It is the fundamental right of people to able to lead their lives with dignity, free from mental or physical torture to ensure these transgressors must pay for their unsolicited sexual advances. At the same time organisations such as men against violence and abuse that conduct gender sensitisation programmes and self defence classes to combat sexual harassment at the workplace, must be encouraged.

Importance of Self Defence Training for Women

In today's world women are independent and go out for work. In the same time they also face the problems of stalking molesting, harassment etc., to deal with such problem it is necessary that woman should be trained in self defence. The girls should know how to fight handle themselves without depending on others. She should know her strength and learn to fight against 'he'. In today's world many girls and women face harassment molesting and stalking problems why? Just because every one thinks that she does not have any strength to fight and they start harassing her. There should be a self-defence training in every school in the country to protect themselves. The primary level students can start their training in order to protect themselves. When these children grow up their confident level would be high and would be a better fighter than men. Men are considerd to be stronger than women. But do not think that woman can not fight. Many girls are shy and uncomfortable but this should no longer be there. Girls should know how to fight back if some one tries to do something wrong with her.

Findings

India is rapidly advancing in its developmental goals and more and more women are joining the workforce. It is the duty of the state to provide for the wellbeing and respect of its citisens to prevent frustration low self-esteem, insecurity and emotional disturbance, which in turn could affect business efficacy; leading to loss of production and loss of reputation for the organisation or the employer. In fact the recognition of the right to protect against sexual harassment is an intrinsic component of the protection of women's human rights. It is also a step towards providing women independence, equality of opportunity and the right to work with dignity. The government has also drawn up a draft National policy for the empowerment of women which is a policy statement, outlining the state's response to problems of gender discrimination. As persistent gender inequalities continue, we need to rethink concepts and strategies for promoting women's dignity and rights.

References

- D'Souza, V (1975). Family status and male work participation In: V.D'Souza (ed.), women in contemporary India. India, Monohar; en.m.wikipedia.org/wiki/women-in-india/the free encyclopedia. en.m.wikipedia.org/.....violence-againstwomen-wikipedia.org
- Gupta Manisha and Renu Khanna (2002), Process Documentation of Gender Training of Dilaasa, Mumbai.
- Importance of self Defence for women study. Mode com. Retrieved 06, 2013 from
- http://www.Studymode.com/essay/Importanceofself-Defence-for women-178957.html.
- ncw.nic.in/frmLLawsRelatedwomen.as
- WWW.women empowermentiniindia.com/

14

Gender Sensitisation through Text Books

Dr Chetna Thapa

TGT, Dept. of School Education, Uttarakhand
chetna.ch@gmail.com

Dr Usha Pathak

Dept. of Teacher Education, D.A.V. (PG) College, Dehradun

usha.prof6@gmail.com

Ph No- 08650303009, Ph No- 09760998923

Abstract

In the changing scenario of the modern world where men and women work together and interact in the professional, the social and the domestic front, gender equality is an essential criterion to be observed by responsible human beings. Gender sensitisation is about making people aware of the need to bring about a quantum change in our mindset which sees man as the bread winner and woman as the house keeper. The school being a miniature society, the first step of gender equality should begin at the school level and textbooks play an important impact in it. The present chapter is an attempt to analyse the significance of interdisciplinary perspective and how it can evolve as a means for bridging the gulf which exists across academic disciplines. Social issues such as gender discrimination and gender sensitisation have been addressed by integrating the content of literature and social sciences and cutting across the boundaries of disciplines.

Key words: *Gender sensitisation, Textbooks, Interdisciplinary*

Introduction

In recent times, there has been a paradigm shift in the notion of teaching-learning process which has been articulated in National Curriculum Framework 2005. The five guiding principles of NCF 2005 are connecting knowledge to life outside the school, ensuring that learning is shifted away from rote methods, enriching the curriculum to provide for overall development of children rather than remain textbook centric, making examinations more flexible and integrated into classroom life and nurturing an over-riding identity informed by caring concerns within the democratic polity of the country (p. 5). These principles envision us regarding school education and its significance in students' overall development. In this regard, it is pertinent to understand the role of school education in education in enabling young minds to view social reality as emerging in their context. The present chapter is an attempt to analyse the significance of interdisciplinary perspective and how it can evolve as a means for bridging the gulf which exists across academic disciplines. Of late, it has been realised that over packed school curriculum needs to be replaced by integrating components across various disciplines. Thus, rethinking the significance of interdisciplinary perspective forms the background of the present study.

Understanding Gender Sensitisation

In the changing scenario of the modern world where men and women work together and interact in the professional, the social and the domestic front, gender equality is an essential criterion to be observed by responsible human beings. Gender sensitisation is about making people aware of the need to bring about a quantum change in our mindset which sees man as the bread winner and woman as the house keeper. The home-bound woman of yester years has metamorphosed into the smart, dynamic modern woman who is adept at balancing her professional and domestic lives. She has successfully carved a niche for herself in the scheme of things. Given the increasing number of women who work alongside with men for long hours in the professional field, the need of the hour is to develop a cordial and amiable working environment where there is mutual respect and trust between the sexes, without sexual innuendoes and obstructive chauvinism to mar the atmosphere. The foundation for this changing mindset should be laid right from childhood and that is why the school plays a pivotal role in gender sensitisation. The school being a miniature society, the first step of gender equality and sensitisation should begin at the school level. The purpose of the present chapter is to examine the representation of gender sensitisation across disciplines.

In this regard, it is imperative to understand how such issues have been presented in text books. NCERT text books (based on National Curriculum Framework, 2005) have initiated to bridge the gap between the literature and social sciences. Social issues have been addressed by integrating the content of literature and social sciences and cutting across the boundaries of disciplines. The following section presents a brief text book analysis of NCERT Social Science, Hindi and English text books with regard to understanding the way of representation of gender sensitisation.

Social Science VI and VII Class: *Kanta's story* in class VII, is an example to portray how to gain a deeper insight into equality, the issues of inequality also needs to be understood. It is imperative that the ideas of equality and justice should be implemented practically in order to realise constitutional goals and make India a democratic nation not in words but in spirit and action also. The issues of women inequality have been raised by the references of *Rashsundari Devi* and *Rokeya Begum.* Although the fundamental rights enshrined in the constitution talk about equality, liberty and justice, yet in the present scenario, on analysing Indian landscape, it emerges that there is a huge gap between theory and practice which needs to be bridged down.

VIII Class Civics: In the beginning, the note to teachers articulates the vision with which the book has been written. It highlights the fact that social science should focus on developing an informed understanding about social issues so that students may be able to conceptualise social issues in a holistic manner.

***X Class Hindi*:** In Hindi textbook "*Kshitij*" there is a poem *'Kanyadaan'* written by *'Rituraj'* which gives significant key message of women empowerment. The following lines are noteworthy:

'Maa ne kaha paani mein jhank kar
Apne chehre par mat reejhna
Aag rotiyan sekane ke liye hai
Jalne ke liye nahi
Vastra aur aabhushan shabdik bhramon ki tarah
Bandhan hai stri jeevan ke
Maa ne kaha ladki hona
Par ladki jaisi dikhai mat dena'

The mother's word to her daughter at her wedding farewell are quite significant as it denotes women's status in the society, gender socialisation, gender stereotypes, gender bias prevailing in the society, gender discrimination, violence against women, atrocities and injustice meted out to women, the emerging need of asserting for own rights and standing against oppression and discrimination, belief in self existence, following one's duty as well as awareness about one's rights, knowledge of societal perceptions and conventional attitudes towards women along with the understanding of the crucial need for changing patriarchal mindset and initiating a new change in this direction. Each word has its own significance as it delineates societal reality in a realistic way and encourages the bride to stand for her rights.

The poem denotes that women's qualities such as love, patience, compassion, sacrifice, respect for elders, obligation towards family and home, her ideals, beliefs and values need to be viewed as an obstacle in the path of her empowerment rather patriarchal belief system needs to be questioned and challenged. The last lines are highly connotative as it captures the glimpse of Indian society where girls are neither safe at home nor society. The poem is symbolic as it addresses pertinent issue of women empowerment through certain symbols.

The teacher can weave in ideas of gender discrimination and women empowerment while teaching this poem. In recent times, there has been an increase in crimes against women. *Nirbhaya Case* and so many such cases are a stigma and a shame on our society which shows that it is not a progressive nation rather we are heading towards brutality and a savage state.

There is a lesson *'Stri Shiksha ke virodhi kutarkon ka khandan'* written by *Mahaveer Prasad Dwivedi* which contends that education serves as a significant tool for women empowerment. It is a thought provoking article in pre-independence era which calls upon a radical change in societal perceptions towards women. It argues that women education is very essential for their personal development and society at large. The author criticises age old customs and beliefs which serve as a roadblock in the path of women education. This lesson has been taken from an article which was published in September 1914 in *'Saraswati'* magazine for the first time, entitled as *'Pade likhon ka panditya'*. The lesson strongly advocates the crucial need of women education for bringing out societal change and progression towards a democratic society encompassing a thinking community.

IX Class English: *'Beehive'* has a lesson *'Reach for the top'* depicts the success story of Santosh Yadav. The lesson starts with these lines, *'The only women in the world who has scaled MT. Everest twice was born in a society where the birth of a son was regarded as a blessing, and a daughter, though not considered a curse, was not generally welcome. When her mother was expecting Santosh, a travelling 'holy man', giving her his blessing, assumed that she wanted a son'.*

The above lines present gender discrimination which begins prior to birth of a baby girl in the family and follows her entire life. However, Santosh Yadav's persistent efforts towards her goal enabled her to become a successful name in the man dominated world. *'Santosh was not always content with her place in a traditional way of life. She began living life on her own terms from the start. Santosh's parents were affluent landowners who could afford to send their children to the best schools, even to the country's capital Delhi, which was quite close by. But, in line with the prevailing custom in the family, Santosh had to make do with the local village school. So, she decided to fight the system in her own quiet way when the right moment arrived.'* Her success gets reflected in the lines, *'She then conquered the Everest a second time, thus setting a record as the only women to have conquered the Everest twice, and securing for herself and India a unique place in the annals of mountaineering. In recognition of her achievements, the Indian government bestowed upon her one of the nation's top honours, the Padamshri'.*

Strengthening Links across Disciplines

The above discussion reveals that there have been efforts to intermingle content from other disciplines as in the case of Social Science text books, the excerpts from poems and stories have been presented to provide a detail picture of such issues related to gender discrimination. Similarly, language textbooks have evolved to highlight social issues, the presentation of which is usually considered a prime objective of Social Science discipline. English textbooks have also touched upon the crucial issues of gender sensitisation in the form of narratives and autobiographical accounts of famous persons. This emerging trend of cutting across the boundaries of disciplines is an effective and most subtle way to orient students towards a holistic perspective whereby they can collect, collate and analyse information with their socio cultural contexts and simultaneously, engage in the process of knowledge construction on their own. It is argued that an interdisciplinary perspective is needed to address such issues which would present an integrated approach and cover all related issues in a meaningful way.

Implications for Schools and Teacher Education

- It is imperative to improve the content and relevance of school education through curriculum reforms. It needs to be designed to meet the needs of present times. There is an urgency to apply more dynamic and stimulating approaches for presenting knowledge in an integrated manner whereby children can connect social issues within the ambit of their socio-cultural economic backgrounds.
- Teachers play a crucial role in transacting the curriculum. It is imperative that they need to be given intensive training with regard to pedagogical content knowledge and multidisciplinary perspective to teach their specific subjects. Such type of training needs to be imparted in pre-service teacher education programme as well as in-service teacher education programmes.
- There is a trend of organising faculty meeting in schools. There is an urgent need to shatter pre-conceived notion of compartmentalising knowledge and instead, view knowledge as evolving and emerging, finding its relevance in multidisciplinary perspective. Thus, staff meetings need to be organised which could serve as a way of engaging in meaningful deliberations, generating discussions and immersing in reflective practices. Adequate time for such meetings should be allocated in school time-table.
- It is an irony that during teacher education programmes, theory-practice gap prevails. It is essential that pre methodology courses

need to be taught in such a way that student-teachers are able to connect it with other theory courses. The teachers' beliefs about subjects and students tend to influence their pedagogical practices. Thus, it is important to orient prospective teachers to engage in reflective practices to understand the influence of their beliefs on their teaching practices and teaching learning process.

- School experience has to be perceived and implemented as an internship programme where student teachers would be able to gain a deeper insight into pedagogical content knowledge and applying multidisciplinary approach in teaching subjects.
- Lesson plans need to be re-designed in such a way that there is an ample space for integrating across subjects. There should be scope for flexibility, the lesson plans have to be prepared in a flexible manner, keeping in view the constructivist paradigm and the emerging role of the teachers as reflective practitioner.
- The activities such as maintain reflective journals, peer observations and observations of regular faculty have to be given due significance, so that student teachers may understand the way of presentation of content in effective manner.
- Teachers need to be oriented about the complex issues such as gender discrimination and sensitisation. Such an understanding would enable them to handle issues which emerge from diversity inside the classroom.

Conclusion

It emerges that school curriculum needs to evolve to impart knowledge, developing skills and inculcating proper interests, attitudes and values. In this regard, multidisciplinary perspective presents a way to present social issues related to women and gender sensitivity. It is need of the hour to internalise the fact that school education should serve as a means for holistic development of the child, preparing her to face the future challenges. Thus, school curriculum also needs to be revamped according to the emerging circumstances and expectations of the society. As proposed by National Curriculum Framework 2005, teachers need to be prepared to view knowledge not as external reality embedded in text books, but as constructed in the school content of teaching – learning and personal experience.

References

- Beehive (2009), *Main Reader in English for Class IX,* New Delhi, NCERT.
- Kshitij (2009), *Main Reader in Hindi for Class X*, New Delhi, NCERT.
- NCERT (2000), *National Curriculum Framework for School Education*, New Delhi, NCERT.

- NCERT (2005), *National Curriculum Framework*, New Delhi, NCERT.
- NCERT (2005), *Position paper, National Focus Group on Teacher Educction for Curriculum renewal,* New Delhi, NCERT.
- NCTE (2005), *National Curriculum Framework for Teacher Education*, New Delhi, NCTE.
- Social and Political life (2009), *Civics textbook for class VIII*, New Delhi, NCERT.

15

Women as Agents of Peace

Dr Vanita Malewar

Lecturer, Lalitha College of Education
Venkatapur (V), Ghatkesar (M)

(Ph. 9701288383, Email-vanita777@rediffmail.com)

Abstract

Over the past decade there has been growing recognition of the importance of women's engagement in all aspects of conflict and post-conflict societies, including: accessing the peace table, rebuilding war-torn societies, standing for parliament and redefining gender-specific security needs. Women's rising position as "agents of change" rather than merely as "victims" can be seen through the numerous women worldwide who—as government representatives, activists, leaders of nongovernmental organisations (NGOs) and women's networks—have persevered to initiate transformative change within their societies. Undeterred by rebel groups, authoritarian regimes, cultural restrictions or resource limitations, and often at great personal risk, these countless women continue the work of promoting peace and security in their communities. Asha Hagi Elmi Amin, on behalf of the NGO Working Group on Women, Peace and Security has said, "Women's participation in peace processes is not optional: it is a requirement. Women are often confronted with challenges including cultural barriers, traditional patriarchal structures, minimal legislative support and lack of resources. This creates critical barriers inhibiting the transfer of their learned knowledge and first-hand experiences into a recognised and formal environment. However, many women's organisations have developed informal and innovative community-based responses that are transforming attitudes (of men and women) and reshaping women's roles in their communities. Some of the women have achieved observer status at local government meetings, and others have been elected to office at the provincial level. Furthermore, these women have become well positioned as role models to other women in their communities and also to serve as moderators within their neighbourhoods. With international support and strong and courageous advocacy from local women's organisations, tangible victories for women have occurred. The present chapter is an attempt to highlight the role of women as agents of peace.

Keywords: *nongovernmental organisations, environment, communities*

Introduction

Women have historically been under represented and sidelined in peace processes. According to Womenpeace.org, "women have represented fewer than eight per cent of participants and fewer than three per cent of signatories, and no woman has ever been appointed chief or lead mediator in UN-sponsored peace talks". Since the adoption of UN Security Council Resolution 1325 however, the issue of female visibility and participation is slowly beginning to take centre stage. Secretary Clinton, who herself is not unlike her female fictional counterparts in being the token Wonder Woman among her male colleagues on the world stage, has said, "for years, many of us have tried to show the world that women are not just victims of war; they are agents of peace. And that was the wisdom behind the historic UN Security Council Resolution 1325, which was adopted a decade ago but whose promise remains largely unfulfilled".

We are living in an exciting time where the new measures to ensure female participation in peace processes encourage us more than ever before to actively play a part in peace and security issues. One way in which we can help hasten this change in roles of women in peace and security is by changing the way we are perceived and represented in popular culture. We can fight for more accurate representation of our strengths and abilities in bringing about peace and stability in our fictional counterparts. It is now more than ever that we need to see greater numbers of strong, smart capable female superheroes joining the ranks of their male counterparts that have dominated popular culture since the 1930s. We need our female superheroes to inspire us, to be our muses, to be the female fictional agents of peace that make us believe that we the women too, can save the world.

International Scenario for Peace Building

In 2011, the United States established a national action plan to implement a U.N. resolution that calls for the equal participation of women in resolving conflicts and building peace. The U.S. National Action Plan on Women, Peace, and Security reflects that countries are more peaceful and prosperous when women have equal rights and opportunities. The plan ensures that gender concerns are fully integrated into diplomatic, military and development activities.

The plan specifies how U.S. international engagements involve women — half the world's population — as equal partners in preventing conflict and building peace in countries threatened by war, violence and insecurity.

According to President Obama's executive order establishing the plan, achieving this equality is critical to U.S. and global security. The United States joined more than 30 countries that have adopted similar plans. These are among the U.S. plan's guidelines:

- Promote gender equality and advancement of women and girls in areas facing conflict.
- Support the full participation of women in preventing and resolving conflict and building peace.
- Protect women and girls, who are disproportionately affected by conflict, from gender-based violence, exploitation, discrimination, trafficking and other abuse.
- Promote stability by investing in health, education and economic opportunity for women and girls.
- Provide for disaster and humanitarian responses that respect the specific needs of women and girls.

Implementing a Vision

In October 2000, the U.N. Security Council adopted Resolution 1325 to recognise "the important role of women in the prevention and resolution of conflicts and in peace-building … and the need to increase their role in decision-making with regard to conflict prevention and resolution".

Lessons from Northern Ireland, Liberia and other areas already had shown that, when involved, women are more likely to support agreements that restore security and services to their communities, without regard to "winning" or "losing".

Women participants tend to focus on issues critical to peace but sometimes overlooked in formal negotiations, including human rights, justice, national reconciliation and economic renewal. They tend to build coalitions across ethnic and provincial lines and speak for other marginalised groups. They may act as mediators and foster compromise during the rebuilding process.

Early Lessons

The significance of including women in peace and security issues has been demonstrated in many places. Women from rival communities in Northern Ireland built bridges through the Northern Ireland Women's Coalition and contributed to the end of a decades-long conflict. Rwandan women helped put their communities on the road to peace and prosperity after the horrific violence between Hutus and Tutsis, and they laid the foundation for the highest percentage of women in parliament in the world.

U.S. Approaches

The U.S. plan requires government agencies working with other countries to help increase women's skills for political peacemaking; this includes training women to take active roles in their local and national governments. Other tasks include helping develop laws and policies that promote women's rights; increasing the capacity of U.N. systems (law enforcement, military and others) to prevent and respond to conflict-related violence against women; and helping ensure women's equal access to aid distribution and other emergency services.

The State Department is helping to implement the U.S. plan by supporting the roles of women in peace-building and recovery in Afghanistan, South Sudan and Burma, among other countries. In "Arab Awakening" countries, the State Department is supporting women's participation in politics and promoting their roles in reforming security.

In the Democratic Republic of the Congo, Nepal and El Salvador, the State Department works with women's groups to pursue justice for survivors of gender-based violence related to conflict. In addition, the U.S. Agency for International Development (USAID) builds women's negotiation skills in the Mindanao region of the Philippines, trains police in Nepal, and increases the number of registered women voters in Yemen, among other initiatives.

Guiding Beliefs

The United States recognises that millions of women and girls worldwide are excluded from public life, subjected to violence or barred from education. Such exclusions inhibit economic growth and opportunity in the countries where they are practiced. They defy America's sense of justice — the belief that no country can advance when it suppresses half its population and fails to apply those talents, energies and gifts in building a future. The United States will continue to empower women as agents of peace.

Women Across the Globe

Women leaders from Liberia, Pakistan, Tunisia, Libya, Egypt, Yemen and Samoa shared compelling accounts of their innovative leadership approaches in a two-part panel event, "Women Leading Change in Transitioning Societies". These women, who have just been recognised as the 2012 honorees of the annual Vital Voices Global Leadership Awards, are leading change in their transitioning societies through civil society, political activities, and private business.

What kind of leadership is most effective in societies undergoing upheaval and/or transition? To address this pivotal question, women leaders from Liberia, Pakistan, Tunisia, Libya, Egypt, Yemen and Samoa shared compelling accounts of their innovative leadership approaches in a two-part panel event.

These women, who have just been recognised as the 2012 honorees of the annual Vital Voices Global Leadership Awards, are leading change in their transitioning societies through civil society, political activities, and private business. Such innovative approaches of leadership and decision making are critically important to a process of non-violent change around the world today.

The panel event also reflects the commitment of the Center for Gender and Peace-building at the U.S. Institute of Peace to build the capacity of women leaders in conflict and post-conflict settings. Such strategic goals can be creatively accomplished through the collaboration of civil society organisations and governments. USIP's co-sponsoring partners, Vital Voices Global Partnership and the Royal Norwegian Embassy, exemplify this spirit of women leading change, said Kathleen Kuehnast, director of USIP's Center for Gender and Peacebuilding, in her opening remarks.

In welcoming the group of honorees, Linda Jamison, acting executive vice president at USIP, described Vital Voices as "an important NGO that catalyses women to become agents of change in their own countries". The first panel, made up of women leaders from Pakistan, Liberia and Samoa, emphasised that effective leadership includes bringing innovative ideas and taking bold risks to make change happen in their respective countries. From filmmaking to an NGO focused on rehabilitating girl child soldiers to creating family-based businesses in remote places, each leader illustrated the need for staying grounded at the community level to make sustainable impact.

The second panel focused on women leading change in Tunisia, Egypt, Yemen and Libya. The panelists stressed the importance of supporting young girls' development and encouraging their leadership in order to prevent violence and create a more peaceful and stable society. They also emphasised the importance of remembering that it takes time to change societies that are coming out of dictatorships, and must be done from the citisens themselves.

The moderator, Kathleen Kuehnast, concluded that the panelists had offered clear examples and lessons learned on how women are leading change in their transitioning societies through non-violent and innovative approaches to engage both men and women in a more peaceful society.

Workshop on Women and Peace in India: a Gender Resource Centre and Pakistan India People's Forum for Peace and Democracy:

(PIPFPD- Odisha Chapter)

In Bhubaneswar, India from 27th to 29th March, 2011, under the aegis of PIPFPD- Odisha Chapter and Sansristi, a gender resource centre, a small group of activists, writers and scholars met to discuss UN Security Council Resolution 1325 on Women Peace and Security and its relevance in the Indian context.

The objective was to set the momentum on a National Action Plan (NAP) for the implementation of SCR 1325 in India. Acclaimed academicians and experts (including PIPFPD members) representing the women's equality movement in particular and development in general got together for intense deliberation on the issue. The keynote address was provided by Professor Betty Reardon.

One objective of the conference was to assess how 1325 applies to the Indian context and how it can be used to promote peace through women's full and equal participation in all matters of peace and security. Focus on the understanding and interpretation of UNSCR 1325 included interventions on the resolution as a tool for demilitarising security. Panelists maintained that UNSCR 1325 is in essence a significant declaration on the essential need for women's full political equality and hence concerted efforts need to be put in place for implementation from all quarters. The two-day discussion highlighted especially three concerns.

The first and fundamental one was the question of drawing lines around 'conflict.' What is a conflict area and what is not? What sorts of conflicts fall under the 1325 ambit? The policy-maker's response is likely to draw a narrowly defined circle. The activist's stance is to include the full gamut of conflicts and struggles in society. The scholar's perspective is to recognise the challenges inherent in both views. Participants also saw 1325 as an opening to push the Indian government to recognise the rightful role of women in peace negotiations at all levels.

The second concern relates to increasing the participation of women in the security sector. The discussion was predicated on the existence of an integral and systematic connection between the women's movement and peace movement stemming from the fundamental relationship scholars have long asserted of a relationship linking the exclusion of women from political power to the continual resort to war among most nation states. The problem of including token women who may not make a substantive contribution to the peace process was raised. Why don't we know more about those women who can contribute constructively to peace-building? They are out there, but media, scholars and government seem oblivious. The conference participants did not debate women's participation in the military; this has not been as much of an issue in India as it is in the U.S.

The third concern related to gender violence in conflict contexts. Many of the participants described the incidence of rape and sexual violence and other human rights violations affecting women. But this is another way in which it becomes hard to draw the line between "conflict" and "non-conflict" situations. For women and girls who live with the threat of violence everyday in their homes, schools, workplaces and streets, there is not much difference between the two situations, both of which are manifestations of the gender inequities and violence which serve to perpetuate the patriarchal power order.

The conference discussions wove around these three intertwined concerns, identifying India's current Security Council membership and its quest for a permanent seat as an unusual opportunity for advocacy for a NAP.

Some of the facts and findings that underpin the commitment to women around the globe:

- According to the World Bank, investing in women and girls has a positive correlation with poverty alleviation and a country's prosperity.
- Moreover, women's equality is smart economics. It is estimated by the UN that the Asia-Pacific region is losing over $40 billion in GDP annually due to the untapped economic potential of women.
- Or think about the role of food in human existence: Did you know that women comprise the great majority of small farmers in much of the world? If they have no say in the allocation of agricultural resources, or those resources are trampled by war, what happens to levels of nutrition, hunger, and starvation in a given country or region?
- Here is another fact: studies show that the more educated women are, the more likely they are to make positive contributions to a country's economy, and the single most effective development investment is to educate a girl—with positive consequences for her and her future family.
- Finally, I would point to a World Bank study that found that "where the influence of women in public life is greater, the level of corruption is lower", contributing to greater confidence in governance and less need to resolve disputes beyond the bounds of the rule of law, including through violence.

World Development Report on Gender Equality and Development (WDR2012)

The World Banks "World Development Report on Gender Equality and Development (WDR2012)" identified women's voice, agency and participation as key dimension of gender equality and as a major policy priority. Agency, as defined in the WDR 2012, is the ability to use endowments to take advantage of opportunities to achieve desired outcomes. In particular WDR 2012 focused on five "expressions" of agency: women's access to and control over resources; freedom of movement; freedom from the risk of violence; decision-making over family formation; and having voice in society and influencing policy.

Nobel Peace Prise

Malala Yousafzai

On 10th October, 2014, Malala Yousafzai was announced as the co-recipient of the 2014 Nobel Peace Prise for her struggle against the suppression of children and young people and for the right of all children to education. At age 17, Yousafzai is the youngest Nobel Prise laureate. Yousafzai shared the prise with Kailash Satyarthi, a children's rights activist from India. She is the second Pakistani to receive a Nobel Prise, Abdus Salam being a 1979 Physics laureate, and the only Pakistani winner of the Nobel Peace Prise.

After she won the Nobel Peace Prise, there was praise but also some disapproval of the decision to award it to her. A Norwegian jurist, Fredrik Heffermehl, commented on the winning of Malala's Nobel Prise: "This is not for fine people who have done nice things and are glad to receive it. All of that is irrelevant. What Nobel wanted was a prise that promoted global disarmament".

In October 2011, Archbishop Desmond Tutu, a South African activist, nominated Yousafzai for the International Children's Peace Prise of the Dutch international children's advocacy group Kids Rights Foundation. She was the first Pakistani girl to be nominated for the award. The announcement said, "Malala dared to stand up for herself and other girls and used national and international media to let the world know girls should also have the right to go to school". The award was won by Michaela Mycroft of South Africa.

Her public profile rose even further when she was awarded Pakistan's first National Youth Peace Prise two months later in December. On 19 December, 2011, Prime Minister Yousaf Raza Gillani awarded her the National Peace Award for Youth. At the proceedings in her honour, Yousafzai stated that she was not a member of any political party, but hoped to found a national party of her own to promote education. The Prime Minister directed the authorities to set up an IT campus in the Swat Degree College for Women at Yousafzai's request, and a secondary school was renamed in her honour. By 2012, Yousafzai was planning to organise the Malala Education Foundation, which would help poor girls go to school. In July of that year she participated in the national Marxist Summer School, and delivered a message to the 32nd congress of the Pakistani IMT which thanked them "for giving me a chance to speak last year at their Summer Marxist School in Swat and also for introducing me to Marxism and Socialism".

Mother Teresa

Mother Teresa of Calcutta, a Roman Catholic nun of Albanian stock who has cared for the poor and sick in India for more than 30 years, was named the winner of the 1979 Nobel Peace Prise.

"I am unworthy", Mother Teresa said in Calcutta on hearing that she had been selected by the five-member Nobel Committee of the Norwegian Parliament in Oslo.

But, she said, because she is "more aware of the condition of the poor", she plans to use the money, the equivalent of $190,000, to build more homes for the destitute, "especially for the lepers." The Nobel Committee's announcement said: "This year, the world has turned its attention to the plight of children and refugees, and these are precisely the categories for which Mother Teresa has for many years worked so selflessly." Mother Teresa, who is 69 years old, has been a candidate for the Peace Prise ever since her work first gained worldwide recognition more than two decades ago. Even so, she was a surprise winner today.

Message Sent by President

Among the names more frequently mentioned in recent weeks as possible winners were those of Steve Biko, the black leader who died in a South African prison in September 1977; the Anti-Slavery League in London, and President Carter, who reportedly had been nominated for his efforts to achieve peace in the Middle East.

But doubts about Mr Carter's chances began to circulate this week in Oslo as reports said it was unlikely that the Nobel Committee would award the prise for peace efforts in the Middle East for a second year since it had honoured President Anwar el-Sadat of Egypt and Prime Minister Menachem Begin in 1978.

"Your work on behalf of children, refugees, the poor and the sick has been a great inspiration for many years to those of us who cherish and espouse human rights", the President declared.

"Mankind is in your debt for your fine contributions and for the example you have provided of selfless concern for others".

The award announcement from Oslo noted that Mother Teresa was not directly involved in the struggle to achieve and maintain peace but said, "It is not the first time that the Norwegian Nobel Committee has awarded the Peace Prise for work undertaken in the struggle to overcome the poverty and distress in the world, which also constitute a threat to peace".

Mother Teresa founded her order, the Society of the Missionaries of Charity, in Calcutta's slums in 1948 when she opened her first school with special permission from Rome to live outside a convent. Her work among the poor of Calcutta, where her society's workers collect the dying and destitute from the streets, has spread to 50 Indian cities and more than 25 countries, from Papua, New Guinea to the United States, with a branch also in the South Bronx.

Society has 158 Branches

The society has 158 branches and there are 1,800 nuns and 120,000 co-workers. Her order operates schools, hospitals, youth centers and orphanages, and 53,000 lepers are among the patients treated at medical centers in Africa and Asia.

Mother Teresa refuses direct financial assistance from the Indian Government but has accepted an occasional gift of land for a new project. Among the prises she has won for her work are the Jawaharial Nehru Award of India and an award from the Joseph Kennedy Jr. Foundation.

The Nobel Committee said today that it had decided to honour her as much for her organising and managerial skills as for her compassion and dedication to the poor.

International Day of Peace

On twenty-first September International Day of Peace, however, we need to remember the fundamental role of women in countries affected by conflict. Remember women not as hapless victims, but as agents of change who invest in their families and communities and who have the potential to build peaceful and prosperous societies.

The international community can do more to support women in accessing employment, property, markets and new skills. Supporting their financial independence may go a long way towards giving women a voice and the power to negotiate when it comes to making decisions within families and communities in even the most remote, war-torn corners of the Earth.

Improving women's access to education, capital, jobs and markets promotes balanced and inclusive growth. The Asia-Pacific region loses $42 billion to $47 billion per year because of restrictions on women's access to employment opportunities. This hurts social cohesion, stability and trust in institutions, which are fundamental for long-term peace.

Women with jobs are also far more likely than men to invest their income in food, education and health care for their families. With healthier and better educated children, societies can begin to end cycles of poverty and violence. These goals are not unattainable. UNDP has long been focusing on empowering women to actively help prevent conflicts and equally participate in the process of recovering from crisis situations. In Burundi, after decades of civil war, UNDP helped more than 7,000 people — of whom 47 per cent were women — invest their savings in small businesses in 2012. The project not only increased household incomes but gave these women an economic stake in long-term peace. Across the world, women already play a fundamental role in advocating change. They just need to be supported and acknowledged.

Conclusion

Women are important agents for creating stability in the lives of their families and to promote reconciliation and peace even under very difficult and traumatic situations. However, women's peace building potential have had no significant impact on policies and decision relating to conflicts because of their absence from the decision making processes and bodies in the region. Women have a crucial place in traditional society, determining kinship ties and land inheritance, and also have played an important role in the search for peace. Women's groups have helped in creating and sustaining pressure for peace through marches, vigils, petitions and mass meetings and conferences. However, women's participation in the formal peace process and political arena was limited. Women's organisations have to address the conflict issues such as development and women's education and seek long-term changes for further empowerment and peace. The participation of women in conflict resolution and mediation efforts around the world is a very significant one. Some of the women have achieved observer status at local government meetings, and others have been elected to office at the provincial level. Furthermore, these women have become well positioned as role models to other women in their communities and also to serve as moderators within their neighbourhoods. Better educational and training opportunities must be cultivated, greater financial and technical assistance must be obtained for grassroots women's organisations, larger forums and networking venues must be established to enable the formulation of common agendas, there must be greater cultivation of local female leadership, and more supportive men must be integrated into these processes. The women are always at a mission to work and to keep connecting with each other around the world to grow their capabilities, leadership, and opportunities for creating a peaceful environment to live. Empowerment of women has begun and the road to peace is clear in the step they proceed to change the world wherever they find themselves. We are at a critical juncture in marshalling humanity's best efforts so that we can march ahead toward equality, justice, peace and prosperity. It's up to all of us to keep succeeding in peace as each and every one of us does each day in order to create a better world. As women leaders in their own right are dedicated to ensure a world at peace and they would make this happen.

Bibliography

- "A Look at the Top 10 Youngest Nobel Laureates". Yahoo!-ABC News Network. 10 October 2014. Retrieved 11 October 2014.
- Cowell, Alan; Walshoct, Declan (2014). "Nobel Peace Prise for Malala Yousafzai and Kailash Satyarthi". *New York Times*. Retrieved 10 October 2014
- Frank J. Prial (1978). Mother Tresa of Calcutta wins Peace Prise. Oct, 18, 1978. The New York times on the Web.
- Honoring Women Leaders as Agents for Change and Peace. June 5, 2012. Gender and Peacebuilding. United States Institute of Peace.
- Kavitha Suthanthiraraj (2011). Promoting Women's Participation: How Women Are Building Peace. Women Building Peace. January Issue.

SGI Quarterly. A Bhuddist Forum of Peace, Culture and Forum.

- "Le prix Nobel de la paix attribué à Malala Yousafzai et Kailash Satyarthi". *Ijsberg Magazine* (in French). 10 October 2014. Retrieved 10 October, 2014.
- "Malala Yousafzai becomes youngest-ever Nobel Prise winner". *The Express Tribune*. 10 October, 2014. Retrieved 10 October, 2014.
- "Malala Yousafzai: Mixed Reaction in Pakistan to Teenage Activists Nobel Prise Award". IBTimes. 11 October, 2014. Retrieved 11 October, 2014.
- Melanne Verveer (2011). Women as Agents of Peace and Stability. Ambassador-at-Large for Global Women's Issues. Sea Service Leadership Association's 24th Annual Women's Leadership Symposium. San Diego, CA. March 15, 2011. Diplomacy in Action.
- "Michaela Mycroft winner of International Children's Peace Prise 2011". International Children's Peace Prise. 21 November, 2011. Retrieved 25 July, 2013.
- "Nobel peace prise decision is highly political". The Guardian. 10 October 2014. Retrieved 11 October 2014.
- Roma Bhattacharjea 2013. Women can be the best agents of peace — if we let them. Sep 20. United Nations Development Programme.
- "The Nobel Peace Prise for 2014" (Press release). Oslo: Nobel Media AB. 10 October, 2014. Retrieved 10 October 2014.
- Susan Markham (2013). Women as agents of change: Having voice in society and influencing policy. Gender Equality and Development. National Demogracratic Institute. Women's Voice, Agency and Participation. Research Series. No. 5. World Bank.
- Walsh, Declan (10 October, 2014). "Two Champions of Children are Given Nobel Peace Prise". *The New York Times*. Retrieved 11 October, 2014.
- Women as Agents of Peace. 11 December, 2012. IIP Digital, U.S. Department of State.
- Workshop on Women and Peace, Organised by Sansristi: a gender resource centre and Pakistan India People's Forum for Peace and Democracy (PIPFPD- Odisha Chapter) was posted on Friday, June 24th, 2011 at 3:44 pm. Peace Education News Blog news, events, research & jobs from around the world.

16

Gender Development and Complexities

Priyanka Sanguri Fulara

Abstract

Change is the law of nature. Development, progress and evolution are different concepts to denote different modes of change. The word 'development' has various meanings like human well being and welfare, freedom and liberties, equality, higher income, greater and more equal opportunities. The term gender refers to an individual's anatomical sex, and the cultural and social aspect of being male and female. Mostly the concept of gender development is attached to the development of women. Gender development is an issue with other development as there is a wide gap in social aspect of male and female.

Women from the ancient time to modern era have been gone through various process of development in various fields of life. But still the development of women is very slow. In modern India there is sufficient development of education of women but even after achieving this development of education, there is no change in views of people for the status of women. In twenty-first century women are benefitted with more freedom but at the same time it has increased their problems. Their responsibilities have been increased very much. They are doing jobs or running business like men and performing their household duties as a wife, mother etc. The development has enhanced them with mental barriers but they are losing their softness. Their life is becoming more complicated. They can cope up with these complexities by becoming aware of the right and laws made for their protection and progress.

Introduction

Change is the law of nature. Development, progress and evolution are different concepts to denote different modes of change. The word 'development' contains many ideas such as progress, human well-being and welfare, freedom and liberties, equality, higher income, greater and more equal opportunities. Also it can be defined as improvement and upliftment of the quality of life of people, that they are able to attain their potential, build and acquires self confidence, and manage to live lives of reasonable accomplishment and dignity. The term gender refers to an individual's anatomical sex, and the cultural and social aspect of being male and female. Gender is a social construct that outlines the roles, behaviours, activities and attributes that a particular society believes are appropriate for men and women. Mostly the concept of gender development is attached to the development of women. With the passes of time and circumstances the status of women faces ups and down due to various factors. Since independence, Indian women have got right to equality by the constitution, but in practical sense the situation is quite miserable. Women constitute about 50 per cent of the total population but still the disparity in literacy rate between males and females is very wide. For instance, the low literacy or high mortality rate among females depicts a poor status whereas the gap between men and women in literacy levels or mortality rates signifies gender-based discrimination in society. Women are subjected to discrimination and violence within the household, at the workplace and in the society. Their inferior status can be traced to the patriarchal values entrenched in the society which keep women subjugated, assigns them a subordinate and dependent role, and, prevents them from accessing power and resources. Men hold the power and resource within families and control any property and family income. Women are considered as men's property, their sexual activity, income and labour being systemically controlled by the men in their family. Men have been socially conditioned to genuinely believe in their own superiority. From childhood they are treated differently from their sisters. They grow to believe that they are more valuable and more deserving than women, and that their opinions and views should have more weight than any woman's. Furthermore, predominant religious misinterpretations have further legitimised these feelings. Women's participation in the total workforce is increasing in quantity but the quality is decreasing.

Women in modern era sharing the economic burden of males even then they are not achieving the status which they deserve. Although the development levels by the state levels by the state are exemplary, the status of women continues to be a cause of concern. Discrimination against girls and women seems to be woven into very socio-cultural fabric of the society. Gender development is an issue with other development as there is a wide gap in social aspect of male and female. The status of women had always been lower than men, but the extent of the gap between the sexes varies across cultures and time. As such, gender is as a social construct specifying the socially and culturally prescribed roles that men and women are to follow or biological distinction between males and females. Hence, the extent to which the society views women's roles or women are engaged in domestic activities as against gainful employment outside of the home has inverse relation to their status. In Indian Society, men are perceived to be assertive and commanding, whereas women are expected to comply, obey and be submissive and docile. The large proportion of women reporting "home duties" as their main activity was common across all age groups, except for elderly women aged 65 and over, who as expected, more than 50 per cent listed "retired or too old to work".

Education is the most important instrument for human resource development. Education of women, therefore occupies top priority amongst various measures taken to improve the status of women in India. Education expands opportunities for women, equips them to be more informed, empowers them to resist oppression and enables them to claim their rights. Women presence and participation are now recognised as an essential condition for the development in some soft sectors like primary education, health, sanitation etc., empowerment of women through education, economic freedom and entrepreneurship can lead to the revolutionary era of development of human resource. The education system must be transformed to ensure that the content and process of education reflect gender equality. Education enhances the brain's powers of concentration and its ability to quickly change it train of thoughts. Education in India is constrained by the socio- economic conditions of the people, their attitudes, values and culture.

The Government of India has taken several measures to empower women including giving them educational facilities, employment and entrepreneurship opportunities. There has been increasing worldwide recognition and effort to improve and enhance the creativity, ability and contributions of women to the society; improve literacy among women; and reduce gender based inequalities. Women's education thus influences and is influenced by the context in which it is developed. The programmes for women's education will have to be implemented as a priority so that women attain a comparable level of education by 2020 A.D. In view of the social and cultural handicaps that have operated against women's education and taking account of the multiple roles that women are required to play, the need for adopting set of objectives specific to women's education is imperative. The education of the women should usher in an era of complete rationalism and equality. Equality between men and women means equality in their dignity and worth as human beings as well as equally in their rights, opportunities and responsibilities. Recognising women's rights and believing their ability are essential for women's empowerment and development. Indian society is male dominated society but now the society has started realising women's importance and accepted their empowerment, women as an active agent for development, participation in and guiding their own development. Women achieve more development within two three decades due to gaining proper education. They have achieved good status in society but it is not sufficient for the gender development. There are many complexities in their overall development. They have proved themselves in the various fields of society but they have not attained the proper status in the society.

Gender Development in India

There is a glimpse of development of women from ancient period to the modern era. Indian society came into existence during Indus valley civilisation. When human being came into existence there was no difference in the work of men and women. During the initial phase of human development women enjoyed due respect and status. During this phase each society of world was converted into matriarchal society. During the subsequent period women have undergone a steady deterioration in their social status. There subsequent periods impaired their identity and relegated them to an inferior, inhuman and loathsome place in society. In Vedic period the status of women in society was good. In spite of the attitude of indifference towards female child, once born the daughter was entitled to all the privileges given to a son. In matter of education there was no distinction between son and daughter. Even at that time we can find out a class of women who can continued their studies even for the lifetime. In the religious life, which was very important aspect of life of people during this period, women actively participated in it. Further, there are special sacrifices which were exclusively performed by women. As regard the other aspects of women's life she seemed to exercise good deal of influences in the matter of selecting the partner. On the whole in the Vedic period, within the patriarchal society the position of women was high. In epic age the status of women was not so good. It was changed after the Manu Shamhita in which Manu thus lays down a theoretical basis for the social and legal subordination of women. In this period marriage based on free selection of the husband by a woman was popular among the royal families as in case of Sita, Draupadi and others. At this time the movement of women was restricted in normal days. Manu prepared a mental outlook for the future subordination of women. Buddhism emphasised the superfluity of any intermediary between God and man further opened the portals of religion to all human beings.

Though woman can reach the highest state but she is inferior to male Bhikku in status. During Buddhism the position of women in society was considerably good. The age of marriage was generally believed to be within sixteen to twenty. In puranic period women could join the religious order and become a nun, threatened the dominant position of the Brahmins in the Hindu society. Whatever mobility castes possessed was destroyed and rigidly demarcated castes with unequal rights were established. The position of woman became more and more servile. This was thus an era of the increasing subjection of woman. This enslavement of her to man was by a brutal irony of life glorified as "Pativrata Dharma". The religious life of woman was restricted to the observance of some "vratas". There is no freedom for girls to choose to remain unmarried for the whole life. Widow remarriage is prohibited during this period. The instances of Jauhar and Sati pratha was practiced by women. These practices show deterioration of the position of woman and her subjection.The invasion of the country by the Muslims brought about further deterioration of position of woman. The post- puranic phase was one of the darkest periods for woman in Indian history. The steady deterioration of her status continues till ninteenth century. When the Indians came in vital contact with the British in the latter half of the eighteenth century, the position of the Indian woman had reached the maximum degree of deterioration. Ideologically woman was considered a completely inferior species, inferior to male, having no significance, no personality; socially she was kept in a state of utter subjection, denied any right, suppressed and oppressed. Thus not only social institutions and customs thwarted the free growth of her personality, but the prevailing ideology also assigned the Indian woman an inferior status. She was denied independent personality. She had no separate as a member of the family or society. Her existence was taken as granted. Her opinion, her desires, her likes or dislikes were never to be considered. The women of India have indeed achieved their success in half a century of Independence, but if there is to be a true female, independence, much remains to be done. The fight for autonomy remains an unfinished combat.

Role of Education in Gender Development [Chapter]

Education is widely recognised as the gateway to economic security and opportunity- particularly for girls and women. Their education leads them to independent thinking for which their family and society become intolerant of them. This is true not only because education is an entry point to other opportunities, but also because the educational achievements of women can have ripple effects within the family and across generations. Investing in girls' education is one of the most effective ways to reduce poverty. They struggle between tradition and modernity. Education forms a very basic indicator for women's equality and empowerment. Levels of female literacy, gender gaps in literacy levels, enrolment and dropout rates at the primary school level are relevant indicators. From the beginning of the planned era, education along with health and social welfare were accepted as crucial services for women's development. Literacy is the first step towards formal education. It refers to the ability to read and write. Female literacy has been improving over the years. The proportion of women who are literate has increased by 15 per cent over the last decade from 39 per cent in 1991 to 54 per cent in 2001. Of the 130 million 6-11 year-old children not in school, a majority i.e., 60 per cent are girls. The figures only go to show how in most regions of the world, specially the developing societies, gender bias impinges on girls' education. The foremost factor limiting female education is poverty. Economics plays a key role when it comes to coping with directs costs such as tuition fees, cost of textbooks, uniforms, transportation and other expenses. Wherever, especially in families with many children, these costs exceed the income of the family, girls are the first to be denied schooling. All this despite the fact that educating girls is one of the best investments a society can make. An educated woman has the skills, the self-confidence and the information she needs to become a better parent, worker and citisen. Girls' lack of access to education isn't always related to scarcity of places in schools. It also emerges from expectations, attitudes and biases in communities and families. Economic costs, social traditions, and religious and cultural beliefs limit girls' educational opportunities.

Whatever the underlying reasons, having large number of girls outside the formal schooling system brings developmental challenges to both current and future generations. Individuals, families, communities and nations are affected. Inability to read, write and calculate complicates a girl's efforts to engage in both market-focused production and household activities as effectively and efficiently possible. This affects her family's welfare and diminishes her potential contribution to the development of the household, local and national economy. Despite reported progress, there is still a persistent gap between women and men's access to education. Combating the high rate of illiteracy among women and girls remains an urgent global need. According to the UNESCO Institute of Statistics, it is now estimated that two-thirds of the world's 875 million illiterate adults are women. In Southern Asia, nearly three in five women are illiterate and it is estimated that half of all women in Africa and in the Arab region are still illiterate. However, gender disparities and literacy rates are less marked among young adults. There is now, little or no gender difference in the literacy rates of 15-24 year olds in several regions of the world. Over the past 20 years, significant progress has been made with regard to higher education. It is of particular interest that in countries where tertiary education has expanded significantly, women's school enrolment has increased more than men's. But this is not all and enough to ensure that women get equal employment opportunities. Thanks to the fight for women's rights, increasing participation of women in the job market and to the right to vote, women have emerged from the strictly private sphere to which they were formerly restricted. Women have broken the implicit social contract that for more than hundreds of years confined them to home, child rearing, household tasks and fieldwork, while men worked outside the home.

In India, more and more young women have been joining the official workforce in recent years and are experiencing some of the benefits - financial independence, higher status and lower fertility rate through delaying the age of marriage. Children also benefit because women usually devote more of their income to the family's welfare compared to men. However, in the context of the developing world, lack of education has forced many women into the risky "informal" economy as street traders, domestic servants, home workers and seasonal labourers. This in turn reflects a continuing belief that there is little benefit in educating a girl when she could be working in the market place or fields. Boys are affected by this thinking, too, though not to the same extent.

Although economically productive to society, once again, women's work, if they get the opportunity at all, is rarely recognised in official statistics and the women often get no protection from unions or employment legislation. Just as women's domestic work is undervalued, so are their skills in the world of employment. Most are concentrated in the poorly-paid, low-skilled "women's" sectors of the economy like Free Trade Zones set up in many developing countries to attract foreign companies. Exhausting 18-hour days in unsafe and unhealthy conditions are the norm, along with sexual harassment and lack of job security. As more women are entering the workforce, conflict is growing between the patriarchal social norms and women's urge for economic independence. In recent years there has been a significant change in the attitude towards women taking up outside employment. With the breakup of the extended family, greater numbers of women are seeking employment.

Complexities

The gap separating men and women in the job market remains wide in many countries, whether in the North or the South. With marginal variables between most countries, women have a lower employment rate, are unemployed longer, are paid less and have less secure jobs. Young women, particularly pay the price of job market flexibility. They suffer double discrimination. First for being young, in the difficult phase of transition between training and working life, in an age group that has, on an average, twice the jobless rate or older workers and are at the mercy of employers who exploit them under the pretext of enabling them to acquire professional experience. Secondly they are discriminated against for being women and are more likely to be offered low paying or low status jobs. Women, from time immemorial, especially in our society, have been ill – treated and discriminated. Since independence lots of changes have been observed in the status of women, but their exploitation is still at alarming state. Inequalities, sexual discrimination, violence are still stopping women in coming forward, the result of which is gross human rights violation of women every day. Patriarchal form of society has been spread its root deeply in our society. Due to this women are not getting the full freedom of thinking, acting and decision making. Up to now women support physically mentally to their family but in the present scenario she is indulged in economic activities. On the one hand women have been reached to space but on the other they are not safe in buses, and trains. A woman could still bear up with these problems if she had control over the money she earns. But in most families even now her salary is handed over to father, husband or in-laws. So the basic motive for seeking employment of getting independence is nullified in many women's case. In India men do not share on most of the household chores, it is women who have to cook, clean the house, do the dishes, wash clothes, get their children ready for school etc. Men just took care of few chores that are to be dealt outside the house. So the major burden of running the family is on the shoulders of women. It was alright for women to handle all the chores as long as they were homemakers. Now with their increasing need for getting some income for the family, they have to work all the more harder. They have to take up a 9 to 5 job plus handle all the household chores that they handled as a homemaker. Men's role has not changed much. In the Indian context the roles that men and women play in society are socially determined but not biologically. From the moment of birth, gender expectations influence how boys and girls are treated. India is a multifaceted society where no generalisation could apply to the entire nation's various regional, religious, social, and economic groups. Nevertheless, certain broad circumstances in which Indian women live affect the ways they participate in the economy. The stereotyping continues to prevail in technical and professional fields. Even where women have open access to all professions, they overwhelmingly opt for traditionally female occupations. The workplace is a setting where gender inequalities can be noticeable and sustained. Work plays a significant component in shaping power and status for both women and men. This generates gender inequalities in the distribution of everyday jobs. In the post-modern era, strategies have been designed to deal with situations of gender discrimination. However, gender inequality in the workplace is an acute and persistent problem, especially in developing countries. Women continue to face many barriers on their way to the top, that are unique to their gender. Efficiency and success of women is widely acknowledged all, but despite this woman in the Indian scenario are often exposed to some form of gender discrimination or other. Although laws have been enacted to provide equal opportunities in the workplace for both men and women, the fact is that 'women and glass ceiling still exists'. The reasons behind the complications faced by women are just due to some factors like sociologically-driven role specifications that are prevalent in India, patriarchal form of social structuring which is also reflected at workplace, stereotyping image of female, confined to family roles and which directly leads to role conflict if they opt for employment. Discrimination is still very much in evidence and education and training policies specially targeting young women are needed to restore a balance. Although young women are increasingly choosing typically 'male' professions, they remain over-represented in traditionally female jobs, such as secretaries, nurses, and under represented in jobs with responsibility and the professions. In the Indian context, the discrimination begins at an early stage of socialisation and becomes reflected in every aspect of life. Trafficking of women and children is a significant problem in developing countries around the globe, and particularly in South Asia. In the absence of social protection, economic security and legal support, an alarming number of women and children from the poor, marginalised and disenfranchised sections of the community (an overwhelming majority of the population of South Asia) become easy victims of trafficking. In India, a victimised woman usualy tries to avoid the legal process as she becomes more stigmatised by the society. She dares not file complaints; fearing negligence and harassment in police station, courts and society. Daily news reports are filed with atrocities including physical and psychological torture, sexual harassment, sexual assault, rape, dowry related violence, trafficking, forced prostitution, coerced suicide and murder. Domestic violence, or violence perpetuated in the home or family environment, is a major social problem.

Domestic violence incidences are fairly common and widespread across the country. Women of al economic strata are vulnerable to maltreatment and abuse by husbands, in-laws, and other family members. Available data suggests that the number of cases of domestic violence is increasingly being reported in the newspaper. In the new and upcoming sectors too, there is an imbalance in the representation of men and women. An instance is ICTs where, despite their rapid growth, where women generally occupy positions towards the bottom of hierarchy. And even in female dominated sectors like health, women work as nurses, but a large majority of hospital directors and department heads are men.

Views and Suggestions

Gender development is being a sensitive issue and it needs realistic views for its solution. There are various aspects of dependence of women so it is quite difficult to face the complexities. In Indian scenario, if women show their independency then there is a certain probability to destruction of family. Gender development movement causes to evolve consciousness in women but the problems faced by them are as it is. Even today women want to take privilege in society by giving birth to boy. Even today thousands of girls sit within the four walls of their houses and wonder why they do not have the right to choose their own lives, decides for themselves whether they want to be homemakers or more. Marriage is still the reason for their birth. Freedom is more than just being aloud out for shopping with friends.

From epic age, the women are deteriorated long time so women are not able to seek knowledge and information in order to make informed choice at the own pace. Therefore, it is necessary to create such environment for women. We have to evolve educational institution which cater underprivileged group of women.

In modern India there is sufficient development of education of women. But even after achieving education there is no such change in the views of people for the status of women in society. Men and women must work together to ensure rights and freedom for all citisens. Parents must change their attitude towards their daughters and bring them up in a way that reflects equality. Daughters must be given opportunities to develop their decision making skills and leadership capacities. What we need today are trends where girls are able not only to break out of the culturally determined patterns of employment but also to offer advice about career possibilities that look beyond the traditional pale of jobs. In many countries, special initiatives have been taken to direct girls to non-traditional fields of study. In Austria, special computer and Internet courses have been offered to increase the number of girls enrolled in technical courses. In India can such efforts be initiated for the girls and women? Perhaps yes. And here I would like to point attention to some efforts where women are being trained for IT jobs. I would like to mention here briefly some projects that have shown that women too can harness the potential of the ICTs. The M. S. Swaminathan Research Foundation, MSSRF, in Chennai, India has piloted a path-breaking project, in the tiny coastal state of Pondicherry. The project, being run by the foundations Rural Technology Centre, has helped local women become computer-literate and in the process, empowered them. The programme has taught them how to download the latest weather reports from the US Oceanographic department on the Net. The women broadcast these reports on the public address system - information that is often crucial to their husbands out fishing on the high seas. They have earned respect from the community that once looked down upon them. Encouraged by this, the women have also started accessing information on issues crucial to them - reproductive health, basic education and so on. And this is just the beginning. In another effort, Nari Raksha Samiti (NRS), an Indian social welfare organisation devoted to improving the lives of poor and destitute women founded fifty years ago to help women in distress, NRS focuses on promoting the safety and security of women, family welfare, employment, health, and training in job-oriented professions. The Samiti has twenty centres headed by volunteers. Under the leadership of Vandana Sharma, NRS has begun using twenty-first century technology to address the wrongs that result from the age-old traditions associated with the dowry system. Vandana recognised the impact that computers are having on the changing Indian economy and established a small computer education centre in the NRS building. Vandana and the NRS volunteers are now training 250 young women — 60 of whom are dowry victims and have a history of harassment and exploitation — in basic computer literacy as well as office software such as MS Excel, Word, and Power Point. This IT training programme joins training programmes in tailoring, interior decoration, cooking, food preservation, and weaving in providing needy women with the job skills necessary to break out of the cycle of poverty and abuse which affects so many women in India. The NRS computer centers not only provide job training, but have also allowed NRS to establish an online complaint system for solving dowry and family dispute issues. Women can confidentially lodge complaints through the system and receive assistance from NRS and police and government authorities. NRS has been successful in training more than four hundred dowry victims and poor women in the community. One of the main reason is that the policy makers either do not feel it is necessity, or do not want to make public itís failure to provide necessary protection to women.

There is no systematic documentation of women's status due to a lack of proper survey or research methods and the tendency to concentrate.

Conclusion

A fundamental change is required in the attitudes of the employers, policy makers, family members and other relatives and the public at large. Technological advancement results in retrenchment of women employees. No one thinks of upgrading their skills. Traditionally men are seen as the bread winner and women as the house-keepers, child bearers and rearers. This typecast role model continues to put obstacles before the working women. Maternity leave is seldom given. The psychological pressure of all this can easily lead to a woman quitting her job. Most of the problems that beset working women are in reality rooted in the social perspective of the position of women. It is much easier to terminate the woman's employment and hire someone else. Trade Unions do little to ameliorate the lot of women workers. Women's issues do not occur on the priority list of most of the trade unions. Women going to work are often subject to sexual harassment. Public transport system is overcrowded and men take advantage of the circumstances to physically harass women. Colleagues offer unwanted attention which can still be shaken off but a woman is placed in a difficult situation if the higher officer demands sexual favours. If it is refused, the boss can easily take it out on the woman in other ways to make life miserable for her. There have been several cases of sexual harassment recently involving even the senior women officials. On the other hand, if a woman is praised for her work or promoted on merit, her colleagues do not hesitate to attribute it to sexual favours. Education is a potent source of socio-economic and political changes. The government has to take actions to ensure that the female teachers and professors have the same opportunities as and equal status with male teachers and professors, in view to support and develop gender studies and research at all levels of education. The mass media has not any concerted efforts to discuss serious issues that concern women and prepare the women to plan their rightful and equal role in the society. To change the situation we will have to regularly monitor that media and point out the merits as well as demands on continuous basis. Adequate and quality women's education is considered as an essential prerequisite for economic independence of women.

References

- Sharma, B.M., "Women and Education" (2008); Commonwealth Publishers, New Delhi.
- Sharma Rama and Mishra, M. K., "Mahila Vikas" (2012), Arjun Publishing House New Delhi.
- Singh, Trilok "Essentials of Women Resource Development", (2011), Cyber Tech Publications, New Delhi.

- Soni, J.K., "Women's Education – Harnessing the Gender Power"; Authorspress, New Delhi.
- Rao, B. D. and Latha, D.P., "Education for Women"; Discovery Publishing House, New Delhi.
- Rao, V.K., "Higher Education", (2008), APH Publishing Corporation, New Delhi.
- http://www.oneworld.net
- www.dise.in
- www.pintersociety.com
- www.shareyouressays.com

17

Gender Equity in Education for Promoting Peace

Ms Gagandeep Kaur Chatrath
Assistant Professor Khalsa College of Education
Ranjit Avenue, Amritsar

Abstract

Gender-based discrimination in education is both a cause and a consequence of deep-rooted disparities in society. Harmful practices such as early marriage and pregnancy, gender-based violence, and discriminatory education laws, policies, contents and practices still prevent millions of girls' form enrolling, completing and benefitting from education. In the last decade, there has been progressive improvement in overall literacy levels across the country. This has also been a decade of extensive research and documentation in elementary education and gender and social equity issues. Although our country has made impressive progress on the primary education front, the same cannot be said for secondary education or post-secondary education. The women participation in research work is less and there is also a distinctive dispersion and variance concerning the representation of women at professorial level. The women need to empower in their careers by building up their professional confidence and self-belief. These measures like policy awareness, training and engagement, and monitoring and evaluation needs to be taken. At the international level UNESCO and other allied bodies work to promote equal opportunities to quality learning, free from gender-based or other forms of discrimination. The research institutions should demonstrate significant gender awareness and competency to use gender as a resource to create new knowledge and stimulate innovation by modernising their organisational culture. The ultimate objective should be a change process that is to work towards a better gender relation and equal representation of both sexes in education and in all staff categories of the institutions.

Keywords: *Empowerment, Discrimination, women literacy*

Introduction

Gender equality means that males and females have equal opportunities to realise their full human rights and contribute to and benefit from economic, social, cultural, and political development. World Bank 2005 mentioned that a basic principle of equity is equality of opportunity among people: "that a person's life achievements should be determined primarily by his or her talents and efforts, rather than by pre-determined circumstances such as race, gender, social or family background". Equity does not imply treating all learners the same because many factors could disadvantage them in having a chance to achieve equitable outcomes. ILO (2000) mentioned that responses may include "equal treatment or treatment that is different but which is considered equivalent in terms of rights, benefits, obligations and opportunities" (as cited EQUATE Project, 2008). According to Jena (2014), the Constitution of India guarantees to all women, equality (Article 14), no discrimination by the state (Article 15 (1)), equality of opportunity (Article 16), equal pay for equal work (Article 39 d), renounce practices derogatory to the dignity of women (Article 51 (a) (c)).

Education is important for everyone, but it is very much significant for girls and women. The 1994 Cairo Consensus recognised education, especially for women, as a force for social and economic development. This is true not only because education is an entry point to other opportunities, but also because the educational achievements of women can have ripple effects within the family and across generations. Closing the gender gap in education is a development priority. Universal completion of primary education was set as a 20-year goal, as was wider access to secondary and higher education among girls and women. Closing the gender gap in education by 2015 is also one of the benchmarks for the Millennium Development Goals (*United Nations Population Fund, 2008)*.

In the last decade, there has been progressive improvement in overall literacy levels across the country. In spite of the number of legislation and policies government adopted for promoting gender equality, gender inequalities persist vigorously. Gender-based discrimination in education is both a cause and a consequence of deep-rooted disparities in society. The gender inequality index in the "The Human Development Report 2013 of UNDP" indicated that there is loss in a country's progress and human development because of gender inequality in three sectors: reproductive health, women empowerment and labour market participation (Jena, 2014). Gender-based violence in schools undermines the right to education and presents a major challenge to achieving gender equality in education because it negatively impacts girls' participation and their retention in school. In addition, ineffective sexual and reproductive health education inhibits adolescents' access to information and contributes to school dropouts, especially among girls who have reached puberty (Karam, 2013).

The Human Development Report 2013 of UNDP titled "The rise of the South: Human Progress in a diverse World" mentioned that India ranks 132nd position out of 187 countries on the Gender Equality Index. The condition is such that India is far behind than all nations in South Asia in many respects (Jena, 2014). Parity and equity are the building blocks of equality in education. Morrison and Jütting (2005) (as cited Cerise & Francesca, 2012) mentioned that there are challenges related to measuring discriminatory social institutions. One challenge is endogeneity, the difficulty in differentiating between 'underlying factor' and 'outcome' in relation to gender inequality. Klasen and Lamanna (2009); OECD (2012) (as cited Cerise & Francesca, 2012) further mentioned that the discrimination against women is multi-faceted, inter-related and self-reinforcing. For example, the lower status of girls in the family leads to practices such as early marriage which in turn limits the educational attainment of girls. Lower educational attainment limits employment opportunities which in turn have an influence on women's decision-making power in the household. Several studies have found that expanding women's access to quality employment opportunities is important for economic growth and development. Gertler and Alderman (1989) (as cited Moheyuddin, 2005) that there are three major reasons for low investment in girls' education are: Low Return from Girls' Schooling, No (or Low) Direct Benefit from Investing in Girls' Education, Social Preferences regarding the lower investment in girls' education. The gender inequality reflects some different social, cultural or regional preferences about gender roles. Poverty, geographical isolation, ethnic background, disability, traditional attitudes about their status and role all undermine the ability of women and girls to exercise their rights. Harmful practices such as early marriage and pregnancy, gender-based violence, and discriminatory education laws, policies, contents and practices still prevent millions of girls form enrolling, completing and benefitting from education (EQUATE Project, 2008). Investing in girls' education is one of the most effective ways to reduce poverty. Investments in secondary school education for girls yield especially high dividends. Girls who have been educated are likely to marry later and to have smaller and healthier families. Educated women can recognise the importance of health care and know how to seek it for themselves and their children. Education helps girls and women to know their rights and to gain confidence to claim them. However, women's literacy rates are significantly lower than men's in most developing countries (*United Nations Population Fund, 2008*).

Equity is the strongest framing principle of a post-2015 rights-based agenda, and underlines the need to redress historical and structural inequalities in order to provide access to quality education at all levels. This implies that all aspects of education should be considered from a rights perspective, including structural features of education systems, methods of education, as well as the contents of the education curricula (Karam, 2013). There are four main dimensions of gender equality: equality of access, equality in the learning process, equality of educational outcomes, and equality of external results (Subrahmanian N.D.). Karam (2013) mentioned that inequalities in general, and particularly gender equality, need to be addressed simultaneously on multiple levels—economic, social, political and cultural. A response on behalf of the International Women's Health Coalition maintained that "all girls, no matter how poor, isolated or disadvantaged, should be able to attend school regularly and without the interruption of early pregnancy, forced marriage, maternal injuries and death, and unequal domestic and childcare burdens".

EQUATE Project (2008) highlighted that the Quality and equality in education are inextricably linked. Poor or marginalised children, who are more likely to have illiterate parents and less access to reading materials in the home, are more dependent on their teachers for their learning than are better-off children. As a result, poor instruction perpetuates inequities because it is more often the most marginalised children who become school leavers, either through failure or voluntary termination. Research has shown that girls seem to be more sensitive to school quality than boys and that the quality of teachers has a greater impact on the demand for girls' education than for boys' (Kane 2004).

This has also been a decade of extensive research and documentation in elementary education and gender and social equity issues. Although our country has made impressive progress on the primary education front, the same cannot be said for secondary education or post-secondary education. However, there is some indication that secondary level education may provide higher returns, especially for girls. "The economic returns to schooling at the secondary and tertiary levels are consistently high (and differentially high for young women). The gap between the returns to higher and lower levels of schooling is widening. The women participation in research work is also less and there is a distinctive dispersion and variance concerning the representation of women at professorial level. The women need to empower in their careers by building up their professional confidence and self-belief.

The Human development Report 2013 of UNDP reiterates the reasons for low participation in labour force (only 29 per cent of Indian women, above the age of 15 in 2011 were a part of the country's labour force, compared to 80.7 per cent men (Jena, 2014). There can be various reasons of this low participation of women in jobs. Alexander (2011); Kimerling et al. (2009); Meisel et al. (2003) (as cited Cerise & Francesca, 2012) mentioned that the Violence against women has also been negatively associated with female employment. Similarly, restrictions on women's access to public space such as the law providing that husbands have the sole authority to choose the place of residence, or women's limited access to economic resources such as land or credit can influence women's employment opportunities.

Discriminatory social institutions often reflect social norms that reinforce stereotypes of women as inferior, less able or less deserving of quality jobs. Thus, in countries with higher gender discrimination, it can be expected that women may be relegated to jobs or sectors that offer lower opportunities, poor working conditions and lower remuneration. Government funded paid maternity leave has greater effect on female employment in countries with higher levels of discrimination (Cerise & Francavilla, 2012).

There are many benefits of promoting equity in education because educated mothers are more likely to be in the labour force, allowing them to pay some of the costs of schooling, and may be more aware of returns to schooling. And educated mothers, averaging fewer children, can concentrate more attention on each child. There is strong link between education, increased women's (as opposed to girls') labour force participation, the wages they earn and overall productivity, all of which ultimately yields higher benefits for communities and nations. Particular emphasis is given to expanding and improving the quality of education for girls and women at the secondary level and in the area of literacy, to take successful initiatives to scale, to replicate good practice and to engage new actors. According to Summers (1992) "Educating girls quite possibly yields a higher rate of return than any other investment available in the developing world" (as cited EQUATE Project, 2008). Educating girls achieves even greater results. When girls go to school, they tend to delay marriage, have fewer but healthier children, and contribute more to family income and national productivity. Female education level is also linked with fertility and thus with population growth, and this linkage is reinforced through the linkage with under five (child) mortality, which by itself is linked to fertility too. Population growth has a negative linkage with economic growth, although growth of labour force can be positively linked to economic growth (Moheyuddin, 2012). Investing in girls' education is one of the most effective ways to reduce poverty. Investments in secondary school education for girls yield especially high dividends. Girls who have been educated are likely to marry later and to have smaller and healthier families. Educated women can recognise the importance of health care and know how to seek it for themselves and their children. Education helps girls and women to know their rights and to gain confidence to claim them. However, women's literacy rates are significantly lower than men's in most developing countries (*United Nations Population Fund, 2008)*.

UNESCO works to promote equal opportunities to quality learning, free from gender-based or other forms of discrimination. In particular, UNESCO mobilises additional funds through the 'Better Life Better Future' initiative, aimed at expanding learning opportunities for girls and women seeks to address obstacles to learning such as gender-based violence and HIV & AIDS promotes gender equality in national education laws, policies and plans seeks to expand access to learning opportunities, in particular for girls and women. UNESCO launched the Global Partnership for Girls' and Women's Education, known as 'Better Life, Better Future', in 2011 guided by the conviction that educating girls and women can break the cycle of poverty and foster greater social justice. The Partnership seeks to increase learning opportunities for adolescent girls and women and to find solutions to some of the biggest challenges and obstacles to their education. Other projects like Malala Fund for Girls' Education, UNESCO/HNA partnership, Girls' and women's education using ICTs in Senegal and Nigeria are working in this regard.

Translating the concept of gender equality in education into a practical framework will assist education programmers in better designing, managing, and evaluating education projects. To be practical, this framework must draw clear distinctions and demonstrate interrelationships among the concepts of gender parity, gender equity, and gender equality. In addition to drawing out the nuances between equity and equality, the framework also reinforces other key issues in education such as access, quality, continuity, and relevance. The future development agenda should include the dimensions of gender inequality such as violence against women; women's status and role in the family; and women's access to and control over assets and various access like access to Land , Women's legal and *de facto* access to agricultural land, access to Credit Women's legal and *de facto* access to bank loans, access to property other than Land, Women's legal and *de facto* access to other types of property, especially immovable property, access to public space, accessing public space political voice (Cerise and Francavilla, 2012).

Conclusion

The women need to empower in their careers by building up their professional confidence and self-belief. These measures like policy awareness, training and engagement, and monitoring and evaluation needs to be taken. The research institutions should demonstrate significant gender awareness and competency to use gender as a resource to create new knowledge and stimulate innovation by modernising their organisational culture. The ultimate objective should be a change process that is to work towards a better gender relation and equal representation of both sexes in education and in all staff categories of the institutions.

References

- Cerise, S & Francavilla, F (2012). *Tackling the root causes of gender inequalities in the post-2015 development agenda*. Retrieved from http://www.oecd.org/dev/poverty/Tackling_the_root_causes_of_gender_inequalities_OECD_DEV.pdf
- EQUATE Project: Achieving Equality in Education (2008). *Education From A Gender Equality Perspective*. Retrieved from http://

www.ungei.org/resources/files/ Education_from_ a_ Gender_ Equality_Perspective.pdf

- Jena, P.P. (2014). Considering Gender Inequality: A necessity for Inclusive Growth. *University News, 52*(43), 11-16.
- Karam, A (2013). Education as the Pathway towards Gender Equality. *US Chronicle, L*(4), Retrieved from http://unchronicle.un.org/article/ education-pathway-towards-gender-equality/
- Moheyuddin, G. (2005). Gender, Economic Development and Poverty Reduction. *MPRA Paper No. 685 posted 7*. Retrieved fromhttp:// mpra.ub.uni-muenchen.de/685/1/MPRA_ paper_685.pdf
- UNESCO. (2014). *Gender Equality in Education*. Retrieved from http:/ /www.unesco.org/new/en/education/themes/leading-the-international-agenda/gender-and-education/
- *United Nations Population Fund (2008). Empowering Women through Education*. Retrieved from www.unfpa.org/gender/ empowerment2.htm

18

Peace Education: An Approach to Eradicate Gender Violence

Dr (Mrs.) Srutirupa Panda

Lecturer in Education, Nabakrushna Choudhury College of Teacher Education Utkal, University, Angul, Odisha

Email - srutirupa.panda@gmail.com

Abstract

We have already seen two World Wars and several other international and home wars what already destructed some of the part of earth vigorously. International terrorist attack, violence, sexual attacks, conflicts, naxallets problems have made the society threatened. Each human of earth is now realising the life threatening impact of crime and attacks on weak gender, on human population, on their life as well as society. Thus for building a harmonious future planet earth, it's the responsibility of its each inhabitant to realise the dangerous impact of sexual violence and gain knowledge, understanding as well as skill relevant to avoid sexual offence and gender violence so that they could be able to plan and practice strategies to live harmoniously not only in present but also in future. This goal of human society can only be achieved without establishing Peace Education which can inculcate the basic relevant knowledge related to importance of each gender for human society to children, adolescents, and adults from their initial stage of learning who would hold the responsibility of future planet earth. In this context the role of teacher, planner, administrators in providing adequate peace education linked with prestige to eradication of gender biasness is really beyond doubt. Therefore to inculcate and expand the importance of each gender through peace education in recent days it's an urgent demand. Therefore the system should merge peace education in schools, colleges, as well as pre- service and in-service teacher instruction to achieve the mission appropriately.

The chapter intends to explore the relation between arousing safety, respect for individual gender and establishment of peace in earth as well as

objectives, strategies and challenges related to eradicate gender violence through peace education.

Introduction

The planet earth holds the major responsibility of nurturing and providing shelter for all organism of this world as it serves as the natural habitat of all living beings. Its survivals determine the existence, growth as well as continuation of each race of future world. The laws, principle of the nature controls each aspects of the life through several continuous essential physical biological phenomena. Similarly in turns, the activities as well as habits of each living specimen affects the structure, function of the nature. The role of human being in creating an appropriate environment in planet earth is really important. The social, political, economical dimensions of human civilisation have a significant role in constructing peaceful future. Being the most intelligent creature of this planet it has the capacity to lead the world either in positive direction or in negative direction. It is the need, intelligence; interest, attitude as well as aptitude of human being to plan, design, and implement activities which may create either construction or destruction of planet earth. However to achieve some self centred goal few individuals of this human society never hesitate to apply their ability in a wrong way to destruct the world in terms of war, conflicts, terrorist activities, mass murder which not only affect the physical environment of the earth but also affects the social, political, economical and psychological world of planet earth. These days peace of the world is really in danger. One of the causes for it is the brutal attack of the dominant male gender on the weak females in terms of murder, rape, sexual harassment, sexual torture, psychological pressure, domestic violence, dowry, killing female foetus, forcing for prostitute activity, girls trafficking, sexual biasness, child rape, transmission of sexual diseases etc. These incidents are destroying the peace of women mind and creating fear, shame, anger, violence in the society. It is clear from recent Delhi gang rape case what created bursting environment throughout the country. If we try to understand and analyse the reason behind this type of problematic peace less situation it is quite apparent that lack of proper gender education is making people ignorant for marinating proper sensitivity, attitude, respect towards women. Improper knowledge about status and importance of each sex type is creating several sexual crimes in the society which are absorbing the peace of the humans and producing unhappiness, tragedy.

Conceptualisation of Peace and its Promotion through Gender Education

Peace is a state of harmony characterised by the lack of violent conflict. Commonly understood as the absence of hostility, peace also suggests the existence of healthy or newly healed interpersonal or international relationships, prosperity in matters of social or economic welfare, the establishment of equality, and a working political order that serves the true interests of all. In international relations, peacetime is not only the absence of war or conflict, but also the presence of cultural and economic understanding.

Peace education is an attempt to respond to problems of conflict and violence on scales ranging from the global and national to the local and personal. It is about exploring ways of creating more just and sustainable futures — R. D. Laing (1978). Peace education is holistic. It embraces the physical, emotional, intellectual, and social growth of children within a framework deeply rooted in traditional human values. It is based on a philosophy that teaches love, compassion, trust, fairness, co-operation and reverence for the human family and all life on our beautiful planet — Fran Schmidt and Alice Friedman (1988). Peace education is skill building. It empowers children to find creative and non-destructive ways to settle conflict and to live in harmony with themselves, others, and their world...... Peace building is the task of every human being and the challenge of the human family —Fran Schmidt and Alice Friedman (1988).

Thus peace education mainly deals with the instruction, training on how to create, maintain, sustain harmony and peace in each situation and condition whether favourable or unfavourable in life of the individual as well as society and to avoid violence, conflicts by nurturing relevant knowledge, understanding, skill, attitude, interest of the learner. The main objectives of peace education is to develop cooperation, fellow feeling, brotherhood, fundamental freedom, coexistence, humanity, ethical and moral thinking among the citisen of country. Peace education cannot attain its goals unless and until it promote gender education as these days attacks and conflicts related to gender making the situation most worst.

For the adequate promotion of peace it is necessary to spread gender education in the society so that people would be free from wrong knowledge, attitude, practices related to gender that is disturbing the harmony of the world.

Controlling Gender Violence through Peace Education

Gender means the state of being male or female, what it means to be a man or a woman, and its social context it refers to the social differences between men and women. People usually use 'gender' as synonym of sex. But sex is something one is born with whereas gender is imbibed and learnt through a process of socialisation. Sex does not change and is constant whereas gender and gender roles and norms change and vary within and between the culture. Social construction of gender determine attitude about what man and women are capable of and how they should have, what kind of role model and images are presented for men and women and who will occupy the positions of power. Gender affects almost all aspects of womens and mens' lifes, their needs, opportunities and access to resources. While sex and its associates biological functions are programmed genetically, gender roles and power relations across cultures and through time, and thus are amenable to change.

Gender violence refers to any action done by a specific gender group/ individual against opposite gender in terms of hurting emotionally or physically. It includes murder, rape, torture, blackmailing, sexual harassment, gender biasness etc.

Through peace education gender violence can be removed from the society. This education has objectives to:

- Provide knowledge and understanding
- Meaning and uniqueness of each gender
- The role of each gender in the society
- Responsibility of each gender for society
- Gender equality
- Develop attitude of respecting each gender
- Removing superstition, biases
- Abolishing superstitions, biases related to gender

Develop life skills of:

- self control
- coping with emotion
- decision making
- critical thinking
- problem solving
- negotiation/refusal
- empathy
- tolerance
- cooperation and coordination
- interpersonal skills
- stress management
- self evaluation
- effective communication

Target Groups

Gender based peace education can be taught to several subjects such as:

- school and college students
- adult persons of the society
- illiterate worker and labourer
- office personnel
- teachers

Gender oriented peace education can be imparted to each citisen of the country by several educational institution as well as social activist and organisations.

Teacher education institutions, schools, colleges, NGO should take active part in spreading gender education.

Strategies for Imparting Education for maintaining Peace Related to Gender

Thorough the following strategies educational institution can impart peace education:

- Lectures
- Seminar
- Conference, Discussion, Debate, co-curricular activities
- Conducting Case Studies
- Projects relevant to peace education
- Orientation course for in-service teachers
- Organising Work shops
- Conducting Research Activities
- Showing movies, documentaries, Power point presentation
- Organising drama, role play on peace education
- Supply of books, magazines related to gender based peace education
- Giving Projects on gender based peace education
- Continuous illustration and frequent example of great persons who practiced peace in classroom, school, society and for nation
- Creating adequate attitude, confidence, behaviour, act of people through continuous inspiration
- Construction of disciplined and ideal environment in the campus education institutions
- Frequent orientation by college , university as well as guest lecturers/ professors, social activist

- Training on self control, tolerance, life skills for peace education
- Creation of favourable attitude, views , appreciation and interest towards gender among the teachers and people by conducting several activities
- Frequent evaluation of each students attitude, view, behaviour towards gender and construction of peaceful environment
- Designing remedial activities to modify indiscipline and negative plus inadequate attitude as well as behaviour of students of gender oriented peace education

Challenges

While providing peace education to citisens of country there lies several obstacles and challenges with respects to availability of competent resource person, designing of curriculum, use of relevant strategies, availability of appropriate text books, teaching learning materials etc. However, these challenges can be overcome by taking adequate educational planning, administration and management programmes relevant to gender education for maintenance of peace.

Conclusion

In India the crime against women, the so called weak gender is increasing day by day. It is tremendously shaking the future of society and its harmony. Now it's time to awake the spirit of the country to irradiate such a situation by lightening the candle of knowledge in every citisen of country to make a prosperous and peaceful nation. This approach cannot work without implementation of gender oriented peace education. Administrators, teachers, intellectual must take some steps to remove all the obstacles in the path of gender based peace education to establish heavenly harmony.

References

- Peace Education: Frame work for Teacher Education (2005) UNESCO, New Delhi
- Gender Equity in Education: A review of Trends and Factors (2008): NUEPA, New Delhi

19

Schooling and Skill Development: Enroute to Gender Equality and Inclusive Development

Anand Valmiki

Asst. Professor Regional Institute of Education, Bhopal (NCERT)

Valmiki2009@gmail.com

Abstract

We must equip and nurture our youth with the right kind of education, skill-set and opportunity to reap this demographic dividend (Address of President of India to the Parliament on 09.06.2014). Skills and knowledge are the driving forces of economic growth and social development for any country. As India moves progressively towards becoming a 'knowledge economy' it becomes increasingly important that the nation must focus on advancement of skills and these skills have to be relevant to the emerging economic environment with the twin targets of achieving the economic growth and inclusive development. The present chapter attempts to explore the inter-linkages between schools, skill development and gender equality in twenty-first century by highlighting the prominence of 'capabilities approach'. Thus, the chapter revolves around the central theme of promoting gender equity through skill development in schools to achieve the goal of inclusive development. Various sections of this chapter deliberate the concept of gender equality in brief; conceptual understanding of skills; and the rationale behind the skill development to attain gender equality to sustain inclusive development.

Keywords: *Gender Equality, Skill, Capabilities Approach, Inclusive Development*

Introduction

In the pre-independence era skill was usually transferred from father to son. This informal method of skill acquisition continued for centuries. With the advent of industrialisation the need for more skilled workforce became enormous in nenteenth and twentieth century. Independent India during Nehruvian era underwent rapid industrialisation process that demanded more and more skillful workforce. Was this demand for skilled workforce undermined in policy making and practice? Did schooling in Independent India ever imparted "skills" to the children that enabled them to make their 'career choices' as well as facilitate 'vertical mobility' in higher education? Have we ever attempted to impart "skills" to our children that would empower them to be 'employable' in the market in their future? Are educators aware of the fact that "skills" are gateway to 'social inclusion' and 'employment' that eventually carve a path to 'equality' and 'inclusive development'? This chapter conceives the answer to the above questions as big YES.

After independence, as a matter of policy, a number of committees and commissions recommended the vocational education system inextricably interlinked with common school curriculum. National Policy of Education (1968), Kothari Commission (1964) and Central Advisory Board of Education in 1975 emphasised the need for (pre)vocational skills in schools and diversified vocational training at secondary schools. The focus of such initiatives was to build a sustainable skill based education system. The Kothari Commission on Educational Reforms, 1966 had visualised that 25 per cent of the students at the secondary stage would go for the vocational stream.[1] Scholars and educators of Nehruvian era predicted that 'skill development' in the nation will have to be in consonance with the wheels of modernisation that are rolling through the industry, agriculture and tertiary sector. Nevertheless, current scenario in India is that only five per cent of the population of 19–24 age group has acquired some sort of skills through vocational education, while the corresponding figure for Korea is as high as 96 per cent.[2] Experts estimate that 32 per cent of its current population is under the age of 15.[3] India with more than 1.2 billion citisens has the second largest education system in the world (after China). However, the National Knowledge Commission and the Planning Commission reiterate lack of skill to be a major hurdle in nation's inclusive development.

In such a context of inclusive development, this chapter takes a position that socialising school children into skills and facilitating them to acquire skills becomes central to schooling. Furthermore, in order to achieve the goal of inclusive development, this chapter perceives that skills have to be imparted in schools so as to empower both girl students and boy students to achieve the immaculate goal of gender equality and eliminate the remnants of historical marginalisation, social exclusion and oppression of one the sub-categories of gender, i.e., women. The subsequent sections deliberate the concept of gender equality in brief; and the rationale behind the skill development to attain gender equality and sustain inclusive development. It also highlights the contextualisation of capabilities approach to attain gender equality through skill development in schools. The perspective that this chapter adheres to is to permeate vocational training in schools as a part and parcel of integral/common curriculum for schools.

Gender Equality via Right to/within/through Education

The term gender equality is reflected in one of the six Education for All (EFA) goals elucidated in the Dakar Framework for Action [2000][4]4 which envisages 'eliminating gender disparities in primary and secondary education by 2005, and achieving gender equality in education by 2015, with a focus on ensuring girls' full and equal access to and achievement in basic education of good quality'. Goal 3 of the Millennium Development Goals i.e., *Promote Gender Equality and empower women*[5] Targeting Development: Critical Perspectives on the MDGs [London: Routledge]. is incorporated as major socio-political agenda of the state in India.

Gender equality refers to the equal rights, responsibilities and opportunities of women, men, girls and boys. Gender equality is achieved when the different behaviours, aspirations and needs of women and men are equally valued and favoured and do not give rise to different consequences that reinforce inequalities[6]. As such, gender inequalities arise from the unequal power relations between women and men. For women in particular, equality means the realisation of rights that have been denied as a result of cultural, institutional, behavioural and attitudinal discrimination. Equality is both a goal and a means whereby individuals are accorded equal treatment under the law and equal opportunities to enjoy their rights and to develop their potential talents and skills so that they can participate in national political, economic, social and cultural development and can benefit from its results[7]. Consequently, a need is felt to develop workers into knowledge workers who will be more flexible, analytical, and adaptable as well as multi skilled. In the new knowledge economy (of twenty-first century) the skill sets will include professional, managerial, operational, and behavioural, inter personal and inter functional skills.[8] For this purpose, this chapter draws on Duncan Wilson's (2003) three-fold characterisation of 'rights in education'[9] and adapts the characterisation of rights in the context of skills and gender equality. The three-fold characteristics of 'rights in education' are:

1. Right to Education
2. Right within Education
3. Right through Education

The Right of children for Free and Compulsory Education Act, 2009 (Act

No. 35 of 2009) is already in vogue as a state agenda for universalisation of school education between age of six to fourteen years. However, the standpoint of this chapter moves beyond the concept of free and compulsory education and advocates 'Rights within Education' which means every childwill have to be endowed with the right to get imparted with the skills that are required for her/him to function successfully in twenty-first century. Furthermore, Right to Education will also have to ensure 'Rights through Education' whereby a child is instilled with skills that are necessary to legitimise and institutionalise equality, more specifically gender equality. Thus skill becomes central to achieve gender equality which is quite substantive and perpetuates and reinforces inclusive development. The sections below will deliberate on skills; skill development and twenty-first century skill for gender equality.

Skills: What Body of Literature/Research Says?

As the concept of "skill" is gaining its prominence tremendously due to various forces such as globalisation of 'Market Economy', inclusion, equality and development, it is pertinent to overview the literature pertaining to skill to develop a conceptual understanding of skills. Skill may be defined as "the ability to do something well". It has various synonyms such as "expertise, skillfulness, expertness, adeptness, adroitness, deftness, dexterity, ability, prowess, mastery, competency, capability, efficiency, aptitude, artistry, art, fitness, flair, virtuosity, experience, professionalism, talent, cleverness, smartness, ingenuity, versatility, knack, readiness, handiness"[10].

For Some, the ability to use one's knowledge effectively and readily in execution or performance dexterity or coordination especially in the execution of learned physical tasks a learned power of doing something competently. Skill is "an ability and capacity acquired through deliberate, systematic, and sustained effort to smoothly and adaptively carryout complex activities or job functions involving ideas (cognitive skills), things (technical skills), and/or people (interpersonal skills)".[11] This section briefly reviews the historical genesis of the skill; its contextual usage in scholarly/research works.[12]

Skill was characterised by Pear (1927) as being concerned with the quantity and quality of motor output: 'skill is the integration of well-adjusted muscular performances' (Pear, 1948, p. 92). While for Pear the emphasis was on manual, motor skills, his contemporary Hans Reynold in 1928 defined skill as 'any combination, useful to industry, of mental and physical qualities which require considerable training to acquire' (More, 1980, p. 15). While Reynold was therefore, introducing a cognitive dimension alongside the manual, his emphasis on training ignores the fact the skills may equally be acquired through practice, without training. Usually the term skill is used to refer to a level of performance, in the sense of accuracy and speed in performing particular tasks (skilled performance). Skilled performance has long been a subject of psychological enquiry and is of obvious interest to employers. In Cox's (1934) study of manual skill, which was not defined but involved both physical psychomotor abilities and mental cognitive abilities, performance in terms of speed and accuracy was measured in experiments with repetitive assembly operations. Hence, the concept of skill acquired enormous significance with industrialisation process across the globe in nenteenth and twentieth centuries.

Another strand of skills research has concerned transfer of training, particularly the extent to which proficiency and experience in one task helps performance in another. In general, transfer of motor skills has only been found to occur where the tasks have particular elements in common, undermining the argument for developing general abilities that will improve performance in various activities (Adams, 1987; Gagné, Foster and Crowley, 1948). This observation has been shown to apply equally to the transfer of cognitive skill (Singley and Anderson, 1989). One conclusion of Cox's studies was that 'skill developed by the mere repetition of one manual operation confers little advantage in the performance of other operations that may be subsequently undertaken' (Cox, 1934, p. 176).

Welford (1968, p. 12-13), who defined skill as a combination of factors resulting in 'competent, expert, rapid and accurate performance', regarded this as equally applicable to manual operations and mental activities. Welford's (1968; 1976) work focused on perceptual-motor performance, as has much of skills research since the two are intimately linked in practice (Fuchs, 1962; Lintern and Gopher, 1978). Welford's work shows how actions are selected and coordinated at different levels of skilled performance and the conditions of practice and training that promote the acquisition and transfer of skill.

More recently, research into skilled performance has increasingly taken into account broader cognitive skills such as problem solving and decision making. This demonstrates the difficulty in regarding such cognitive competences as knowledge rather than skill. Indeed, there is substantial evidence that acquiring skill and demonstrating skilled performance involve a combination of underlying perceptual, cognitive and motor skills (Carlson and Yaure, 1990; Salthouse, 1986). Also, retaining even relatively simple motor skills appears to depend upon understanding of results (Lavery, 1962) and verbalised knowledge (Berry and Broadbent, 1984), or knowledge that is articulated in the course of developing such skills. Moreover, knowledge and working memory play a major role in acquiring skills (Chase and Ericsson, 1982) including procedural skills (Carlson, Sullivan and Schneider, 1989), problem-solving skills (Carlson et al., 1990) and complex cognitive skills (Logie et al., 1989; McKeithen et al., 1981).

Fitts and colleagues (Fitts et al., 1961; Fitts and Posner, 1967) developed a three stage framework for skill acquisition: (i) the cognitive phase of understanding the nature of the task how it should be performed involves conscious cognitive processes; (ii) the associative phase involves inputs linked more directly to appropriate actions and reduced interference from outside demands finally and (iii) the autonomous phase occurs when actions are automatic requiring no conscious control.

Proctor and Dutta (1995, p. 18) in what is arguably the most authoritative text on skill acquisition and performance, define skill as 'goal-directed, well-organised behaviour that is acquired through practice and performed with economy of effort'. Each element of this definition is important: first, skill develops over time, with practice; second, it is goal-directed in response to some demand in the external environment; third, it is acquired when components of behaviour are structured into coherent patterns; and finally, cognitive demands are reduced as skill develops. In further articulating their conception of skill, Proctor and Dutta (1995) distinguish perceptual skills, response selection skills, motor skills and problem-solving skills. Perceptual skills are concerned with the ability to make distinctions and judgements; more complex situations require attentional control for processing but many tasks that initially require attention become automatised. Skill in selecting the appropriate response can be developed with practice; reaction time is affected by the number of alternatives and can be accelerated by providing advance information, thereby reducing the alternatives. Motor skills are the manual aspects of performance such as speed and accuracy of physical movements or dexterity. Problem-solving skills, while dependent upon intellect and mental models, can be acquired and developed through practice.

Skill Development and Schooling: Capabilities Approach

The 11th Five Year Plan (2007-12) has recognised India's massive need to skill millions of formal and informal workers in the next ten years. In response, the government developed an ambitious scheme of increasing the proportion of formal and informal skilled workers in its total workforce from a mere two per cent now to 50 per cent by 2022, thus creating a 500 million strong resource pool"[13]. Improved training and skill development is critical for providing decent employment opportunities to the growing youth population and necessary to sustain the high growth momentum[14]. The 12th Five Year Plan (2012-17) envisages that "while skill formation has to be mainstreamed in the formal education system right from class X onwards, skill creation outside the formal education needs coordinated action and innovative approach"[15]. Planning Commission (2011) opines that children acquire skills faster if taught earlier. It goes on to say that it is important to offer pre-vocational courses in classes IX and X either as an add-on or as an alternative to work education or third language, where applicable. Furthermore, students opting for such pre-vocational courses could be encouraged and facilitated to take up advanced vocational subjects at the higher secondary level. Providing vertical mobility options for students opting for vocational courses, to pursue undergraduate and postgraduate level, if they so desire, appears imminent, failing which the vocational courses at the school-level may not pick up. For a high quality vocational education at school level to evolve and grow in the country, there is a need to train and equip our teachers on a continuous basis with latest skills and the vocational pedagogy itself.

Gender and Economic Policy Discussion Forum which deliberated on Empowering Women through Skill Development—-Challenges and Opportunities[16] identifies that low social value is attached to girl's education, and as they are considered secondary income earners, lower importance is given to training of girls for employment. It also goes on to say that much focus has to be given on improvements in access to education and training for girls, including the provision of services, such as transport, hostels, scholarships, and other incentives to encourage women to enrol for education and training[17]. It is in such a context, this chapter argues that skill development programs have to be initiated in schools with an emphasis on skilling girl children for more employability in the market with in a broad framework of *capabilities approach*[18]. Elaine Unterhalter (2003) interprets that "the key idea of the capability approach is that social arrangements should aim to expand people's capabilities – their freedom to promote or achieve 'functionings' which are important to them". According to Sen (1992) the foundational idea is that what matters to people is that they are able to achieve actual functionings that is 'the actual living that people manage to achieve'. Walking is a functioning, so are eating, reading, writing and talking. The concept of functionings reflects the various things a person may value doing or being varying from the basic (being adequately nourished) to the very complex (being able to take part in the life of the community). Sen argues that when we make interpersonal comparisons of wellbeing we should find a measure which incorporates references to functionings, that is what has been achieved, but also reflects the intuition that what matters is not merely achieving the functioning but being free to achieve it. So we should look at 'the freedom to achieve actual livings that one can have a reason to value' (Sen, 1999, 18) or, to put it another way, 'substantive freedoms' or 'the capabilities' to choose a life one has reason to value (Sen, 1992, 40). "A person's capability refers to the alternative combinations of functionings that are feasible for her to achieve". The Capability Approach considers development through education to be understood not only as increasing income or better access to resources, but as the enhancement of people's freedoms to do and be what they have reason to value (McCowan 2011, p. 285). This capabilities approach goes beyond economic development and rights and broadens the perspective of enabling people's freedom and choices to function in the society. In the light of the above discussion, this chapter argues that skills are such capabilities that can be nurtured through schooling where the future citisens 'freedoms to do and be' are enhanced.

NCERT's position paper on 'Gender Issues in Education' by National Focus Group acknowledges that substantive gender equality in education is a more complex notion that relates to the nature and quality of education, and has to focus on how education can enables girls to exercise their choice and claim their rights[19]. Hence, it is argued in this chapter that skills will enable girls to exercise their choice in market spaces as well as private spheres. The following section explicates the skills that are required for young generation to exercise their choices and rights, specifically girl-students in the twenty-first century.

Gender and twenty-first Century Skills

With the realisation that school education is increasingly becoming academic-oriented; the government has decided to revive skill development programmes in schools to ensure 'all-round development' of students. We must equip and nurture our youth with the right kind of education, skill-set and opportunity to reap this demographic dividend[20]. A well educated population, adequately equipped with knowledge and skill is not only essential to support economic growth, but is also a precondition for growth to be inclusive since it is the educated and skilled person who can stand to benefit most from the employment opportunities which growth will provide[21]. It is by providing skill training in schools, a strong foundation can be built for students which can later be put to use for entrepreneurship and also in their everyday life. Besides the demographic dividend, another factor that adds to the urgency for improved skill development is the increasing number of newly educated youth, especially women, who are willing to seek employment in the service sector school curriculum and schooling become active instruments of cultural reproduction and social control without seeking to alter the informal and the formal processes of socialisation. This chapter argues that education and skill development sector has to adequately respond to this emerging need, making it imperative to provide skill development and training in marketable skills and services.

The most recent developments in the knowledge society and the subsequent changes in the world of work at the global level are raising skill/qualification requirements for job entry and subsequently demand for a more knowledgeable and skilled workforce[22]. In this context, this chapter explicates that there is a dire and urgent need for a paradigm shift in the skill development sector, in favour of innovations, improvements and high quality training. Furthermore, the chapter expounds that it is very pertinent that the concept of training and skill development will have to move beyond the conventional goal of imparting technical and managerial competencies, to playing a broader role of even including basic literacy, numeracy, critical social and political awareness, awareness about gender, and enhancing life skills. Such interventions by their nature will encourage higher self-esteem among girl children and overall personality development. This chapter is in consonance with the exposition that for skill development to be more effective, training needs to bend towards developing the kind of skills women and men already knows[23]and move towards the skills unknown to boys and girls previously. This chapter broadly categorises the skills that are required for gender equality to become more inclusive in twenty-first century and these skills can be incorporated under an umbrella term known as twenty-first century skills. The term twenty-first century skills refers to a broad set of knowledge, skills, work habits, and character traits that are believed—by educators, school reformers, employers, and others—to be critically important for success in today's world, particularly in contemporary careers and workplaces. Generally speaking, twenty-first century skills can be applied in all academic subject areas, and in all educational, career, and civic settings throughout a student's life. It should be noted that the "twenty-first century skills" concept encompasses a wide-ranging and amorphous body of knowledge and skills that is not easy to define and that has not been officially codified or categorised. While the term is widely used in education, it is not always defined consistently, which can lead to confusion and divergent interpretations. In addition, a number of related terms—including applied skills, cross-curricular skills, cross-disciplinary skills, transversal skills, non-cognitive skills and soft skills that are widely used in reference to the general forms of knowledge and skill commonly associated with "twenty-first century skills". While these different terms may not be strictly synonymous, and they may have divergent or specialised meanings in certain technical contexts, these diverse sets of skills are being addressed in this one entry for the purposes of practicality and usefulness.

Generally speaking, the twenty-first century skills concept is articulated, in this chapter, by the belief that teaching students the most relevant, useful, in-demand, and universally applicable skills must be prioritised in today's schools and by the related belief that many schools may not sufficiently prioritise such skills or effectively teach them to students. The basic idea is that students, who will come of age in the twenty-first century, need to be taught different skills than those learned by students in the twentieth century discussed in earlier sections on this chapter, and that the skills they learn must reflect the specific demands that will placed upon them in a complex, competitive, knowledge-based, information-age, technology-driven economy and society. While the specific skills deemed to be "twenty-first century skills" may be defined, categorised, and determined differently from person to person, place to place, or school to school the term does reflect a general—if somewhat loose and shifting—consensus. The following list provides a brief illustrative overview of the knowledge, skills, work habits, and character traits commonly associated with twenty-first century skills:

Types of Skills:

A. ***Technical/ Work-specific Skills*** (Vocational Skills) are specific to a job and are not easily applied in other environments or situations. These skills tend to be technical and specialised.These skills can be imparted/acquired through vocational training. Vocational training is about imparting of specialised skills and knowledge, instilling social and political attitudes and behaviour patterns for successful economic activities by people engaged in dependent employment, self-employment in both Formal as well as Non-formal trainings. Integration of vocational education at the school level is the only practical way of imparting basic technical skills to a large number of new entrants to the labour force.[24] Planning Commission Task Force on skill development further goes on to recommend that "Vocational Education can be provided in schools either by 'weaving' the subjects into the curriculum or by providing separate 'optionals' at the School and College level. The Planning Commission affirms that software aspect can be looked at by the National Council of Education Research & Training (NCERT) and the *extent* to which these subjects can be covered should be largely left to the Secondary School Boards and Universities (2007, p.i). Highlighting the role of NCERT The following recommendations are made by the Task Force of the Planning Commission (2007) to integrate technical skills in schools:

a) Flexibility should be provided in the school curriculum to give weightage to vocational subjects during the examinations and for the grant of credits.

b) VT and VE programmes can be made available to students after Class VIII at any time and after Class V for those over 15 years of age in order to cater to dropouts from the formal education system. As regards 'streaming' of students into VT, this could begin after class X, given the Government of India's mandate to universalise elementary education and expand opportunities for secondary education.

c) The Pundit Sunder Lal Sharma Central Institute of Vocational Education (PSSCIVE) should become the coordinating agency for VE and promote the interface between education and industry. It can be designated as the National Institute for Vocational Education Planning and Development.

This chapter advocates close linkages between various institutes such as Institute for Applied Manpower & Research (IAMR), The National Council of Vocational Training (NCVT), Industrial Training Institutes (ITIs), NCERT, PSSIVE and evolve strategies to integrate Vocational Education and Training at school level for the purpose of providing exposure to school students about various skills and train them in one or two skills of their choice, propensities, proclivities and inclinations. Furthermore, Polytechnics should only be opened in those areas where there is a public demand and a likelihood of employment. National Mission on Skill Development, Skill Development Council and Skill Development Centre's need to provide incessant inputs to schools and the Polytechnics. Keeping in view importance of skill development in *agriculture* and its vast potential, this chapter is of the view that agriculture training institutes have to be set up all over the country, to empower persons dependent on agriculture.

Following are the technical/work-specific skills[25] suitable for twenty-first century:

1. Commerce Based

- Office Secretaryship
- Accounting and Auditing
- Marketing and Salesmanship
- Banking
- Retail
- Financial Management
- Business Administration

2. Engineering Based

- Electrical Technology
- Automobile Technology
- Civil Engineering
- Air Conditioning and Refrigeration Technology
- Electronics Technology
- Geospatial Technology
- Foundry
- IT Application

3. Health and Paramedical Based

- Ophthalmic Technique
- Medical Laboratory Techniques
- Auxiliary Nursing and Midwifery
- X-ray Technician
- Healthcare Science
- Health and Beauty Studies
- Medical Diagnostics

4. Home Science Based

- Fashion Design and Clothing Construction
- Textile Design

- Design Fundamental
- Music Technical Production
- Beauty Services

5. Agriculture Based

- Poultry and Farming
- Horticulture
- Dairying Science and Technology

6. Hospitality and Tourism Based

- Food Production
- Food and Beverage Services
- Mass media Studies and Media Production
- Bakery and Confectionaries
- Front Office
- Travel and Tourism

7. Others

- Transportation System and Logistic Maintenance
- Life Insurance and Related Sector
- Library & Information Sciences

B. *Life skills/functional/transferable skills/self-* management skills can be applied in most environments and situations. "Life skills" are defined as psychosocial abilities for adaptive and positive behaviour that enable individuals to deal effectively with the demands and challenges of everyday life. There are many different understandings of life skills but no definition is universally accepted. Different organisations attach different meanings to the term. The International Bureau of Education (IBE) derives its understanding from the Delores four pillars of learning - learning to know, learning to do, learning to be and learning to live together - and defines life skills as personal management and social skills which are necessary for adequate functioning on an independent basis.[26] For instance, meaningful targets for an overall goal aimed at "improving all aspects of the quality of education and ensuring excellence of all so that recognised and measurable learning outcomes are achieved by all, especially in literacy, numeracy and essential life skills (EFA Goal 6). Additionally, it is essential to ask how life skills are defined in particular life situations

> and throughout life (Ouane 2002; Goody 2001). It is believed that life skills are developed as a result of a constructive processing of information, impressions, encounters and experiences, —- both individual and social -—- that are a *part of one's daily life and work* and the rapid changes that occur *in the course of one's life.* The social dimensions are particularly important as they condition life itself and compel individuals to purposefully acquire skills, develop attitudes and values in order to face and master real life situations (Ouane 2002).

Life skills can be loosely grouped into three broad categories of skills: cognitive skills for analysing and using information, personal skills for developing personal agency and managing oneself, and inter-personal skills for communicating and interacting effectively with others[27]. Essentially, there are three kinds of skills:

"Thinking skills"-those related to thinking and these skill relate to reflection at personal level,

"Social skills"-skills related to dealing with others and include interpersonal skills,

"Emotional skills" can be perceived as a skill not only in making rational decisions but also in being able to make others agree to one's point of view. Elaborate list of life skills[28] are presented below that are essential in twenty-first century to ensure gender equality:

"Decision-making and problem-solving; creative thinking and critical thinking; communication and interpersonal skills; self-awareness and empathy; coping with emotions and coping with stress; Perseverance, self-direction, planning, self-discipline, adaptability, initiative; leadership, teamwork, collaboration, cooperation, civic, ethical, and social-justice literacy; economic and financial literacy, entrepreneurialism dealing with conflict that cannot be resolved, dealing with authority, solving problems, making and keeping friends/ relationships, cooperation, self-awareness, creative thinking, decision-making, critical thinking, dealing with stress, negotiation, clarification of values, resisting pressure, coping with disappointment, planning ahead, empathy, dealing with emotions, assertiveness, active listening, respect, tolerance, trust, sharing, sympathy, compassion, sociability, self-esteem; critical thinking, reasoning, analysis, interpretation, synthesising information; personal expression; public speaking and presenting, listening; health and wellness literacy, including nutrition, diet, exercise, and public health and safety; environmental and conservation literacy, ecosystems understanding".

This chapter maintains that an eclectic approach is required to evolve school programs that integrate vocational and life skills with the core curriculum. This chapter emphasises that NCERT, NCTE and CBSE will have to advance a liaison with Skill Development Council and evolve curriculum on skills for various stages of schooling which is intricately integrated with the core curriculum of schools.

Conclusion: Gender, Skills and Inclusive Development

Skills, knowledge and innovation are driving forces of economic growth and social development in any country of the world. Countries with higher levels of education and highly skilled citisens are not only more competitive in the global economy, but can also quickly respond to challenges and seise opportunities[29]. There is a dual rationale for promoting gender equality. Firstly, that equality between women and men - equal rights, opportunities and responsibilities – is a matter of human rights and social justice. And secondly, that greater equality between women and men is also a precondition for (and effective indicator of) sustainable people-centred development. The perceptions, interests, needs and priorities of both women and men must be taken into consideration not only as a matter of social justice but because they are necessary to enrich development processes[30]. All in all, this paper foresees the synergy between schools and skill development to promote gender equality from the perspective of inclusive development.

References

- Adams, J.A. (1987). Historical review and appraisal of research on the learning, retention and transfer of human motor skills. Psychological Bulletin, Vol. 101, p. 41-74.
- Chenoy, D (2012), “Empowering Women through Skill Development: Challenges and Opportunities”, Power Point Presentation at the GEPD forum II, Institute of Social Studies Trust and Heinrich Boll Foundation, at the India Habitat Centre, 24 April, 2012.
- Government of India (2011). Faster, Sustainable and More Inclusive Growth: An Approach to the 12th Five Year Plan, Planning Commission. Retrieved from www.planningcommission. nic.in
- King, K (2012), “The Geopolitics and Meanings of India’s Massive Skills Development Ambitions”, in International Journal of Educational Development, 32, 2012, pp. 665–673.
- Faster, Sustainable and More Inclusive Growth: An Approach to Twelfth Five Year Plan. Planning Commission, Government of India, 2011.
- Berry, D.C.; Broadbent, D.E. (1984). On the relationship between task-performance and associated verbalised knowledge. Quarterly Journal of Experimental Psychology, Vol. 36a, p. 209-231.
- Chase, W.G; Ericsson, K.A. (1982). Skill and working memory. In Bower, G.H. (ed.). The psychology of learning and motivation. New York: Academic Press, p. 1-58.

- Carlson, R.A., Sullivan, M.A.; Schneider, W. (1989). Practice and working memory effects in building procedural skill. Journal of Experimental Psychology: Learning, Memory and Cognition, Vol. 15, pp. 517-526.
- Carlson, R.A., Khoo, B.H., Yaure, R.G.; Schneider, W. (1990). Acquisition of a problem-solving skill: levels of organisation and use of working memory. Journal of Experimental Psychology: General, Vol. 119, pp. 193-214.
- Carlson, R.A.; Yaure, R.G. (1990). Practice schedules and the use of component skills in problem solving. Journal of Experimental Psychology: Learning, Memory and Cognition, Vol. 16, pp. 484-496.
- Cox, J.W. (1934). Manual skill: its organisation and development. Cambridge: Cambridge University Press.
- Empowering Women through Skill Development Challenges and Opportunities. Forum II, Briefing Note 2, April, 2012. Retrieved from http://in.boell.org/sites/default/files/downloads/Briefing_note_2.pdf
- Fitts, P.M.; Bahrick, H.P.; Noble, M.E.; Briggs, G.E. (1961). Skilled performance. New York: John Wiley.
- Fitts, P.M.; Posner, M.I. (1967). Human Performance. Belmont, CA: Brooks/Cole.
- Fuchs, A.H. (1962). The progression-regression hypothesis in perceptual-motor skill learning. Journal of Experimental Psychology, Vol. 63, pp. 177-182.
- Gagné, R.M.; Foster, H.; Crowley, M.E. (1948). Measurement of transfer of training. Psychological Bulletin, Vol. 45, pp. 97-130. Gender and Economic Policy Discussion Forum.
- GoelP. Vijay Technical and Vocational Education and Training (TVET) System\ In India for Sustainable development. Retrieved fromhttp:// www unevoc.unesco.org/up/India_Country_ Paper.pdf, Ministry of Human Resource Development, Government of India.
- Goody, J. (2001) *Competencies and Education: Contextual Diversity.* In: Rychen, D.S, Salganik L.H. (eds.) (2001) *Defining and Selecting Key Competencies*, Göttingen, Hogrefe and Huber Publications.
- Lavery, J.J. (1962). Retention of simple motor skills as a function of type of knowledge of results. Canadian Journal of Psychology, Vol. 16, pp. 300-311.
- Lintern, G.; Gopher, D. (1978). Adaptive training of perceptual-motor skills: issues, results and future directions. International Journal of Man-Machine Studies, Vol. 10, p. 521-551.
- Logie, R. et al. (1989). Working memory in the acquisition of complex cognitive skills. Act a Psychologica, Vol. 71, pp. 53-87.

- McCowan, T. (2011), Human Rights, capabilities and the normative basis of 'Education for All'. Theory and Research in Education. Vol. 9, No. 3, pp. 283-298.
- McKeithen, K.B. (1981). Knowledge organisation and skill differences in computer programmers. Cognitive Psychology, Vol. 13, pp. 307-325.
- More, C. (1980). Skill and the English working class, 1870-1914. London: Croom Helm.
- OSAGI (2001). "Important concepts underlying gender mainstreaming", factsheet by the Office of the Special Adviser on Gender Issues and the Advancement of Women.
- Available online: http://www.un.org/womenwatch/osagi/pdf/factsheet 2.pdf.
- Ouane, A (2002) Key competencies In Lifelong Learning. *Institutionalising lifelong learning: Creating Conducive Environments for Adult Learning in the Asian Context*, UNESCO Institute for Education, Hamburg.
- Pear, T.H. (1927). Skill. Journal of Personnel Research, Vol. 5, pp. 478-489.
- Pear, T.H. (1948). Professor Bartlett on skill. Occupational Psychology, Vol. 22, p. 92-93.
- Position Paper -National Focus Group on Gender Issues in education. Retrieved from http://www.ncert.nic.in/rightside/links/pdf/focus_group/gender_issues_in_education.pdf.
- Report of the Task Force on Skill Development, Planning Commission Government of India New Delhi May, 2007.
- Salthouse, T.A. (1986). Perceptual, cognitive and motoric aspects of transcription typing. Psychological Bulletin, Vol. 99, p. 303-319.
- Sen, A. (2001), Development as freedom. Oxford: University Press.
- Sen, A. (2005), Human Rights and Capabilities. Journal of Human Development. Vol. 6, No. 2, July, 2005, pp. 151-166.
- Singley, M.K.; Anderson, J.R. (1989). The transfer of cognitive skill. Cambridge, MA: Harvard University Press.
- Targeting Development: Critical Perspectives on the Millennium Development Goals [London: Routledge].
- Wilson, D [2003] Human Rights: Promoting gender equality in and through education. Background paper for EFA GMR 2003/4.
- Welford, A.T. (1968). Fundamentals of skill. London: Methuen.

20

Role of Transgender in Violence of Trilokpuri Area: A Case Study

DrLokanath Mishra

Principal Vivek College of Education Bijnor

Ms Shalini Research Scholar Dr Harsing Gour University Sagar

Abstract

Transgender is the state of one's gender identity or gender expression not matching one's assigned sex. From the mythology transgender are playing a vital role to stop violence. The transgender of Trilokpuri have set an example as to how even a small group of people can bring about a change even while communal tension is flaring all around. This chapter highlights about how the so called hinjiras *are come forward for stopping the communal violence in trilokpuri area of New Delhi.*

Keywords: *Violence, Transgender, community*

Introduction

For centuries, transgender people in India have been treated with a mixture of fear, mockery and confusion. While the "*hijras*" blessings are sought at the time of a birth, it is believed they also have the power to make a curse. Many transgender people are effectively ostracised. Transgender is independent of sexual orientation; transgender people may identify as heterosexual, homosexual, bisexual, etc; some may consider conventional sexual orientation labels inadequate or inapplicable to them. The definition of *transgender* includes:

- "Of, relating to, or designating a person whose identity does not conform unambiguously to conventional notions of male or female gender roles, but combines or moves between these.
- "People who were assigned a sex, usually at birth and based on their genitals, but who feel that this is a false or incomplete description of themselves."

- "Non-identification with, or non-presentation as, the sex (and assumed gender) one was assigned at birth."

A transgender individual may have characteristics that are normally associated with a particular gender and identify elsewhere on the traditional gender continuum, or exist outside of it as other, a gender, gender-neutral, gender queer, non-binary, third gender, etc. Transgender people may also identify as big ender, pan gender, or along several places on either the traditional transgender continuum or the more encompassing continuums that have been developed in response to recent, significantly more detailed studies. Furthermore, many transgender people experience a period of identity development that includes better understanding one's self-image, self-reflection, and self-expression. More specifically, the degree to which individuals feel genuine, authentic, and comfortable within their external appearance and accept their genuine identity is referred to as transgender congruence.

Society generally mocks at transgenders, but they have made a huge contribution in restoring peace in the riot-hit Trilokpuri in New Delhi. As per a TOI report, "A mob armed with swords and stones charged towards Block 35, the eunuchs stood at the entrance and threatened to start taking off their clothes if the angry men didn't turn back". Because of this threat the angry mob backed off. This threat is often used by eunuchs to extort money from people on various occasions but this time it was to stop the violence in the riot-hit area of Delhi. Not only this, they were seen removing stones from the road which people hurled at each other while the fight between Hindus and Muslims was on in the area. As the sanitation staffs are not coming in the area after the violence, these eunuchs have also started a sanitation drive to clean the streets. As per the report, they also guard the gates of the blocks by taking turns so that no more incidents of violence take place. According to eminent social activist and Shahdara MLA Jeetendra Singh Shanty, when he went there to appeal for peace in the region, he saw how these eunuchs were cleaning the roads along with the police. Residents of the riot-hit Trilokpuri area say that people don't even like to talk to these eunuchs in normal days but now they have emerged as real heroes for people in the area.

Causes of Violence

"The three-day spiral of violence originated from a spot in Block No. 20 which came into sudden prominence before Dussehra when some locals organised a 'Mata ki chowki' (Bhagwati Jagran). The spot, where the entire paraphernalia came up, is right opposite and barely 50 steps away from a mosque which has been there for years". Cots were placed and speakers were also installed at the spot which led to rising of a few eyebrows. "When even after Dussehra, there was no sign of the congregation being wound up; those who visited the mosque began to get anxious. Old fault lines, prejudices or genuine nuisance, whatever may be the reason, the Muslims began to complain that the bhajans, allegedly being played at a high volume, were disturbing their *namaz* and *azan*. They also alleged that there was much carousing and dancing. The Hindu residents say no assurance had been given and there was no such deal. Tension further built up and led to a brawl but it was sorted with the help of elders living in the area. From the very day the locals could smell the possibility of a bigger problem in future. But none, neither the government nor the police took charge of the situation which took shape of a big violence on the Diwali night.

Role of Transgender

Transgender people, who sometimes collect money in the street, often threaten to strip or raise their skirts to intimidate people into offering a few coins. As communal clashes gripped the Trilokpuri neighbourhood of Delhi, the group of local transgender people went out to confront a mob that was advancing on local homes armed with swords and stones.

The Times of India a national newspaper in English said the group stood in front of the mob and threatened to start taking off their clothes if the angry men did not turn around and go back the way they had come. The newspaper said the group then set about organising local people to get involved in a clear up of the bricks, stones and other debris, that had been hurled during the clashes. "The condition of the area was so bad that people weren't able to even walk on the roads", the group's leader, Laila Sa, told the newspaper. "Sanitation staffs haven't come after the riots. Someone has to clean these streets as we all have to live here in the end". Though police have been deployed to the area, Trilokpuri remains tense and the group has helped out as volunteer guards. "We sit outside on the benches all the time. Iron gates are installed at the entrance, segregating one block from another. We take turns to guard the gate", said Laila Sa.

When asked to Laila Saji she said when she was going to take meal heard a noise in the Trilokpuri area. Stones ad bricks are thrown from each side of the community. She astonished and think it should be stopped. So she came foward and stand in between two groups of people and started soughing. She said I use my formula to stop violence. She said to two groups of people come forward to fight with me not in the groups. She said while *Shrikhandi* was standing in front of Bhisma Pitamah in the battle field of Mahabharat, Pitamaha Bhisma not wanting to fight 'a woman', lowered his weapons. Knowing that Bhishma would react thus to Shikhandi, Arjuna hid behind Shikhandi and attacked Bhishma with a devastating volley of arrows. Thus, Shikhandi's role was instrumental in Bhisma's death. And also opined that we are born and brought up in India, we are adopting Gandhian principles of non-violence, love, unity etc.

While asking Mohini another one said we all are equal , "*Dharma to pakhija he*" if people believe separate Dharma then why there are no seven moon seven sun seven earth. Though we are living under one sky we all are one. God has not created separate Sun separate Moon separate earth separate tree for different religion, so we should live together with harmony.

Conclusion

From the above discussion right from Mahavarat to till now we observe transgender play a vital role in mitigating the violence and conflicts in the society.

References

- http://news.oneindia.in/feature/trilokpuri-riots-area-was-on-the-boil-since-dusshera-what-were-authorities-doing-1547038.html
- http://en.wikipedia.org/wiki/Arjuna
- http://www.youtube.com/Watch?v=cR_S0MHq0jk& noredirect=1
- http://www.independent.co.uk/news/world/asia/indian-transgender-group-disperses-rioting-mob-by-threatening-to-strip-9823338.html

21

Gender Equality: Meeting the Needs of Peace, Development and Education

Dr Preety Agarwal

Asstt. Prof. Deptt.of Teacher Edu. D.A.V.P.G. College, Muzaffarnagar,

Dr Dharmendra Kumar

Asstt Professor Deptt.of Teacher Edu.Vardhman P.G. College, Bijnor

Abstract

Gender equality means that males and females have equal opportunities to realise their full human rights and contribute to and benefit from economic, social, cultural, and political development. Parity and equity are the building blocks of equality in education. It is well established that a significant amount of occupational gender segregation exists in all societies, though the extent varies. That is, to varying degrees women and men work in different occupations. By and large, the induction of women into skilled and professional jobs, political bodies has not made any significant change in their traditional image as house-wives. Most of our employed women are concentrated in low paid, semi-skilled and unskilled jobs. Those who have secured unconventional roles as engineers, doctors, police and defence personal are usually assigned tasks which are less challenging. For instance, our women minister would normally get the portfolios of health, family welfare education environment, cultural affairs etc. Since women's resource position is inferior to that of men, and they have greater chances of losing out to men in the field of employment. Multinational Corporation has been found to prefer female worker because they are cheaper then male worker. Women are the last to acquire skills which falls outside the traditional skills allotted to them. Also with the increased competition for unskilled jobs, globalisation is likely to throw unskilled women workers in fierce competition with men. Consequently, women who are the last in the house hold to enter the work force, happen to be the first to be thrown out in the event of market contraction. The present chapter attempts to highlight the gender inequalities in employment. Hence, the urgent need for intervention to safe guard and improve women's employment conditions.

Keywords: *Women's Work and Economic Empowerment, Types of Gender Discrimination, Girls' Education at a Crossroads, Actions to Promote Gender Equality, Policies to Promote Gender Equality, Interventions*

Introduction

Employment puts a women to a double disadvantage working women, before going to work has to complete several tasks, e.g., cooking, preparing the children for school, sending the husband to work, washing clothes, setting the house in order. Even when she is at her work place, she often keeps worrying about things that need to be done urgently at home. The moment she comes home, she again starts her domestic work. Such process within the family and beyond leads to compartmentalisation of gender roles. Society not merely accepts the hierarchical arrangement, but even encourages it instead of granting facilities for child care to pregnant and lactating mothers, women in the unorganised sector are often kicked out, thus the biological 'qualities' are often turned into 'Biological handicaps'. Men are more favourably placed than women in their respective strata and regions due to the unequal distribution of resources. This systematic differentiation in terms of access to resource and status between men and women leads to the popular view that there ought to be equality of opportunity for both the genders. When girls and boys from the very birth, are prepared for different kinds of role how can they be expected to show a similar out in employment? The gender bias often extends to work place, industry, school, college, university, professional institutions etc. Even if a large number of women especially in the villages, work outside the house and bring in money they are seldom treated as "workers" as par with men. At no point is a woman treated as an individual, with abilities similar to those of as a man. Consequently, even employment has not granted women an independent status. "Work" has an altogether different meaning in the case of female employment, her first priority being the "house".

At the work place, she is, time and time again, made to realise by her supervision colleagues and even juniors that she needs protection. The differences in the work patterns of men and women, and the 'invisibility' of work that is not included in national accounts, lead to lower entitlements to women than to men. Women's lower access to resources and the lack of attention to gender in macro-economic policy adds to the inequity, which, in turn, perpetuates gender gaps. For example, when girls reach adolescence they are typically expected to spend more time in household activities, while boys spend more time on farming or wage work. By the time girls and boys become adults; females generally work longer hours than males, have less experience in the labour force, earn less income and have less leisure, recreation or rest time. This has implications for investments in the next generation. If parents view daughters as less likely to take paid work or earn market wages, they may be less inclined to invest in their education, women's fastest route out of poverty. The general lack of publicity of this advantage to women is surprising. There was not always this advantage to women; it is part of a significant change in industrialised societies in the last 50 years. The change results from changes in the occupational structure. Formerly women were more likely than men to be in manual occupations, but as manual work has declined it is predominantly women who have moved into non-manual jobs, so that now it is men who are more likely than women to be manual workers. Initially, in the change from manual to non manual work, women tended to be employed in low level non-manual occupations, especially clerical work. More recently, however, they have contributed to the expansion of professional employment. Although this development can be expressed in terms of changing labour markets and social processes (Blackburn et al., 2002) it has probably, in part, also been influence despite flooding the workplace since the 1970s and 1980s, women still face many institutional challenges to equality in the workplace. The most obvious and publicly condemned example of inequality in the workplace is the prevalence of occupational sexism, or any discriminatory practice, statement, or action based on a person's sex that occur in a place of employment. One typical manifestation of occupational sexism is sexual harassment—the intimidation, bullying, teasing, or coercion of a sexual nature, or the unwelcome or inappropriate promise of rewards in exchange for sexual favours. Sexual harassment may be a particular offer extended to an individual (i.e., a promotion in return for sexual rewards) or the general atmosphere created within a workplace. If a workplace engenders an environment that is hostile to women, that workplace is in violation of employment law that bans sexual harassment. However, sexual harassment is not synonymous with workplace inequality. Legally, sexual harassment can be directed by one person of either gender towards another person of either gender. However, inequalities in the workplace typically refer to institutional barriers placed in the way of professional success for women.

Beyond sexual harassment, the most obvious instance of inequality in the workplace is wage discrimination. Frequently referred to as the gender pay gap, this phenomenon observes that women are consistently paid less for performing the same tasks as men. While the exact figure varies in response to a variety of factors, there is little debate that women earn less than men. Women are estimated to earn 76 per cent of what men earn for the same work. In other words, women make 76 cents for every dollar men earn for performing the same task. Part of the pay gap can be attributed to the fact that, more often than men, women tend to engage in part-type work or work in lower-paid industries. This explanation of the pay gap invokes the notion of the pink-collar worker. A "pink-collar worker" is a term for designating the types of jobs in the service industry that are considered to be stereotypically female, such as working as a waitress, nurse, teacher, or secretary. The term attempts to distinguish this type of work from blue-collar and white-collar work. However, not even this acknowledgement explains the entirety of the wage gap, for even women working full time in higher-paid industries earn less than their male colleagues Gender Equality Intergenerational gender gaps.

Women's Work and Economic Empowerment

In nearly every country, women work longer hours than men, but are usually paid less and are more likely to live in poverty. In subsistence economies, women spend much of the day performing tasks to maintain the household, such as carrying water and collecting fuel wood. In many countries women are also responsible for agricultural production and selling. Often they take on paid work or entrepreneurial enterprises as well. Unpaid domestic work – from food preparation to care giving – directly affects the health and overall well being and quality of life of children and other household members. The need for women's unpaid labour often increases with economic shocks, such as those associated with the AIDS pandemic or economic restructuring. Yet women's voices and lived experiences – whether as workers (paid and unpaid), citisens, or consumers – are still largely missing from debates on finance and development. Poor women do more unpaid work, work longer hours and may accept degrading working conditions during times of crisis, just to ensure that their families survive.

Types of Gender Discrimination

Sex discrimination, or gender inequality, is unequal treatment based solely on gender. Treatment must be unequal, not simply different. Providing separate restroom facilities is not discrimination, but using separate criteria for promotions is discriminatory. Failure to provide equal pay for equal work is discrimination, as are criteria for bonuses based on gender. Job offers and hiring based on gender — or stereotypes or assumptions about gender — are discriminatory, for example, in professions such as nursing that are traditionally associated with one gender. Discrimination against women because of pregnancy is not legal; pregnancy and giving birth must be treated the same way as any temporary condition.

Harassment

Harassment in the workplace is a form of gender discrimination and takes many forms, including bullying and sexual harassment. The latter includes off-colour jokes, suggestive photos, and inappropriate physical contact and unwanted sexual overtures. Promises of promotion or other benefits made to an employee by an upper-echelon employer or manager in return for sexual favours is sexual harassment, as are threats of job loss if the favours are not granted.

Girls' Education at a Crossroads

The barriers that keep girls out of school are well known, and solutions for lifting them exist. However, governments and donor agencies have focused primarily on increasing female access and enrollment, with insufficient attention paid to the quality or relevance of education for girls or their retention and achievement rates (Sibbons, et al. 2000). If primary school enrollment and completion rates are high, but the quality of education is low, then "education has not conferred the skills and knowledge that are the source of the hoped-for greater earnings, better health, and more engaged citisenship" (Levine et al. 2003). Access, duration, and quality are all critical variables in realising educational benefits. With most efforts focused on closing the primary school enrollment gap between girls and boys, insufficient attention has been paid to the gender dynamics that affect children's larger participation in school. The relationship between gender and educational inputs, such as curricula, textbooks, pedagogy, and teacher training, are rarely made explicit. Similarly, the links among gender inequities, inputs, and outcomes are not sufficiently acknowledged.

Actions to Promote Gender Equality

Step 1

Provide training on gender equality to management personnel. Educate managers in both the obvious and the subtle discrimination that takes place in business. Teach them how to identify discrimination when it takes place among their staff, how to deal with the situation and how to prevent it from happening in the future.

Step 2

Provide employees with quality, on-site child care facilities for both mothers and fathers that work at your company. Work with your human resources department and management personnel to make sure that family leave is available to both.

Step 3

Showcase your company's successful women. There is nothing as demonstrative of your efforts to promote equality as the women who have achieved success because of it, whether they hold management positions or are rank-and-file employees.

Step 4

Publicise your efforts to promote gender equality. Whether it's on your company website, in newspaper editorials or advertisements, let other companies, your vendors and the local workforce know about your dedication to equality in the workplace. Become a role model for other businesses.

Policies to Promote Gender Equality

Step 1

Establish a policy that ensures that men and women are compensated equally for performing the same work. Beyond equal pay for equal work, the policy should also ensure that both genders are treated equally in recruitment, training, hiring and promotion.

Step 2

Establish a policy that allows both men and women to balance their work lives with their personal lives. This guideline would ensure that management supports employees' pursuit of further education to advance their careers, as well as family counseling, family time or other related efforts that assist employees in maintaining healthy and positive family relationships.

Step 3

Establish a policy that strictly and specifically forbids any form of sexual harassment. Either in the policy itself, or in a related human resources procedure, describe in detail the professional consequences that will result from harassment. Provide employees with an avenue for reporting such activity directly to the human resources department without fear of retribution.

Step 4

Establish a policy that ensures the nondiscriminatory policies that apply to the company's employees also apply to all levels of company management. Gender equality means nothing in the workplace if it is not followed to the letter by all management personnel. Encourage managers to act as role models for non-discrimination.

Be Assertive

In the workplace, women tend to issue requests, while men issue directives. Both expect compliance and cooperation, but in a hierarchical workplace, the man sends a message of strength, while the woman unintentionally sends one of weakness. Eliminate this by using direct, assertive statements. "I need your sales figures by the end of tomorrow" conveys strength better than "Do you think you can get me your sales numbers by tomorrow?"

Structure Meetings

Women and men often operate under different rules in meetings. For men, competition for position and power might mean monopolising speaking time and interrupting others. Women, intent on collaboration, might yield the floor to give everyone a chance to speak. Women managers can develop their own rules for meetings that ensure everyone gets their say and make productive use of communication time.

Listening Cues

Gauging a male colleague's understanding according to a woman's way of reacting won't work. Men listen passively, without as many nods and verbal acknowledgements. A woman might assume he doesn't understand, or isn't paying attention, and repeat herself. The man then stops listening. Before repeating herself, the woman should first ask, "Do you understand?" Women should also adjust their own listening behavior since men sometimes interpret women according to the way men behave. When she nods, he might perceive agreement or permission when she's only signaling acknowledgement.

Spur Improvement

Men tend to tune out criticism and let in praise, while women do the opposite. This accounts for why men sometimes fail to make improvements after discussing their job performance shortcomings. Women managers should develop an action plan for men with specific instructions on how to improve performance.

Skip to the End

Faced with a problem, women are thorough in overcoming it. They consider it from all sides, solicit information, and then take action. To men, problems are like flies to be swatted and killed. Discussion is an obstacle to the solution. The same thing goes for decisions: men don't want discussion, only the outcome. When speaking to male associates, women should do their best to get as quickly to the point as possible.

Skip Relating

Women build relationships to work together, falling back on their language strength to do it. Men would rather skip that, preferring that women managers just give them goals to work on. Given goals, men typically work in a straight line, concentrating on one thing at a time.

Prohibited Behaviour

Women can take legal action for acts such as unwanted sexual leering, touching, gestures or communications at work. Employers and their supervisors cannot demand sexual favours from women in exchange for conditions of employment. For example, a woman's boss cannot threaten termination for refusing his sexual demands. The law also protects women from work-related retaliation because they report sexual harassment. Women cannot be fired because they complain their co-workers are sexually harassing them.

Employer Responsibilities

Generally, the law allows employers to limit their liability for sexual harassment by offering women and men reasonable channels to report workplace sexual harassment. Employers must provide detailed information to employees regarding the company complaint processes and must also define the types of behaviours that constitute sexual harassment. Employees may lose certain, legal protections if they fail to follow reasonable complaint processes. Employers must investigate complaints and take action to stop sexual harassment when it occurs.

Legal Action

Women who are victims of workplace sexual harassment may file complaints. Filing deadlines are short. Generally, a complainant has 45 to 300 days to file following the harassment, depending on the state in which it occurred and whether it involves a private or government employer. State employment commissions have separate complaint processes governed by individual state law. Victims may also pursue private lawsuits in most circumstances.

Legal Consequences

Employers who are found liable for sexual harassment can face stiff liability. Victims can sue for compensatory damages, which include things such as physical pain and suffering, and emotional damages. Compensatory damages are dependent on factors such as the severity and frequency of the harassment. A victim can also recover pecuniary damages, which cover actually money lost due to harassment, such as lost wages from job termination or counseling fees relating to the harassment.

Interventions

- Enact and enforce labour laws that ensure equal opportunity and pay equity.
- Conduct social mobilisation campaigns aimed at increasing women's and girls' status and value in society.
- Promote legal reforms that ensure women and girls have equal protections and rights with regards to family law, citisenship, property ownership, political participation, inheritance, and the financial sector.
- Provide leadership training for women.
- Promote infrastructure enhancements that encourage economic growth, reduce poverty, and improve families' health and well-being, and ease the burden on women and girls.
- Develop programmes to remove implicit or explicit barriers to women's participation in nontraditional sectors, including targeted recruitment, training, and support initiatives for women.
- Ensure that gender concerns are identified and addressed at the

highest level of politics and public policy.

- Recognise that there are myriad entry points for addressing gender inequalities, which include enrollment policies and practices, curriculum relevance, teacher deployment, learning environments, security, new technologies, and resource allocation.
- Ensure that gender concerns are identified and addressed in activities focusing on global issues such as HIV/AIDS and education in emergencies or post-conflict situations.
- Analyse how specific educational programmes and policies impact girls and boys differently, taking into account different roles, responsibilities, needs, and interests and address them during the project design process.
- Integrate gender awareness components into pre- and in-service teacher training.
- Incorporate gender considerations into activities to develop curricula and learning materials.
- Identify and report on indicators such as girls' and boys' net and gross enrollment, gender parity in enrollment, equality in educational outcomes, and girls' and boys' completion rates.
- Make interventions for girls more effective by integrating them into a coherent overall strategy for education reform.
- Develop practical tools to support programming staff in designing, implementing, reporting on, and evaluating programmes that address equitable access and quality from a gender perspective.
- Develop indicators to better identify and measure progress towards gender equality in education.

Conclusion

In order to ensure a more effective implementation of the preventive measures, intervention strategies should include the creation of a supportive environment for all population groups. Sustainable behaviour change and attitude must be determined by men and women their communities. Community leaders, media should sensitise and made aware of the negative implications of some of the traditional stereotypes. Since many of these are seen as role models in families and communities, they also have a major role in influencing community opinions and ideas. Never the less the communities should take the initiative in implementing the conducive ideas. The larger schema into which the gender pay gap fits is the notion of a "glass ceiling" for women in the workplace. The term refers to institutional barriers for which there is little hope for legal redress and, thus, appears to be as invisible as glass but that nevertheless limit the rise of women in the workplace. Women have made great strides in the workplace, but inequality persists. On average there's still a gender gap that needs to be rectified.

References

- Anker, R. (1998). *Gender and Jobs: Sex Segregation of Occupations in the World.* Geneva: International Labour Office.
- Blackburn, R. M., Brooks, B. and Jarman, J. (2001). "Occupational Stratification: The Vertical Dimension of Occupational Segregation". *Work, Employment and Society*, pp.15(3): 511-538.
- Blackburn, R. M. and J. Jarman (2004). "Segregation and Inequality' in European.
- Commission, 25th CEIES Seminar - Gender statistics - Occupational segregation: extent, causes and consequences". Luxembourg: Office for Official Publications of the European Communities.
- Blackburn, R. M. and Jarman, J. (2006). "Gendered Occupations: Exploring the Relationship between Gender Segregation and Inequality". *International Sociology*, 21(2): pp. 289-315.
- Blackburn, R. M., Jarman, J. and Siltanen, J. (1994). "Gender in the Labour Market:
- Occupational Concentration and Segregation." Report prepared for the United Nations, July.
- Blackburn, R.M., Browne, J., Jarman, J. and Brooks, B. (2002). "Explaining Gender Segregation". *British Journal of Sociology*, 53: pp. 513-536.
- Levine, R., N. Birdsall, A. Ibrahim, and P. Dayal. 2003. "Background paper of the Task Force on Education and Gender Equality: Achieving universal primary education by 2015". n.p.: Millenium Project.
- Sibbons, M., D. Swamfield, H. Poulsen, A. Giggard, A. Norton, and A. Seel. 2000. *Mainstreaming gender through sector wide approaches in education: Synthesis report.* London: Overseas Development Institute/Cambridge Education Consultants.

22

Role of Peace, Gender –Equality and Women Empowerment in twenty-first Century

Aareen Aayushman

Student, 4 year, B.A.LL.B., I.M.S.

Unison School of Law, Dehradun

"*You* can tell the condition of a nation by looking at the status of its women"

———Jawaharlal Nehru

Abstract

Human capital is the main asset of India in its drive to become the most competitive and dynamic knowledge based economy in the world. Indian higher education system /sector has great potential to be NEW ENGINE of growth in the background of the competitive global scenario. It is necessary to promote peace, gender equality, valuable education and sustainable development, international exchange and uniting the strengths of every country to cope with the reform process of Globalisation and changing pattern of education sector on world panorama.

The rise and development of higher education, equal gender education, and development of Indian education system, promotion of Women Educational Institutions, Peace and Sustainable Development and Constitutional Response is the central theme of this research.

Education is considered as the tool, and a weapon of a man through which he/she can change the world but in our country it is still considered male dominant canvas. Although in the modern era specially in urban areas and sub-urban areas the picture has changed but in the Rural areas and Remote areas it can be seen easily. Means... a Discrimination in Providing Education between Male and Female.

Women are like wheel of the society and should get equal importance, value, respect as men get. They should be treated as men are. Women are playing an important role in corporate, media, politics, sports, entertainment industry, defence, space in the era of globalisation. They have proved themselves in the all field of professions. They have broken the the barrier's of society and hurdles of Male dominations.

Every coin has two faces, same thing is here – Partiality in providing education, discrimination in society, physical and mental exploitation and exploitation at workplace are the broad categories of womens exploitation and are the dark-side of the coin.

The research is investigating in particular the responses of higher education sector, gender education, current government policies, women's scholarships and schemes, ways to promotion of women's empowerment and development to the changing environment due to the forces of globalisation. A number of future scenarios related to the Indian Higher education sector as well as economic significance of gender-education in the era of Globalisation are discussed in this chapter.

In this research author seeks to examine in detail causes of Gender-inequality, discrimination with women, government policies, and its all impact on higher education in India in comparative manner. Contradictory and critical issues have been also examined in this chapter. The ways of promotion of women education, empowerment and development, and valuable remedial reformations has also been discussed.

Keywords: *Twenty-first Century and Women, U.N. Approach, Indian Position, Constitutional Response, Remedial Reformation*

Introduction

In my textbooks I learned that only men
Are kings and soldiers.
Till I read a book in which famous,
Queens ruled and fought against enemies.
In my textbooks I learned that only men
Are doctors.
When I went to a doctor I saw that
She was a woman.
In my textbook I learned that only men
do farming in my country,
Until, on a train journey I saw women
Working in the fields.
I have learned that I have a lot to learn by seeing.

—Utkarsh Ramaya

In the history of humanity and its development, woman had been an important factor as man, yet she has always been looked down as an inferior creature. The womens' inferior positions throughout the ages prevail not merely in family, society but also in the matter of privileges and rights . For centuries woman all over the world have been denied full justice, personal, social, economical and largely ignored as the weaker sex. Gender–based violence is the most enduring and universal phenomenon in the world today. The present fact of physical and mental form of violence has an overwhelming influence on feminine identity formation. Violence affects the lives of millions of women worldwide, in all social, economic and political spheres of life and this violence cut across the rights of the women to participate fully in the activities in the society. Social justice being one of the dimensions of justice stands for the removal of all kinds of inequalities based on caste, race, Sex-Gender etc[1]. Gender equality is a means to achieve social justice. Discrimination against women inflicts certain disabilities on women, which prevents her to develop and utilise her potential in normal social life.

Gender justice, a facet of social justice is a composite concept. In general the term "Gender-Equality" refers that women and men should be treated alike and it stands for the wiping out of male domination. Gender justice also demands preferential treatment of women[2].

The aim of gender justice is to remove all kinds of inequalities based upon caste, race, sex, power position and wealth and brings about equal distribution of the social, political, and material resources of the country. Male dominations perpetuated and coupled with patriarchy resulted in the need for extending the special protection to women in all spheres of her life.

Due to scientific and technological development, States are becoming globalised, society is moving gradually to modern changes. Technology renders the world smaller each day, bringing traditional and modern lifestyle in tense, unresolved proximity. On the other hand, the drastic change in the natural laws and deterioration in cultural values has been impacting man and woman relationship. Half of the generation on this universe is still suffering systematic violence, indirectly condoned by existing societal attitudes. The world is still a long way from gender parity with evidence suggesting that while women may be visible in large numbers in the global workforce, the disappear as they climb up the ladder towards empowerment. Male-violence against women remains general. Taking into consideration the gravity and varying forms of abuse that women are being subjected to, it is apparent that acts of violence against women are not isolated events in a particular society or culture but are, in fact a global phenomenon, which circumvent social economic structures and educational classes[3].

Women make a significant impact both nationally and internationally in changing discriminatory policies and practices. Though women are represented in international power position, yet their increasing presence is severely limited in numbers, this reflects the historical practice of discrimination against women. Upwards of 3 billion people are subject, systematically and casually, to a wide verity of violations because of being female. There is , at last unprecedented acknowledgement that women universally do not enjoy and exercise their full and fundamental freedoms and human rights on an equal and equitable basis with men.[4]

The protection of women against sexual harassment and right to work with dignity are universally recognised rights under the various international protocols, such as, the convention on the elimination of all forms of discrimination against women (CEDAW)1979, which has been ratified by India in the year 1993. The convention gives positive affirmation to the principle of equality by requiring states parties to take all appropriate measures, including, enactment of legislation for guaranteeing women the exercise and enjoyment of rights and fundamental freedoms at par with men.

The women in our country are in a disadvantageous position because of several social problems and lack of protective legislations. Sexually harassment and other cruelties and violations is a violation of women rights to equality, life and liberty. It creates an insecure and hostile work environment, which discourages women participation in work, thereby, adversely affecting their social and economic empowerment and the goal of inclusive growth. The evil of sexual harassment permeates all strata, ranging from the unorganised sector to corporate.

This chapter is an attempt to show the need for gender awareness among the international community to make suitable interventions for the needy groups of women in each country. Despite the advances in Law, violence against women is rampart across the globe due to the gap between legal principles and reality on the ground.

The chapter investigates the developments took place in international law on gender justice, local activism by women group in various countries, as well the resistance such groups face, within their own communities.

Twenty-first Century and Women

Inequalities of access to rights are widening. Inequalities between men and women, rich and poor, and between different ethnic groups, among others, have spurred conflict, violence against women. The structural inequalities that give rise to abuse such as violence against women or ethnic cleansing are in themselves a fundamental injustice. Significant efforts have been made in many parts of the world in securing liberty and democratic freedoms, the egalitarian aspiration of the rights agenda remains largely neglected and unrealised. When violence against women is described in international work it is seen as women rights issue. When violence against women is described in the

United States it is typically framed as a " personal issue" to be addressed as criminal matter.

Violence against women is an obstacle to achievement of the objectives of equality, development and peace. Violence against women both violates and impairs or nullifies the enjoyment by women of their rights and fundamental freedoms. The long standing failure to protect and promote those rights and freedoms in the case of violence against women is a matter of concern to all states and should be addressed. Knowledge about its causes and consequences, as well as its incidence and measures to combat it, have been greatly expanded in the women protocols.

In all societies, to a greater or lesser degree, women and girls are subject to physical, sexual, psychological abuse that cuts across lines of income, class and culture. The low social and economic status of women can be both a cause and consequences of violence against women. Women have inherent right to dignity. Women are human beings. So every rights pertaining to human beings is not alien to women. Women have right to live a dignified life.

Discrimination against women violates the principles of equality of rights and respects for human dignity, is an obstacle to the participation of women , on equal terms with men, in the political, social, economic and cultural life of their countries, hampers the growth of the prosperity of society and family and makes more difficult the full development of the potentialities of the women in the services of their country and humanity. Women all over the world have not only been denied full justice , social, economic and political but as weaker sex they have been used, abused, exploited and then discarded to lead immoral, street vagrant and destitute life till their death.

Nowadays, however, women have broken their ill-social shackles and are ready to face the contemporary challenges without any help and hesitation and consequently, 8th March, is formally observed and celebrated in several countries, including India as a mark of integrated achievements towards the equality of rights, status and dignity of women and their equal participation in economic, social and cultural development in the contemporary world scenario[5].

The concept of equality between male and female was almost unknown to us before the enactment of the constitution of India. Of course, the preamble of the constitution, which is the supreme law of the land, seeks to secure to its citisens, including women folk, justice –social, economic and political, liberty of thought, expression, belief , faith and worship, equality of status and opportunity, and promote fraternity assuring the dignity of the individual in this twenty-first century[6].

United Nations Approach

For the advancement of the women United Nations has focused its initiations. United Nations expressed the determination of the peoples of the

United Nations "To reaffirm faith in fundamental rights, in the dignity and worth of the human being, in the equal rights of men and women[7]. The purposes of the United Nations is "To achieve international co-operation in solving international problems of an economic, social, cultural and in promoting and encouraging respect of human right and fundamental freedoms for all without discrimination as to race, sex, language or religion"[8]. The provision for equality of women with men has been enshrined in the charter that "The United Nations shall place no restrictions on the eligibility of men and women to participate in any capacity and under cnnditions of equality in its principal and subsidiary organs"[9]. The charter provides for co–operation that "Promoting international co-operation in the economic, social, cultural, educational and health fields and assisting in the realisation of women rights and fundamental freedoms for all without distinction as to race, sex, language, religion and specially on Gender – matters[10.]

Notes

1. According to Ronald Dworkin , Social justice may be natural and distributive in nature.
2. B.K. Ghatak , Dr Ambedkar Thought (New Delhi, APH Publishing corporation , 1997) at p. 121.
3. Vaishali Gupta, Sr. Lecturer, faculty of law, N.R.E.C. College , Khurja, Ford Fellow.
4. Supra n. 2.
5. Awasthi, S. K., and Kataria , R.P. , Law Relating to protection of Human Right (New Delhi , Allahabad : Orient Publishing Company, 2001) at p. 2.
6. Supra n. 2 at p. 2.
7. Preamble , Charter of the United Nations, 1945.
8. Id. , Article 1 (3).
9. Article 8 , Charter of the United Nations , 1945.
10. Id ., Article 13 (1)(b).

23

Mental Health of Women Experienced Domestic Violence

Mehfooz Ahmad
Research Scholar, Department of Psychology,
Jamia Millia Islamia, New Delhi
Mrs Najmunnisa
Assist. Professor, Department of Education
R.B.D. Women's College, Bijnor

Abstract

Violence against women is a universal phenomenon that persists in all countries of the world. Women and girls are vulnerable to several forms of violence throughout their life. The most prevalent form of violence against females worldwide is domestic violence. Domestic violence can take a number of forms including physical, emotional, verbal, economic and sexual abuse, which can range from subtle, coercive forms to marital rape and to violent physical abuse that result in disfigurement or death. Globally, a wife or female partner is more commonly the victim of domestic violence, though the victim can also be the male partner, or both partners may engage in abusive or violent behaviour, or the victim may act in self-defence or retaliation. Many studies have shown the nexus between domestic violence victimisation and mental health problems. Domestic violance may cause various psychological problems to the women i.e., depression, anxiety, anger and Post-traumatic Stress Disorder (PTSD) etc. Protection of the rights, Psychological counseling and sensitisation towards women mental health issues can curb the menace in the present situation.

Keywords: *Mental health, domestic violence, women*

Introduction

Mental health is defined by the World Health Organisation (WHO report, 2005) as a state of well-being in which the individual realises his or her own abilities, can cope with the normal stresses of life, can work productively and fruitfully, and is able to make a contribution to his or her community. According to Skalski and Smith (2006) mental health like physical health, may be viewed as existing on a continuum from healthy living to chronic illness.

Jahoda came up with a list of six criteria you need to meet in order to not be "abnormal":

- Self attitudes – Having high self-esteem and a personally identity.
- Personal growth and self actualisation – How much you develop to you full capabilities.
- Integration – Being able to cope with stressful situations.
- Autonomy – Being independent and able to look after yourself.
- An accurate perception of reality – seeing life as it really is, not in a way no one else perceives it.
- Mastery of the environment – being able to adjust to new environments.

Domestic violence (also domestic abuse, spousal abuse, battering, family violence and intimate partner violence) is a pattern of behaviour which involves violance or other abuse by one person against another in a domestic context, such as in marriage or cohabitation.

Mental health for each person is affected by individual factors and experiences, social interaction, societal structures and resources, and cultural values. It is influenced by experiences in everyday life, in families and schools, on streets, and at work (Lehtinen, Riikonen & Lahtinen 1997; Lahtinen et al. 1999). Violence against women is a universal phenomenon that persists in all countries of the world. Women and girls are vulnerable to several forms of violence throughout their life. The most prevalent form of violence against females worldwide is domestic violence (Sarkar 2009). Domestic violence is a major contributor to the physical and mental ill health of women, for the effects of violence can be devastating. Negative consequences extend beyond women's sexual and reproductive health to their overall health, welfare of their children and even the economic and social fabric of nations (Heise, Ellsberg, & Gottemoeller, 1999). The 1993 Declaration on the Elimination of Violence against Women of the United Nations General Assembly defined such violence as "Any act of gender-based violence that results in or is likely to result in physical, sexual, or psychological harm or suffering to women, including threats of such acts, coercion or arbitrary deprivation of liberty, whether occurring in public or private life".

Domestic violence occurs across the world, in various cultures (Watts, Zimmerman (2002), and affects people of all economic statuses (Waits and Kathleen, 1985). According to one study, the percentage of women who have reported being physically abused by an intimate partner vary from 69 per cent to

10 per cent depending on the country (Heise, L., Ellsberg, M., & Gottemoeller, M., 1999). In a study done in India, on about 10000 women, 26 per cent reported having experienced physical violence from spouses during their lifetime (Jeyaseelan, Kumar, Neelakantan, Peedicayil, Pillai and Duvvury, 2007). The prevalence could be as high as 45 per cent as indicated by data from Uttar Pradesh (Jejeebhoy, 1998).

According to the United Nations, domestic violence is "the most common form of violence experienced by women globally" and can lead to serious health concerns for women even death (United Nations, 2006, p. iii). Violence against women is particularly prevalent in South Asia and throughout the region 50 per cent of women experience violence in their daily lives (Oxfam International, 2004).

Further, women who experienced physical or sexual abuse in childhood also experienced ill health with regard to physical functioning and psychological well-being more frequently than other women (McCauley et al, 1995).

Form of Domestic Violence

The domestic violence can be in the form of physical, sexual and psychological and emotional.

Physical abuse: Most common form of violence in which any body part of victim is partially or completely manipulated or damage that can lead to further physical and psychological problem in future i.e., biting, hitting, kicking, slapping, stabbing, gun shoot, use of belt and stick to harm, use of petrochemical like acid on body parts, pulling, yelling and dragging on the floor (Datton and Gewalt, 2002).

Sexual violence or abuse: It includes various form of sexual harms like forceful sexual intercourse, mutilation of genitalia, painful sex (sadism), forced oral sex, anal mutilation, digital penetration and forced nakedness (Russel, 1982) etc.

Psychological and emotional abuse/violence: This is very complex form of abuse and there is a lot of ambiguity in the definition. Most of time physical abuse leads to psychological sequelae like phobia, guilt feeling, insecurity, poor impulse control, nightmares, impaired sleep, humiliation, shame, isolation of victim, forced weakness (Walker, 1984) etc.

Domestic violence in India is highly under-reported because of the fear among women that if they report such events, it would lead to marital disharmony and broken homes. Women who were poor, less educated were also found to be at increased risk of domestic violence as reported by Kumar S. Jeyaseelan L. Suresh S. et al, 2005).

Mental Health Effects

Psychological health effects are more dangerous than physical health effects. Battered women can experience depression, panic anxiety, nightmares, restlessness, eating problem, psycho-genic diarrhea and other social dysfunction (Ratner, 1993). The most common diagnosis by mental health professionals for battered women is Posttraumatic Stress Disorder (PTSD) (Crowell, 1996). Alcohol and substance abuse are also common among battered women (Golding, 1999). Douglas (1987) interpreted the use of alcohol as an effort by battered women to self-medicate their anxiety. Study reported that battered women also experience suicidal thoughts (Sometimes commit suicide) and homicidal thoughts more frequently than normal women. (Krug EG et al, 2002; The World Bank, World Developmental Report, 1993).

Cognitive problems include a tendency to have perception and memory failures and engage in ineffective and self-defeating problem solving (Vitanza, et al., 1995). Cognitive difficulties result from repeated batterings that lead to the development of perceptions that the victim is unable to successfully resolve her current life situation. The resulting sense of helplessness leads to increased feelings of depression, anxiety, and produces a debilitating effect on problem-solving ability. Obsessive compulsiveness is viewed as an effort on the part of women to defend themselves against anxiety through various respective activities (Gleeson, 1993).

Recommendations

Although domestic violence causes considerable emotional pain, many battered women do not develop-mental health conditions and data indicate that symptoms, particularly of depression, may resolve when social support and safety increase (Campbell, Sullivan and Davidson, 1995; Tan et al, 1995).

Coker et al (2003) found that higher levels of emotional support can modify the effect of intimate partner violence on health, and suggested that interventions to increase emotional and social support to women victims of violence might reduce the negative consequences to mental and physical health.

We can also make people aware about magnitude of problem, training, education, research and preventive approach for prevention of domestic violence (UN Chron 1998).

As reported by one study, many women perceived that education improved women's status and increased their contribution to their households, thereby awarding them more freedom and less dependency (Bates, L.M. et al (2004).

Way to manage violence against women is to increase the number of female officers in the police force and to offer training programmes for officers (WHO, 2010 p.19). Other ways to prevent and manage domestic include the development and implementation of the following law enforcement practices: (WHO, 2010 p. 37-86).

- Code of Conduct for law enforcement
- Police agency guiding policies
- Training programmes, including sensitivity training for domestic violence and gender-neutral application of the laws
- Investigation protocols, including always responding to alleged acts of domestic violence, applying applicable legal remedies, and prosecute criminal acts
- Threat assessment and risk management
- Victim services and witness protection
- Programmes to respond to offenders
- Privacy and confidentiality procedures
- Police accountability and oversight practices

Counseling is another means of managing domestic violence. For the victim of abuse, counseling may include an assessment of the presence (Lawson, 2003), extent and types of abuse. (Lawson, 2003).

Conclusion

In sum, Violence against women is a demonstration of male power juxtaposed against the lesser power of women. Where women have low status they often lack the necessary perceptions of self-efficacy and the social and economic ability to leave a relationship and return to their family or live alone and thus are severely curtailed in their ability to act against an abuser. Domestic violence cause poor mental health of the women, whole family and the whole society therefore only by removing it; we can expect a good mental health of the women and the society at large.

References

- Bates, L.M. et al. (2004). Socioeconomic factors and processes associated with domastic violence in rural Bangladesh. International family planning perspective, 2004, 30(4):190-9
- Coker, A. L., Watkins, K.W., Smith, P. H., et al (2003) Social support reduces the impact of partner violence on health: application of structural equation models. *Preventive Medicine, 37, 259 -267.*
- Campbell, R., Sullivan, C. M., and Davidson, W. S. (1995). Women who use domestic violence shelters: Changes in depression over time. *Psychology of Women Quarterly 19*, 237-255.
- Crowell, N. & Burgess, S. (eds.) (1996). Understanding violence against women. Washington, D.C.: National Academy Press.
- Dattor M. A, Gewalt G. F. (2002). Diagnostic used Intervention. Bem

verlab hans Huber; 2002.

- Douglas, M. (1987). The battered woman syndrome. In D. Sonkin (Ed.), Domestic violence on trial, (pp. 39-45). New York: Springer Publishing Co.
- Gleason, W. J. (1993). Mental disorders in battered women: An empirical study. Violence and Victims, 8 (1), pp. 53-68.
- Golding J M. (1999) Intimate partner violence as a risk factor for mental disorder: A Meta Analysis. J Fam Vol. 1999; 14: pp. 99-132.
- Jahoda, M. (1958). Current Concepts of Positive Mental Health. New York Basic Books.
- Heise, L., Ellsberg, M., & Gottemoeller, M. (1999). *Ending violence against women.* Baltimore: Johns Hopkins School of Public Health, Population Information Programme. Population Reports Series, 11.
- Jeyaseelan L, Kumar S, Neelakantan N, Peedicayil A, Pillai 2. R, Duvvury N. (2007).
- Physical spousal violence against women in India: some risk factors. *J Biosoc Sci*; *39:* pp. 657-70.
- Jejeebhoy S. J. Wife-beating in rural India: a husband's right? Evidence from survey data. *Econ Pol Wkly* 1998; *33*: pp. 855-62.
- Krug EG et al (2002). World report on violence and health. Geneva: WHO, 2002.
- Kumar S, Jeyaseelan L, Suresh S, et al. (2005). Domestic violence and its mental health correlates in Indian women. Br J Psychiatry 2005; 187: pp. 62-67.
- Lawson, D. M. (2003). "Incidence, Explanations, and Treatment of Partner Violence". *Journal of Counseling & Development* 81: pp. 19–99.
- Lehtinen V., Riikonen E., Lahtinen E. (1997). *Promotion of mental health on the European Agenda*. Helsinki, (STAKES), National Research and Development Centre for Welfare and Health.
- McCauley, J., Kern, D. E., Kolodner, K., et al (1995) The 'battering syndrome': prevalence and Clinical symptoms of domestic violence in primary care internal medicine practices. *Annals of Internal Medicine, 123, pp. 737 -746.*
- Oxfam International. (2004). *Towards Ending Violence Against Women in South Asia.* Retrieved October 20, 2012, from http://unpan1.un.org/intradoc/groups/public/documents/apcity/unpan038211.pdf.
- Ratner PA. (1993) The incidence of wife abuse and mental health

status in abused wives in Edmonton, Alberta. Can J Public Health 1993; 84: pp. 246-249.

- Russel, D. (1982). *Rape in marriage.* New York: Mac- Millan, 1982.
- Sarkar M. A study on Domestic Violence against Adult and Adolescent Female in a Rural Area of West Bengal. Indian Journal of community Medicine 2010; 35 (2):pp. 311-15
- UN Chron (1998). Shattering the silence of violence against women; 1: pp. 15-17.
- Skalski, A.K. and Smith, M.J (2006). Responding to the Mental Health Needs of Students. Students Services. PL September 2006. Retrived from:http://www.nasponline.org/resources/principals /School Based per cent 20 Mental per cent 20 Health per cent 20 Services per cent 20 NASSP per cent 20 Sept per cent 20 2006.pdf
- Tan, C., Basta, J., Sullivan, C. M., and Davidson, W. S. (1995). The role of social support in the lives of women exiting domestic violence shelters: An experimental study. *Journal of Interpersonal Violence 10*, pp. 437-451.
- The World Bank, World Developmental Report (1993). Investing in health. New York: Oxford University Press 1993.
- United Nations General Assembly. 1993. Declaration on the elimination of violence against women. 85th Plenary Meeting, A/RES/48/104. Geneva: United Nations General Assembly.
- United Nations. (2006). *Ending Violence against Women: From Words to Action.* United Nations.
- Vitanza, S., Vogel, L. C., M., & Marshall, L. L. (1995). Distress and symptoms of posttraumatic stress disorder in abused women. Violence and Victims, 10 (1), pp. 23-34.
- Waits, Kathleen. (1985). "The Criminal Justice System's Response to Battering: Understanding the Problem, Forging the solution". *Washington Law Review* 60: pp. 267–330.
- Walker L. E. A. (1984). The Battered women syndrome, New York: Springer Publishing House Company
- Watts C, Zimmerman C (2002). "Violence against women: Global scope and magnitude". *The Lancet* 359 (9313): pp. 1232–1237.
- World Health Organisation (2005). *Promoting Mental Health:* Concepts, Emerging evidence, Practice: A report of the World Health Organisation, Department of Mental Health and Substance Abuse in collaboration with the Victorian Health Promotion Foundation and the University of Melbourne. World Health Organisation. Geneva.

- World Health Organisation Fact Sheet No 239; Violence 1. against Women, updated October 2013; Available from: *http://www.who.int/mediacentre/factsheets/fs239/en/*, accessed on November 22, 2013.
- World Health Organisation (2010). Handbook on effective police response to violence against women. Criminal Justice Handbook Series. p. 19.
- World Health Organisation (2010). Handbook on effective police response to violence against women. Criminal Justice Handbook Series. pp. 37-86

24

Importance of Woman Education for Promoting Peace Culture

Dr Alka Saini

Asst Teacher, Basic Education Department,Uttarakhand

Dr Alka

Saini Asst. Teacher, Basic Education Department,Uttarakhand

Abstract

At present, so many countries i.e., from Ukraine to Libya to Central Republic to Iraq, Syria and Afghanistan etc., are facing conflicts and agitation in society where women and children are the worst sufferer. This makes it all the more urgent to explore the women's role to demoralise the forces of terror and violence, in protecting themselves and the community, bringing their sons and daughters to the peace table, and being there to hold them to the purpose of peace, to rebuild peaceful and sustainable societies and economies.

Women can play a vital role in educating young people to value peace and not war being first teachers of children being mothers, grandmothers, and other family members in society. Hence, women and young people are key drivers of the radical change of mind-set, institutions and cultures that we seek. In words of Jane Addams "Peace is not merely an absence of war, it's a nurture of human life and, in time, this nurture will do away with war as a natural process".

Thus Women and their empowerment are crucial to advancing the culture of peace in all its vectors i.e., education, sustainable economic and social development, human rights and equality, democratic participation, advocacy based on true knowledge but also wisdom, tolerance and understanding at all levels in the family, community, country, region and globally. But it is also true that without educating woman, empowerment of women is near to impossible.

Therefore, this chapter is an attempt to explore and analyse the ultimate relation between women education and culture of peace in society being women are natural nurturers.

***Keywords**: Women Education, Peace Culture, Sustainable Development, Women Empowerment, Equality, Natural Nurture*

Introduction

According to UN resolutions: the Programme of Action on a Culture of Peace adopted in 1999; and the 1998 UN resolution on the culture of peace:

"A culture of peace is an integral approach to preventing violence and violent conflicts, and an alternative to the culture of war and violence based on education for peace, the promotion of sustainable economic and social development, respect for human rights, equality between women and men, democratic participation, tolerance, the free flow of information and disarmament".

A culture of peace and non-violence goes to the substance of fundamental human rights: social justice, democracy, literacy, respect and dignity for all, international solidarity, respect for workers' rights and core labour standards, children rights, equality between men and women, cultural identity and diversity, Indigenous peoples and minorities rights, the preservation of the natural environment etc.

Education is the key to uniting nations, bringing human beings closely together. In many parts of the world, civil society suffers because of situations of violent conflicts and war. It is important to recognise the crucial role of education in contributing to building a culture of peace and condemning instances in which education is undermined in order to attack democracy and tolerance. Education is a key tool in combating poverty, in promoting peace, social justice, human rights, democracy, cultural diversity and environmental awareness. Education for peace implies an active concept of peace through values, life skills and knowledge in a spirit of equality, respect, empathy, understanding and mutual appreciation among individuals, groups and nations.

Non-discriminatory education benefits both girls and boys and thus ultimately contributes to more equal relationships between women and men and hence leads to positive social change and equality. Access to and attainment of educational qualifications is necessary if more women are to become agents of social change. Thus it is important to encourage women's education as a consistent strategy towards being one of the ways to attain peace.

At present, so many countries i.e., from Ukraine to Libya to Central African Republic to Iraq, Syria and Afghanistan etc., are facing conflicts and agitation in society where women and children are the worst sufferer. This makes it all the more urgent to explore the wolen'r role to demoralise the forces of terror and violence, in protecting themselves and the community, bringing their sons and daughters to the peace table, and being there to hold them to the purpose of peace, to rebuild peaceful and sustainable sobieties and economies.

Women can play a vital role in educating young people to value peace and not war being first teachers of children being mothers, grandmothers, and other family members in society. Hence women and young people are key drivers of the radical change of mind-sets, institutions and cultures that we seek.

Thus, Women and their empowerment are crucial to advancing the culture of peace in all its vectors i.e., education, sustainable economic and social development, human rights and equality, democratic participation, advocacy based on true knowledge but also wisdom, tolerance and understanding at all levels in the family, community, country, region and globally. But it is also true that without educating woman, empowerment of women is near to impossible.

Let us discuss first of all, the key natural qualities of woman which lead towards peace.

Women: Replica of Mother Earth

Woman creates humans like mother earth creates all creatures. So women have caring attitude by birth and normally avoid conflicts. Women have therefore contributed significant efforts in movements for peace in diverse cultural, social and geographical contexts. Women are highly visible in peace building groups and initiatives (Sylvester, 1992). Polls show that women oppose budget increases in military expenditures and deployment of new weapons more frequently than men (Brock-Utne, 1985). It is therefore common to think of women as being pro-peace. Women in general have sometimes been characterised as "natural pacifists" with a "proverbial" interest in peace (Aronof, 1986). Women's struggle for peace is connected to the concern for human life, for children, for themselves and for other women. Women always strive to reach other women in the opposite camps. Women usually employ a varied set of nonviolent techniques, acts, strategies to resolve issues (Brock-Utne, 1985).

Women: Peace Lover

Are women more peace loving than men? Saraicino (1988) said human aggression is a problem for men, not women; it is men who wage wars, engage in bitter competition fight each other individually and maintain vendettas lasting for years or even decades. Schreiner (1991) said men have made boomerangs, bows, swords or guns with which to destroy one another. There is no battle field on earth which it has not cost the women more in actual bloodshed than it has cost the men who lie there. Women peace efforts are often dismissed as simply part of general softness of women nature or as part of their motherhood role (Vellacott 1988). Women have never institutionalised violence (Brock-

Utne 1985). Girls are taught to be more submissive, less demanding and more nurturing than males. Women fulfill their assigned roles in war as well as in peace sacrificing their sons, husbands and lovers without complaining but mourning their loss (Vellacot 1988). Sylvester (1992) however does not think it is an advantage for women to be so docile. They should embrace classical Marxism which she says has a warrior philosophy to fight patriarchy that has bolstered male supremacy.

Women: Incarnation of Ahimsa

Mahatma Gandhi viewed women as the incarnation of ahimsa and added that due to a different socialisation process, women have tended to grow up more peaceful than men and more capable of solving conflicts in a nonviolent manner. Peace often starts in the minds of women, Mahatma Gandhi added (Gandhi 1992). Margaret Atwood once commented that as far as she heard, war and rape were two activities not extensively engaged in by women (Vellacott, 1985). While most of the world's violence is perpetrated by men, most of its nonviolent nurturing is done by women (Brock-Utne, 1985). Almost all of the women's human rights organisations of the late nineteenth and twentieth centuries saw world peace as part of their vision for a new society (Ruether, 1987). Women usually assume roles of peacemakers in families, in communities and in societies. They are seen as women as saviours of the world (Brock-Utne 1985). Historically women have made efforts in movements for peace. They are considered to be natural peace lovers. Peace Pilgrim the indomitable American Woman (1951-1981) covered 25,000 miles on foot for peace and vowed to continue to walk for peace until human beings have learnt the way of peace (Pilgrim 1982). Betha von Suttner the German actual initiator of the Nobel Peace Prise (1843-1914) without whom there would be no Nobel peace Prise worked relentlessly to promote peace. She was the one who having known and worked closely with Alfred Nobel urged him to set aside some amount as a prise for anyone who worked for peace. Alfred Nobel invented dynamite, a weapon of destruction, but regards himself as a pacifist and made some fortune from the invention. Betha was never mentioned, until she herself got a prise which she should have received much earlier. However, women have traditionally not been well represented at international peace negotiations.

Women: Natural Nurture

As noted in the Declaration on the Participation of Women in Promoting Peace and Cooperation, which was proclaimed by the UN Assembly in December 1982: Although women non-governmental organisations (NGOs) have been working in the field of disarmament and arms control, more opportunity is still needed for women to participate in national and international meetings on peace, conflict resolution, the disarmament and meetings of the Security Council. Betty Reardon (1992), one of the pioneers in education for a culture of peace, has challenged our contemporary realities of a war system as opposed to a peace system using the gender centered concept of nurturing. If we are to think peace, we need a paradigm of peace to move us from a "warring" society to a parenting or caring society, in which all adults parent the young and care for the vulnerable. In this quest for building a more peaceful wnrld, Reardon (1988) equally highlights the crucial contributions of women. She says the acquisition of peace knowledge helps women to become peacemakers and peace keepers, to subvert the "war-system". The war system refers to the practices, institutions and interrelationships which are essentially violent, and which destroy relationships, impede social development and human fulfilment. The alternative is to enthrone a "peace-system" where the society becomes peaceful and the natural order becomes what nature ordains, "... an organic peace that sustains healthy persons and creative societies" (Reardon, 1988 p. 51).

Thus being mother or a natural nurture, woman can play their role more effectively to promote peace culture if they are educated. Now, to recognise importance of women education to promote peace culture, following discussion is being made to know the relation between women education and key vectors of peace culture.

Women Education and Sustainable Economics

W.E.B. Dubois (n.d), a black American scholar, more than 100 years ago believed "education is equated with success, work alone will not do it unless inspired by the right ideals and guided by intelligence. Education must not simply teach work — it must teach Life".

In looking at education as equipping one with life skills, it can be appreciated that without both unbiased formal, non-formal and informal education, progress would take place at a very slow pace. Education makes the social and economic life of the girl-child and the woman significantly better.

An educated woman within society is able to get a better job and therefore be in a better position to fend for her family's needs rather than relying on small businesses that subject the woman to a situation of more often than not abject poverty and that bring in very little income as is the norm currently. Education provides the woman with a way out of the cycle of poverty.

Benavot (1989) conducted a study for 76 countries over the period 1965-1980. He found that, "while the education of both genders had a substantial impact on economic growth, the education of girls was a stronger predictor of growth than that of boys; he also found that this effect was particularly powerful in the poorer countries of sub-Saharan Africa". (Pg. 14)

This shows that if a country is interested in revamping its economic growth in order to have good returns, then it should be willing to pay heed to the factor that the education of girls plays in economic growth and invest in this sector.

"Economic development is enhanced in societies where both girls and boys are educated", Veneman, 2007. The role Education of women plays in the enhancement of the economy cannot be underscored. Knowledge, skills and training that girls and women acquire, facilitates their access to formal decent work and fair wages. Higher levels of education increase their probability to engage in formal paid employment.

In Kofi Annan's address on March 3, 2005, He said, "Education is a key economic asset for individuals and for nations. Every year of schooling lost represents a 10 to 20 per cent reduction in girls' future incomes. Countries could raise per capita economic growth by about 0.3 per cent percentage points per year – or 3 percentage points in the next decade – if they simply attained parity in girls' and boys' enrolments".

According to the United Nations Population Fund, one per cent increase in the number of girls finishing secondary school will boost economic growth by 0.3 per cent. The world over, schooling girls' makes economic sense. A similar increase in the number of boys finishing secondary school doesn't yield the same returns, according to the population fund, or UNFPA. Part of the reason is that women are more likely to invest in their children's health and education, further boosting economic growth.

Even basic education brings benefits. For each additional year a girl is in school, her wages as an adult rise by about 15 per cent, according to UNICEF. (Women's news, 2007)

It must therefore be taken into consideration that if any country wants tn improve its economic situation, then it must be willing to invest in the education of the girl child and reap the benefits. In this day and age of the skilled worker, not educating women is immediately cutting off about fifty (50) per cent of one's economic competitiveness as a country.

Education promotes ownership and control over assets such as land and housing. These provide economic security, incentives for taking economic risks, which lead to growth, and important economic returns including income.

Women Education and Health

Some studies as shown below have indicated that Education has a direct impact on healthcare, infant and maternal mortality. Even if it is informal, education given to the woman on reproductive health, invariably determines the kind of decisions the woman will make with regard to her reproductive health.

"Educated women, it has been shown have not only fewer but also healthier children. When other factors such as access to and affordability of health services and the availability of clean water are included in the equation, the education of mothers is consistently one of the two most powerful determinants of child health, clean water being the other. The effect of mother's education is so strong that, in many cases, it overrides access to health care as a determinant of child survival." (Suttcn. M, 1998; Pg. 391)

Sutton demonstrates that education is important if a nation is to prosper in terms of children being born healthier, children who inevitably form the next generation. Mothers that have received an education are more aware of immunisation services for their children and are likely to use them more than mothers who have not had an education. Women Education would save a lot of money of state in terms of trying to prevent infant mnrtality.

Marphatia A. 2005, states, "Each additional year of schooling helps women combat infant mortality, which drops by 5 to 10 per cent". Educated girls are better equipped to protect themselves against life-threatening diseases such as HIV and AIDS, are more likely to give birth to healthy babies who will survive and grow into adulthood, tend to delay marriage, and are more likely to have fewer children.

Female literacy has also been linked to a drop in infant mortality. Babies born to mothers without formal education are twice as likely to die before age five. Thus a nation with educated women will certainly be a healthier nation.

Women Education and Sustainable Development

The social benefits brought about by education cannot be overlooked. In this day and age of globalisation, skilled labour is essential. The Education of the girl child does not only lead to higher economic growth and better health patterns, but also has a significant impact in positively shaping social relations within society.

In countries where more and more women have reached higher levels of education, women's inclusion into spheres of decision-making is made easier. The representation of the female gender is in this way brought to the fore and development activities tend to take on a multi-dimensional perspective.

As Stromquist (1998), states: "In terms of the social benefits deriving from girl's education, equity at all levels of education appears to have a positive impact. This is a significant finding that suggests the need to look beyond girls' access to primary education. In order for girls to participate fully in primary education, they and their families must ultimately perceive that there are rewards for girls who persist into higher levels of education".

In this way then, it is inevitable that society should not only encourage the education of the girl child at the primary school level but should rather have a higher aim that would lead to greater societal benefits.

A story is told, in a documentary titled 'Tumechoka kuomb omba' of a village in Kenya whereby the State had wanted to initiate a development project.

The Government's representative went to the village to meet the village representatives, who all happened to be male. After some discussions, the men expressed their highest priority as being the need to have electricity – their reason was that in this way, they would be able to walk home safely after their drinking sprees in the evening. This to them was the highest need for that particular community.

None of the women had been consulted. When the Government representative took the initiative to inquire from the women, their priority was quite different – water, so that they would not have to walk long distances to the river and would be home in time to make meals for their children and husbands. They also meant to use the water for irrigation to improve their agricultural produce and to quench the thirst of their domestic animals.

The reason given by the men as to why the women were not involved in the discussions was that first, women were not educated and would not be in a position to take part in discussions with a Government representative; second, women in communities, in accordance with culture, are not allowed to be involved when it comes to the decision-making sphere.

This was interesting to watch, considering that if women had been involved in the decision making process, the whole community would have benefited. If these women would have been "Educated", they would have had a much better chance of being included within the decision making sphere.

The theme for the International Women's Day for the year 2006, was, 'the role of women in decision-making. I believe that one of the ways by which this can be achieved is through educating girl-children and women. Notably, the United Nations, in all its years of existence has never had a woman as Secretary General. In his address during the 2005 International Women's day, Kofi Annan, the immediate former Secretary General, stated that it would be good if the next Secretary General would be of the female gender.

Kofi Annan stated, "As the Beijing Declaration tells us, women's empowerment and their full participation on the basis of equality in all spheres of society, including participation in the decision-making process and access to power, are fundamental for the achievement of Equality, Development and Peace".

Yet, so many women are not included in decision-making due to the fact that those qualified are not considered and the rert simply are not educated to the level that would allow them to be included. So where is society headed in terms of equality, development and peace? Considering that education is one of the ways of empowering women, it would only be fit if the education of the girl children and women was stressed upon and implemented.

Women Education and Empowerment

"Education: the process by which we learn new ways of thinking and behaving, a very significant component of the transition-transformation processes. Education is that process by which we glimpse what might be and what we ourselves can become." (Reardon- Andria Wisler 26th March 2006, Lecture at EPU-Schlaining.).

This particular quotation holds a lot of significance in terms of looking at education as being a life-changing concept, and as the global campaign for education rightly states "Women with education are better able to successfully resist debilitating practices such as female genital cutting, early marriage and domestic abuse by male partners". This means that for women, education is a very vital and significant empowerment tool in terms of giving them the non-violent way of getting out of the abuses that they frequently face in their lives on a daily basis.

Veneman, 2007, says "education is a key to addressing discrimination and violence against girls and helping achieve the Millennium Development Goals."

One of the major differences that education would make, would be in giving the girl children and women a sense of self-esteem that would enable them to fend and stand up for themselves and their rights. Both formal and informal education for the girl –children and women is relevant.

Formal education would equip her with the necessary qualifications required and informal education would empower her to be able to stand up for her rights. It is therefore, important that any form of education should go hand in hand with empowerment and should not just be a structural brainwashing of minds.

That is why we regard education as being a key factor in leading the girl-children and women out of the bondage of structural and cultural violence in society and into empowering roles. Access to and retention of girls and women at all levels of education, including the higher level, and all academic areas contributes to their continued progress in professional activities and thus becomes a huge factor in their empowerment.

"A proper schooling experience, that is cognitive of both genders needs to include: (1) human dignity, a sense of self-esteem and confidence; (2) social legitimacy, belonging to the group on an equal basis; and (3) personal and social power, the capacity to influence decisions and negotiate the transactions of everyday life". (Wyn and Wilson, 1993) These aspects when integrated would lead to the empowerment of women and eventually positive peace in society.

Conclusion

Women are an important part of human society and even we cannot imagine about future of human without women. Women works as a centre in family and all other members linked with them through emotional bindings.

Especially youngsters of family pay more honour to their mother, grandmother, sister etc., over male members and we know the youths are the future. Thus women have natural ability to prevent and resolve disputes/conflicts.

The natural ability of women may be increased by education them. By women education and by women empowerment, women can get an opportunity to be involved in decision making for development of society. Educated women can make the country healthier and disciplined by caring their children in healthier way and teaching them about peace and harmony since beginning. As a replica of Mother Nature, an educated mother always teach to children to care and to cooperate with other vital parts of our environment like ants, birds, plants, water, air etc., which ultimately put a foundation of sustainable development in the brain of youths. Even we can say that educated women not only become a part of conflict solution in society but they prevent disputes in society by teaching youths/children valtes as well as tolerance. Thus we may say that women education plays an important role to promote peace culture among families, societies, counties etc.

References

- Amnesty International. (2005). The Impact of Guns on Women's Lives. Oxford: Alden Press.
- Benavot, A. (1989). "Education, Gender and Economic Development: A Cross-National Study" Sociology of Education. New York: Praeger.
- Biraimah, K. (1982). The impact of Western Schools in Girls' Expectations: A Togolese Case. New York: New York Press.
- Brock-Utne, B. (1981). The Role of Women as Mothers and Members of Society in the Education of Young People for Peace, Mutual understanding and Respect for Human Rights. New Delhi: PRIO Publications.
- Castells, Freire P. et.al, (1999), Critical Education in the New Information Age. Littlefield Publishers, New York.
- Cook, Sharon Anne (2007) 'Sisters are Doing' it for Themselves': The Price of Ignoring Gender in Modern Peace Education The Canadian Journal of Peace and Conflict Studies Volume 39, Numbers 1–2 (2007): 59-74, 2007 Peace Research.
- Duncan, W. (1989). "Botswana". Cited in Gail P. Kelly (ed.), International Handbook of Women's Education. New York: Greenwood.
- Freire, P. (n.d) Philosophy of Education. Retrieved on twentieth Oct 2014 from http://en.wikipedia.org/wiki/Philosophy_of_ education# Paulo_Freire.

- Gender Guidelines: Peace-Building Australian Agency for International Development, Govt of Australia, July 2006.
- Global Campaign for Education, 2004, Learning to Survive: How education for all would save millions of young people from HIV/AIDS, London.
- Human Rights Watch, http://www.hrw.org/
- ICPD, Empowering and Educating Girls and Women, http://www.unfpa.org/icpd_ed.htm
- Kinyanjui, K. (1993) "Enhancing Women's Participation in the Science-Based Curriculum": The Case of Kenya. Michigan: University of Michigan Press.
- Puri, Lakshami,"A culture of peace requires the participation of women" Speech by UN Women Deputy Executive Director Lakshmi Puri at UN Headquarters in New York, 9 September 2014.
- Peace Education; contains Article 26 of the Universal Declaration of Human Rights. United Nations Website : http://www.un.org/sg/
- People's Movement for Human Rights, Reardon, B. 1999, Human Rights as Education for Peace: http://www.pdhre.org/
- Promoting Women's Participation in Peace Negotiations and Peace Processes, Prepared by the programme Promoting Gender Equality and Women's Rights, GIZ is responsible for the content of this publication on behalf of Federal Ministry for Economic Cooperation and Development (BMZ), Division 204 (human rights, gender equality, culture and development) March 2014.
- Structural Violence, Wikipedia, http://en.wikipedia.org/wiki/Structural_Violence.
- Sutton, M. (1998). Girls' Educational Access and Attainment. New York: Garland Publishing Inc.
- Wikipedia, https://www.wikipedia.org/
- Women Peace Education, Retrieved on twentieth Oct, 2014 from http://epu.ac.at/fileadmin/downloads/research/Nzovu.pdf.

25

Education for Social Harmony: A Case Study on Peace Building among the Scheduled Tribes of Birbhum District, West Bengal

Debasis Mondal
Research Scholar Centre for Journalism and Mass Communication,
Debotri Chakraborti
Department of Anthropology Visva-Bharati
University Santiniketan, West Bengal

Abstract

The Present chapter is to examine that what is the significance and importance of education in building peace in the rural society. The main objective of this study: (1) to study the status of education of the Scheduled Tribes of Birbhum District West Bengal,(2) to examine the traditional peace building process of the Scheduled Tribes and (3) analyse the importance of education in forming peace and harmony in the tribal society. Qualitative and quantitative approaches have been used in this research study. A Case Study method and in-depth interview techniques were followed to get the primary data from the field. The present chapter gives the conclusion that despite low literacy, tribal people are being traditionally educated by the community leaders and advice to keep maintained peace and harmony in their society, but peace building process is still be disrupted due to lack of low level of academic achievements.

Key-Words: *Education, Peace, Social Harmony, Scheduled Tribes*

Introduction

"If we are taught real peace in the world we shall have to begin with children".

— *Mahatma Gandhi*

Education in its general sense is a form of learning in which the knowledge, skills, and habits of a group of people are transferred from one generation to the next through teaching, training, or research. Education frequently takes place under the guidance of others, but may also be autodidactic. Any experience that has a formative effect on the way one thinks, feels, or acts may be considered educational. Education is commonly divided into stages such as preschool, primary school, secondary school and then college, university or apprenticeship. The wealth of knowledge acquired by an individual after studying particular subject matters or experiencing life lessons that provide an understanding of something. Education requires instruction of some sort from an individual or composed literature. The most common forms of education result from years of schooling that incorporates studies of a variety of subjects. "Jamie knew the importance of an education, so she chose to go to a four-year university after graduating from high school".

According to some learned people, the word "Education" has been derived from the Latin term "Educatum" which means the act of teaching or training. A group of educationists say that it has come from another Latin word "Educare" which means "to bring up" or "to raise". According to a few others, the word "Education" has originated from another Latin term "Dducere" which means "to lead forth" or "to come out". All these meanings indicate that education seeks to nourish the good qualities in man and draw out the best in every individual. Education seeks to develop the innate inner capacities of man. By educating an individual we attempt to give him some desirable knowledge, understanding, skills, interests, attitudes and critical 'thinking. That is, he acquires knowledge of history, geography, arithmetic, languages and sciences. He develops some understanding about the deeper things in life, the complex human relations, and the cause and effect relationship and so on. He gets some skills in writing, speaking, calculating, drawing, operating some equipment etc. He develops some interests in and attitudes towards social work, democratic living, co-operative management and so on. As an individual in the society, he has to think critically about various issues in life and take decisions about them being free from bias and prejudices, superstitions and blind beliefs. Thus, he has to learn all these qualities of head, hand and heart through the process of education.

Meaning of Peace

Peace is universally referred as a state of harmony in absence of violence, conflict behaviours and to have freedom from fear of violence. In view of Meena Prakash Kute (2014), Peace means much more than the absence of war.

Peace is considered as a set of values, attitudes and modes of behaviour promoting the peaceful settlement, conflict and the quest for mutual understanding. In Oxford Dictionary Peace has defined as freedom from or cessation of, world of hostilities; that condition of a nation or community in which it is not at war with another. The UN Declaration (2000) as the International Year of a culture of peace explained culture of peace as the set of values, attitudes, modes of behaviour and ways of life that reflect and inspire respect for life and all human rights, rejection of violence and devotion to the principles of freedom, justice, democracy, tolerance, co-operation, pluralism, dialogue and understanding among diverse groups of peoples. With references to UNESCO Constitution defined peace is a state of mind. Since wars begin in the minds of men, it is in the minds of men that the defence of peace must be constructed. According to Deepika Sharma (2014), Peace is complementary, fulfilling and most desirable embodiment of reverence, honour, adoration, admiration, dedication and devotion.

Peace is question of feeling and experiencing it, it is a state of mind that has to be experienced for oneself. Reardon insists that Peace is the absence of violence in all forms – physical, social psychological and structural. Peace is social value and remedial measure to protect children from falling into the ways of violence in society. According to Renuka K. Shewkani (2014), Peace is a word that is uttered almost as frequently as truth, beauty and love. Peace follows enlightenment when man establishes peace of heart; no external force can disturb it. Peace is state of harmony with the absence of hostility. Peace is thus, a relationship between two people characterised by respect, justice and goodwill. Albert Einstein remarked Peace cannot be kept by force. It can only be achieved by understanding, therefore we need to create avenues for people to come together, understand participate and contribute to sustainable peace and co-existence. According to Nilima Arvind More (2014), Peace is state of harmony characterised by the lack of violent conflict and the freedom from fear of violence. Its commonly understood as the absence of hostility, peace also suggest the existence of health or newly healed interpersonal or international relationship, prosperity in matters of social or economic welfare, the establishment of equality and a working political order that serves the true intervals of all. In international relations, peace time is not the absence of war or conflict, but also the presence of positive and respectful culture and economic relations.

The very fact you have used the term harmony presupposes that there are many socially discordant groups at work. An ideal society or a nation should find a mechanism for a compromise among all the competing elements within the society and there is a synthesis between different groups' demands and aspirations. Social harmony is a must for the society so that it grows. For incubation and growth of a life, you need to ensure peace. Life cannot grow in constant war and struggle. Life is a way of compromising and making adjustments. Man is a social being as in the case of all living entities including plants and animals. But within each social group there may be heterogeneous traits and features. So each society can be thought of as pluralistic and need social harmony for peaceful co-existence. The aim of social harmony within each group in a society is this peaceful co-existence. Love one another, as one self and rendering help to needy in the group is the mechanics of achieving social harmony within the group. This is not enough. We are living in this planet with other social groups of animals and plants. If we want harmony on this planet we must practice love and consideration mechanism to these other social groups also. In order to achieve harmony on the planet we must practice universal brotherhood with all others. The Universe has countless other planets and star systems with or without earth like social entities in them. Man is now polluting exploiting and destroying the resources of the earth, its atmosphere and bowels. At the rate at which this destruction is going especially by the high consumption patterns of the developed nations we may soon destroy man and his earthly abode. Hence, we must practice love or synergy with all and everything in the World. So for social harmony, we must practice Universal Brotherhood. The term harmony has connotations more than one. Social Harmony should refer to 'peaceful coexistence' of people from different and distinct nationalities/races/religions/creeds/castes... in a given society. A 'pluralistic society' which is more or less universal today with improved transport/communications/opportunities migration and mingling with people of other countries/areas being common the very existence and prosperity of a given society depends on social harmony. Social change in terms of, inter caste marriages, gradual disintegration of rigidity of certain customs and so on did help to certain extent in furthering social harmony.

Literature Review

0. In her paper on 'Peace Education for Cultural and Social Harmony', Kute Meena Prakash (2014) remarked that education can create an environment to overcome conflict although it can carry over from cultural and religious beliefs. In addition to that, she said peace is more effective when cultural context and the needs of a country that it should be encouraged by its cultural and spiritual values together with the universal values. Peace Education empowers children to make the creative and non-destructive path for settled down the conflict and to live in harmony with themselves, others and their world.

1. In his paper on 'Peace Education Through Religion', Nimbalkar Sanjay J (2014) concluded that concept of peace are the inbuilt principles of every religion and it showed that religion helps the individuals to develop head, heart, hand and mind effectively which is ultimately led to develop good conduct of person behaviour in the society and that result in mutual understanding, happy and peaceful life.

2. In his paper on 'Learning to Live Together in Peace and Harmony', Mahesh H. Koltame (2014) pointed out that among the fourth pillar of education learning to live together may persuade populace to implement common projects and to manage the inevitable conflicts in an intelligent and peaceful way. He talked about a form of education which will make it possible to avoid conflicts or solve them in a peaceful way by ushered the idea of learning to live together with others by developing a set of values of pluralism for mutual understanding and peace.
3. In her paper on 'Swami Vivekanand's Man Making Education for Universal Peace and Harmony', Bhardwaj Sonali S (2014) viewed that Swami Vivekanand's man making education helps to increase the mechanisms that will enhance the culture of peace among the people and strengthen people's rights as well as promote their confidence and promote peaceful resolution of conflicts and practice of non-violence through character building education and cooperation.
4. In her paper on 'Women's Education and Communal Harmony: Savitribai Phule's Philosophical Perspective', Goure Archana Malik (2014), assumed that global harmony and social peace are maintained and transforming social conflict by each individual in non-violent ways. Hence, women have a greater role to have special responsibility in conflict management that is directed towards such culture of peace.They are often failed to fill this responsibility at the societal level because of their lack to access to education. She said that only the peace can be meaningful if the educational systems inculcate peace as a value.

Research Question

- How peace and harmony can be maintained in today's tribal society?

Objectives of the Study

1. To study the status of education of the Scheduled Tribes of Birbhum District West Bengal.
2. To examine the traditional peace building process of the tribal Groups.
3. To analyse the importance of education in forming peace and harmony in the tribal society.

Materials and Methods

- *Research Approaches:* Qualitative and Quantitative research, both approaches were employed for picking up the empirical data from the field. Indeed, the secondary data were picked up from various sources like books, journals, articles, conferences, published and unpublished research work etc.
- *Methods and Techniques:* A Case Study method has been applied by

following observation participant and in-depth interview techniques for gleaned up the empirical data from the field. Structure questionnaire and some open ended questions have been used as a tool of data collection.

- *Universe and Population*: The study itself the research universe is scheduled tribes and the population are four sub-caste of scheduled tribes like 'Kol', 'Kora', 'Oraon', 'Santal'. The present study has been made in five tribal villages of Birbhum district, West Bengal. Five villages have been taken such as 'Kurumbo Ghsoh', 'Donaipur', 'Jaljalia', 'Dhultikuri', 'Bondanga', for the fulfilment of purpose of this research study.
- *Sampling*: Non probability sampling like purposive sampling were utilised here as well.
- *Sample Sise*: The total sample sise is 133 out of which 8 'Kol', 17 'Kora', 44 'Oraon' and 64 'Santal' families were the main respondents of this empirical study.

Results and Discussions

The study has been led out in several tribal villages of Birbhum district, West Bengal. The empirical data has been collected by doing hardcore field work in five tribal villages of Birbhum district, West Bengal. Indeed, I have distributed the population of these five villages in various categories. The tables framed out here that such as village wise population distribution, households-wise population distribution, tribes-wise population distribution, and distribution of population by education and sex-wise and one bar chart have been set up for the presentation of literacy rate of the tribal peoples. The empirical data has been framed out and also discussed through the presentation of four tables and one chart. These tables and charts are shown below:

Table No-1

Distributio of households as per Five Villages: Birbhum District, West Bengal

Serial No	*Villages*	*Households*	*per cent*
1	Kurumbo Ghosh	8	6.01
2	Donaipur	12	9.02
3	Jaljalia	17	12.78
4	Dhultikuri	44	33.08
5	Bondanga	52	39.09
	Total	133	99.98

Table-1: The first table indicates the distribution of sample on the basis of households of those villages. There are total five villages. In 'Kurumbo Ghosh' village, there are total 8 Kol households and the percentage is 6.01. In village 'Donaipur', there are total 12 'Santal' households and the percentage is 9.02. In 'Jaljalia' village, there are total 17 Kora households and the percentage is 12.78. In village Dhutikuri' there are total '44' 'Oraon' households and the percentage is 33.08. In Bonndanga village, there are total 52 households and the percentage is 45.21 respectively.

Table No: 2

Distribution of Population of the STs of Five Villages as per Sex, Birbhum District, West Bengal

Serial No	Villages	Male	per cente	Female	per cent	Total	per cent
1	Kurumbo	13	1.9	11	1.71	24	3.62
2	Donaipur	28	4.09	28	4.36	56	8.45
3	Jaljalia	42	6.14	36	5.61	78	11.75
4	Dhultikuri	109	15.94	86	13.39	195	29.41
5	Bondanga	150	21.92	160	24.92	310	46.75
Total		**342**	**49.99**	**321**	**49.99**	**663**	**99.98**

Table-2: In the second table, we have seen the distribution of sample population based on the villages. The village 'Kurumbo Ghosh', consisting of 24 individuals, the total percentage is 3.62, out of which 13 are males (1.9 per cent) and 11 are females (1.71 per cent). In 'Donaipur' village, there are 56 individuals, the total percentage is 8.45, out of which 28 males (4.09 per cent) and 28 females (4.36 per cent). In village 'Jaljalia', there are 78 individuals, the total percentage is 11.75, out of which 42 are males (6.14 per cent) and 36 are females (5.61 per cent). In village Dhultikuri, the number of individuals are 195 and the total percentage is 29.41, in between them 109 are males (15.94 per cent) and 86 are females (13.39 per cent). The village 'Bonldanga', consisting of 310 individuals and the percentage is 46.75. Out of which 150 are males (21.92 per cent) and 160 are females (24.92 per cent). The total numbers of individuals, of those five villages are 663 (99.98 per cent) and out of which 342 are males (49.99 per cent) and females are 321 (49.99 per cent) respectively.

Table No: 3

Distribution of Population in accordance with their Specific Tribes of Five Villages, Birbhum District, West Bengal

Serial No	Specific Tribes	Male	per cent	Female	per cent	Total	per cent
1	Kol	13	1.9	11	1.71	24	3.61
2	Kora	42	6.14	36	5.61	78	11.76
3	Oraon	109	15.93	86	13.39	195	29.41
4	Santal	178	26.02	188	29.28	366	55.2
Total		**342**	**49.99**	**321**	**49.99**	**663**	**99.98**

Table-3: The third table indicates the distribution of sample population in accordance with their specific tribes of those five villages. There are four specific tribes. Here, the percentage of 'Kol' tribes is 3.61 and the percentage of 'Kora' tribes is 11.76 as well. The percentage of 'Oraon' tribes is 29.41 and the percentage of 'Santal' tribes is 55.2 in general.

Table No: 4

Educational Status of the STs of Five Villages, Birbhum District, West Bengal

Serial No	Class Standards	Male	per cent	Female	per cent	Total Population	per cent
1	Illiterate	70	10.23	130	20.25	200	30.16
2	Pre-Literate	61	8.91	44	6.85	105	15.84
3	I-IV	51	7.46	31	4.83	82	12.36
4	V-VIII	58	8.48	43	6.69	101	15.23
5	IX-X	89	13.01	57	8.88	146	22.02
6	XI-XII	5	0.73	5	0.78	10	1.51
7	U.G	6	0.88	11	1.71	17	2.56
8	P.G	2	0.29	0	0	2	0.3
Total		**342**	**49.99**	**321**	**49.99**	**663**	99.98
Literacy Rate		41.02 per cent		28.81 per cent		69.83 per cent	

Table-4: The above table represents the educational status of respondents of the five mentioned villages. In those villages total 200 individuals are illiterate out of which, 70 are males (10.23 per cent) and 130 are females (20.25 per cent) and the total percentage is 30.16. The number of Pre literate individuals are 105, between them 61 are males (8.91 per cent) and 44 are females (6.85 per cent) and the total percentage is 15.84. Now the numbers of individuals those are between class I to class IV, 82. Out of 82 there are 51 males (7.46 per cent) and 31 females (4.83 per cent) and the total percentage is 12.36. In between class V to class VIII, the total numbers of students are 101 and the total percentage is 15.23. Out of which 58 are males (8.48 per cent) and 43 are females (6.69 per cent). In secondary section, between classes IX to class X, there are total 146 students and the total percentage is 22.02. Out of them 89 are males (13.01 per cent) and 57 are females (8.88 per cent). In higher secondary between class XI to Class XII there are total 10 students, out of them five are males (0.73 per cent) and five are females (0.78 per cent) and the total percentage is 1.51. Out of five villages, in UG (Under Graduation) section there are 17 students and the total percentage is 2.56. Out of which, six are males (0.88 per cent) and 11 are females (1.71 per cent). In PG (Post Graduation) out of five villages there are total two students, both are male and the percentage is 0.29. The total number of individuals are 663, out of which 342 are males (49.99 per cent) and 321 are females (49.99 per cent) and the total percentage is 99.98. The total literacy rate of the four villages is 69.83 per cent and the total male literacy and female literacy are 41.02 per cent and 28.81 per cent.

Chart No:1

Literacy Rate of the STs of Five Villages Birbhum District, West Bengal

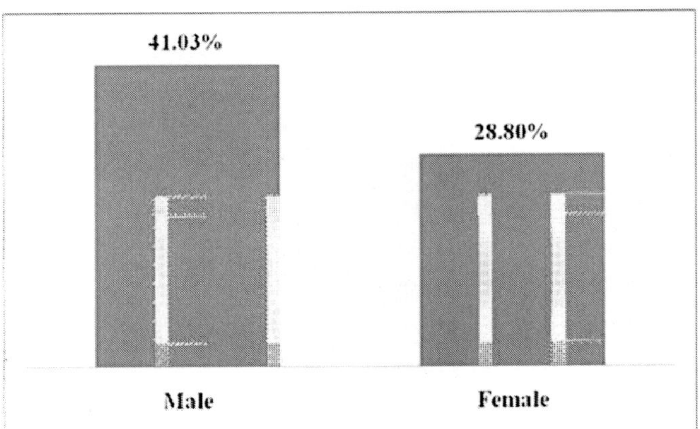

Chart – 1: The chart shows that the literacy rate of the respondents both males and females are 69.83 per cent respectively. Hereafter, the male literacy rate is 41.03 per cent and female literacy rate is 28.80 per cent which is significantly lower among the tribal women of Birbhum district, West Bengal.

The development of any country is reckon upon the inclusive progress of deprived, marginalised and weaker sections of the society such as scheduled tribes in India. The indigenous peoples like scheduled tribes are being counted an important segment of Indian population. A large section of the tribal population mostly lives in isolated hamlets as well as villages. For the development of these indigenous peoples, the role of education has become extremely significant for transforming the country. Education is an important weapon of the individuals to lead the society in right direction. Moreover, education is now considered as an essential instrument for the development of the individuals and further march of the society. It is one of the major factors for measuring the progress of a nation. So, education is much important in bringing positive growth among the tribal groups and overall development of a nation. The leaders of the villages are taking the severe decisions on behalf the community. They have their own customs, law and cultural system. Most of the tribal leaders are illiterate. In spite of illiteracy, they teach their children to make peace within the community as well. The tribal people have their own customs, law and value system. The number of the leaders those are providing their opinion, it varies community to community. They are the main person who can make the decision regarding severe issues whenever any disagreement and conflict are taken place either within the community or outside the community. Social harmony is highly dependent upon education; it's not only in academic sense but also in real sense. It should refer to 'peaceful coexistence' of people from different and distinct nationalities/races/religions/creeds/castes... in a given society. So, from the above discussion we can say that education can change the tribal society and keep them aside from any kind of disagreement or conflict arise in tribal areas. They can understand their needs and fulfil their demands. Education is not only essential for judicial matter it can essential for every sphere of life. Education for peace needs to be seen as an enterprise for healing and revitalising the nation.

Undertaken in this fashion, education for peace could be an effective catalyst in activating a holistic vision for education. This could transform education into a movement for national integration and regeneration, which is the need of the hour. The spotlight of education for peace in the Indian context falls squarely on social justice in education and the need to bridge the aggravating urban–rural divide. An approach to education that erodes social cohesion, aggravates economic inequalities, and undermines ethical foundations needs to be recognised as a threat to peace and a disservice to society. So, education is having a great potentiality to impart knowledge, increasing self confidence, forming encouragement among the tribal groups by which they can overcome their problems and forming peace and harmony in the society.

Conclusion

The present chapter depicted the real scenario that despite low literacy, tribal people are traditionally educated by the community leaders and advice to maintain peace in the society, but peace building process is still disrupted due to lack of low level of academic achievements. Education is very much essential for building peace and establishing harmony in any society. The opinion leaders of the tribal's are the main persons, who can take the decisions on behalf of their community itself regarding any serious matter raised within the villages and also outside the villages. The tribal leader's decisions are final for all peoples of tribal community. They play very crucial role for their community development. So, these persons should have to bring to take part in development process for getting better outputs of tribal education, because these decisions makers know the pulse of the villagers. Moreover, education is the major key factor by which peace and harmony can be established in tribal society. It is also a major factor to create values within the individuals to lead the society in right direction and making a developed a nation.

References

- Burns Robin J. and Aspelagh R. - 1983, Concepts of Peace Education: A View of Western Experience, *International Review of Education, 29(3),* pp: 311-330.
- Boulding E. – 2000, Culture of Peace, The Hidden Side of History, *Syracuse University Press,* New York, pp: 89-106.
- Bekerman, Zvi. - 2009, Peace Education and Contact: Introduction, Claire McGlynn, Zvi Bekerman, and Tony Gallagher, eds. Peace Education in Conflict and Post-ConflictSocieties, *Palgrave MacMillan,* New York.
- Brock B.U. 1998, Peace Education in era of Globalisation (Lecture), *Univertsitat International de Menorca*, Spain.
- Biswas P. 2013, Peace Education and Globalisation in the Present Era, *Golden Research Thoughts, 2(7),* pp: 1-5.
- Barash David P. 2000, Approaches to Peace: A Reader in Peace Studies, *Oxford University,* Oxford.
- Press.Castro A.B. 2004, An Integrated Model of Peace Education: Educating for a Culture of Social and Ecological Peace, Anita L Wanden (Ed), *State University of New York Press.*
- Harris Ian and Synott John. 2002, *Peace Education for A New Century, /Social Alternatives 21(1).*

- Kevin K. 2004, Education for Peace; Content from and Structure Mobilising Youth for Civic Management, *The Peace and Conflict Review, 4(2), Conference Paper.*
- Jassal R.G and Sharma S. 2010, Peace Education: Curbing the Value Crisis: In Bhargava M. And Bhargava R. (Eds), Dynamic of Education, *Vedanta Publications,* Lucknow.
- Kaur B. 2006, Peace Education: New Trends and Innovations, *Deep and Deep Publications Pvt Ltd,* New Delhi.
- Kumar S.P.U–2009, Peace Education in India: A Proposal, *South Asian Journal of Peace Building, II (1).*
- Kirshnamurthy J. 2005, Education and World Peace: In Promila Sharma (Eds.), Problems of Education, New Delhi, pp: 317-328.
- Kumar Shiv. 2006, Education for Peace, *NCERT,* New Delhi.
- Kester K. 2008, Developing Peace Education Programmes: Beyond Ethnocentrism and violence, Peace Prints, *Journal of South Asian Peace Building, 1(1),* pp: 37-64.
- Kamoet, A. S – 2008, Definitions and concepts of peace and conflict: In Peace and Conflict studies in a global context, *P. G. MMUST press,* Okoth.
- PVDT College of Education For women – 2014,One Day National Seminar on Education for Peace, *Aadhar Publication & Aadhar Social Research & Development Training Institute,* Amravati..
- Pandey, S. 2004, Peace Education, Self Instructional Package for Teacher Educators, *NCERT,* New Delhi.
- Reardon B.A. 1988, Comprehensive Peace Education: Educating for Global Responsibility, Teacher College, *Columbia University,* New York and London.
- Saloman G and Nevo B. – 2002, Peace Education: The Concept, Principles and Practices around the World, *Lavrence Erlbaum Associates, Inc Publishers,* New Jersey.
- Udayakumar S.P. 2009, Peace education in India: A Proposal, *Peace Prints: South Asian Journal of Peace building,* Volume - 2, No-1.

26

Promoting Peace: A Case Study

Mr Prateek Chaurasia
Master of Education (Elementary Education)
Regional Institute of Education (NCERT), Ajmer-305004
E mail:prateek.chaurasia100@gmail.com
Mobile: 8765506489

Abstract

In the present time not only education is required but it is required with some special and certain desperate needs and that is peace education, we need to abolish the culture of war and develop the culture of non-violence and brotherhood in our society and especially in our learners. Culture of peace and non-violence goes to the substance of fundamental human rights: social justice, democracy, literacy, respect and dignity for all. For achieving all this, we must have some sustainable sources of promoting peace education. Women are the integral part of our society and in present scenario they are playing a major role in promoting the peace throughout the whole world. Our present study is a case study based on the roles of women's and challenges towards the promotion of peace throughout the whole world. The present study has tried to expose the fact, challenges, and contribution of women's in the present time. Observing minutely we found that women are playing a vital role in promoting the peace as compared to any other agents of promoting peace. But there were also some major social and cultural challenges faced by them during their works. Since women have been a deprived class of most societies due to the male dominancy and social structure, the measures have been taken in filling the gapes of women's development and total social development. Therefore the present study tries to focus on all such agents and issues which effect the overall promotion of peace and peace education in our society.

Key words: Non-Violence, Democracy, Literacy, Sustainable, Integral, Cultural, Deprived

Introduction

"Non-violence is not a garment to be put on and off at will. Its seat is in the heart, and it must be an inseparable part of our being".

..............M.K. Gandhi (Father of Nation, India).

We are living in the world which is full of natural attractiveness and beauty on the other hand it is full of misery and pain. Every day we heard so many horrible news of violence, wars, terrorism and many more painfull stories. No doubt we have created a world of fear around us in which we are bound to live but it is not the end, it is where we can start and think in a direction which can guide our society in a peacefull status. Peace, which is only a five-letter word, plays an important role in our lives. Peace means order, discipline, prosperity and benefits, but there is no single definition of the concept peace. For some people, "Peace" has been understood as the absence of war, violence and hostilities but also the enjoyment of economic and social justice, equality and the entire range of human rights and fundamental freedoms within society. Peace is promoted by equality of the sexes, economic equality and the universal enjoyment of basic human rights and fundamental rights.

According to M.K.Gandhi...............

"Woman is more fitted than man to make exploration and take bolder action in non-violence. There is no occasion for women to consider themselves subordinate or inferior to men. Woman is the companion of man, gifted with equal mental capacity. If by strength is meant moral power, then woman is immeasurably man's superior ... If nonviolence is the law of our being, the future is with women".

In 2011, the United States established a national action plan to implement a U.N. resolution that calls for the equal participation of women in resolving conflicts and building peace.

The U.S. National Action Plan on Women, Peace, and Security reflects that countries are more peaceful and prosperous when women have equal rights and opportunities. The plan ensures that gender concerns are fully integrated into diplomatic, military and development activities.

The plan specifies how U.S. international engagements involve women — half the world's population — as equal partners in preventing conflict and building peace in countries threatened by war, violence and insecurity.

According to President Obama's executive order establishing the plan, achieving this equality is critical to U.S. and global security. The United States joined more than 30 countries that have adopted similar plans. These are among the U.S. plan's guidelines:

- Promote gender equality and advancement of women and girls in areas facing conflict.

- Support the full participation of women in preventing and resolving conflict and building peace.
- Protect women and girls, who are disproportionately affected by conflict, from gender-based violence, exploitation, discrimination, trafficking and other abuse.
- Promote stability by investing in health, education and economic opportunity for women and girls.
- Provide for disaster and humanitarian responses that respect the specific needs of women and girls.

The significance of including women in peace and security issues has been demonstrated in many places. They may act as mediators and foster compromise during the rebuilding process.

Need of the Study

We all are living in a world full of fear and violence. We are creating and producing the violence in immense quantity not only for us also for our upcoming generations. Beside all this, a ray of hope is there which can please and motivate us even in the present violent scenario. Due to all this, I felt need to explore this hope and that is women as active and effective agent of promoting peace in our society. Women have been suppressed since a long time, but today the scenario is changed, they have become spine of most social activities. Our society must be aware of the contributions and challenges that our women are facing in present circumstances. Therefore, I felt a need of the present study.

Objectives

The objectives of the study are:

- To identify the challenges faced by women's in working in our society.
- To diagnose the causes which influence the role of women's in promoting peace.
- To discover the role of women's as an affective agent in promoting peace.
- To create awareness about the women's participation in peace activities.

Review of Related Literature

Biography of Nobel Prise winners in peace.

Methodology

As our present study is a case study, our methodology is basically an inductive reasoning. A qualitative analysis of the available information to reach at conclusion.

Delimitation

The present study has very wide scope it cannot cover all aspects in such a short study. So the study has an introductory aspect of role and challenge of few noble women in promoting peace.

Interventions and Discussion:

- Case 1 Wangari Maathai (Kenya)
- Introduction (life sketch)

Wangari Muta Maathai was born in Nyeri, a rural area of Kenya (Africa), in 1940. Wangari Maathai was the founder of the Green Belt Movement and the 2004 Nobel Peace Prise Laureate. She authored four books: *The Green Belt Movement; Unbowed: A Memoir; The Challenge for Africa; and Replenishing the Earth.* As well as having been featured in a number of books, she and the Green Belt Movement was the subject of a documentary film, Taking Root: the Vision of Wangari Maathai (Marlboro Productions, 2008).

She obtained a degree in Biological Sciences from Mount St. Scholastica College in Atchison, Kansas (1964), a Master of Science degree from the University of Pittsburgh (1966), and pursued doctoral studies in Germany and the University of Nairobi, before obtaining a Ph.D. (1971) from the University of Nairobi, where she also taught veterinary anatomy.

Major Achievements and Honours

0. The first woman in East and Central Africa to earn a doctorate degree, Professor Maathai became chair of the Department of Veterinary Anatomy and an associate professor in 1976 and 1977 respectively. In both cases, she was the first woman to attain those positions in the region.
1. Wangari Maathai was awarded the 2004 Nobel Peace Prise for her "Contribution to Sustainable Development, Democracy And Peace"
2. In 2005, she was appointed Goodwill Ambassador to the Congo Basin Forest Ecosystem by the eleven Heads of State in the Congo region.
3. In 2007, Professor Maathai was invited to be co-chair of the Congo basin fund, an initiative by the British and the Norwegian governments to help protect the Congo forests.
4. In recognition of her deep commitment to the environment, the United Nations (UN) Secretary-General named Professor Maathai a UN Messenger of Peace in December 2009, with a focus on the environment and climate change.
5. In 2010, she was appointed to the Millennium Development Goals Advocacy Group: a panel of political leaders, business people and activists established with the aim to galvanise worldwide support for

the achievement of the Millennium Development Goals (MDGs).

6. 1984: Right Livelihood Award.
7. 1986: Better World Society Award.
8. 1987: Global 500 rolls of Honour.
9. 1991: Goldman Environmental Prise.
10. 1991: The Hunger Projects Africa Prise for Leadership.
11. 1993: Edinburgh Medal (for "Outstanding contribution to Humanity through Science").
12. 1994: The Golden Ark Award.
13. 2004: Conservation Scientist Award from Columbia University.
14. 2007: World Citisenship Award.
15. 2007: Livingstone Medal from Royal Scottish Geographical Society.
16. 2007: Indira Gandhi Prise.
17. 2013: Doctor of Science (honorary degree), Syracuse University, New York.

Contributions towards Promotion of Peace

- Professor Maathai was active in the National Council of Women of Kenya (1976–1987) and was its chairman (1981–1987).
- In 1976, while she was serving in the National Council of Women, Professor Maathai introduced the Idea of Community-Based Tree Planting. She continued to develop this idea into a broad-based grassroots organisation, the Green Belt Movement (GBM), whose main focus is poverty reduction and environmental conservation through tree planting.
- She addressed the UN on a number of occasions and spoke on behalf of women at special sessions of the General Assembly during the five-year review of the Earth Summit.
- Professor Maathai was internationally acknowledged for her struggle for democracy, human rights, and environmental conservation, and served on the board of many organisations.
- She served on the Commission for Global Governance and the Commission on the Future.
- In 2010, Professor Maathai became a trustee of the Karuna Forest Environmental Education Trust, established to safeguard the public land for whose protection she had fought for almost twenty years. That same year, in partnership with the University of Nairobi, she founded the Wangari Maathai Institute for peace and environment studies (WMI).

- Professor Maathai represented the Tetu constituency in Kenya's parliament (2002–2007), and served as Assistant Minister for Environment and Natural Resources in Kenya's ninth parliament (2003–2007).

Even though Maathai has changed the world for many Africans through her hard work and dedication, she cannot save the environment alone. No matter where you live or what age you are, you, too, can make a difference. All it takes is an idea or the desire to change something and the drive to make it happen.

During her Nobel Prise acceptance speech, Maathai said, "I would like to call on young people to commit themselves to activities that contribute towards achieving their long-term dreams. You are a gift to your communities and indeed the world. You are the hope and our future".

Challenges Concerning Promotion of Peace

Land, Politics, and Ethnicity: An Explosive Combination

Maathai explained that in the absence of democratic governance and sustainable environmental management, natural resources have repeatedly ignited conflict in her native Kenya. For instance, the advent of private land ownership during colonialism pitted Maasai herders, who need large tracts of land to graze their cattle, against Kikuyu farmers, who for the first time obtained deeds to their land and began to erect fences to mark the boundaries.

In addition, Maathai noted that politicians often use Kenya's ethnic divisions and land scarcity to whip up animosity towards internal migrants and bolster their own re-election prospects. "If you don't, then, therefore, ensure that the resources within the country are equitably distributed, and you encourage these prejudgments that communities have against each other, you're going to have conflict".

The Three Legs of Stability

Maathai used the traditional African three-legged stool as a metaphor for what she views as the three essential components of a stable society: sustainable environmental management, democratic governance, and a culture of peace. "Those lefs are chiseled by a craftsman [who] chisels all the three legs at the same time, in order to create a balance," she said. "If we don't have these three legs, no matter who comes, and with whatever [loans or aid], we shall never develop".

Case 2 Mother Teresa (Albania)

Introduction (life sketch)

Mother Teresa was born, 1910, in Skopje, capital of the Republic of Macedonia, on August 26, 1910. She was a Roman Catholic Religious Sister and missionary of Kosovo Albanian origin who lived for most of her life in India. Mother Teresa was honoured by both governments and civilian organisations. In 1979, Mother Teresa was awarded the Nobel Peace Prise, "for work undertaken in the struggle to overcome poverty and distress, which also constitutes a threat to peace".

Major Achievements and Honours

- The first Pope John XXIII Peace Prise. (1971).
- Kennedy Prise (1971).
- The Nehru Prise –"for promotion of international peace and understanding" (1972).

Mother Teresa had first been recognised by the Indian government more than a third of a century earlier when she was awarded the Padma Shri in 1962.

Was awarded the Nobel Peace Prise in1979, "for work undertaken in the struggle to overcome poverty and distress, which also constitutes a threat to peace".

Contributions towards Promotion of Peace

Founding the "The Missionaries of Charity". The primary objective of this mission was to look after people, who nobody else was prepared to look after. Mother Teresa felt that serving others was a key principle of the teachings of Jesus Christ.

- Dedication to the very poor.
- Saint Teresa.

Challenges Concerning Promotion of Peace

She experienced two particularly traumatic periods in Calcutta.

0. The first was the Bengal famine of 1943.
1. The second was the Hindu/Muslim violence in 1946 – before the partition of India.

In 1948, she left the convent to live full time amongst the poorest of Calcutta. She chose to wear a white Indian Sari, with blue trimmings – out of respect for the traditional Indian dress. For many years, Mother Teresa and a small band of fellow nuns survived on minimal income and food, often having to beg for funds. But, slowly her efforts with the poorest were noted and appreciated by the local.

Case 3 Shirin Ebadi (The First Female Peace Prise Laureate from the Islamic World)

Introduction (life sketch)

She was born in the city of Hamadan [north-western Iran] in 1947. She began her education at Firuzkuhi primary school and went on to Anoshiravn Dadgar and Reza Shah Kabir secondary schools for her higher education. Shirin Ebadi is an advocate for Iranian women's struggles for equal rights and citisenship. Shirin is a practicing Muslim who believes in an Islam that can be compatible with democracy. She opposes not the religion but its narrow legal interpretation, and the outdated patriarchal traditions that keep the current Iranian order in power.

Major Achievements and honours

0. The selection of The Rights of the Child as Book of the Year by the Culture and Islamic Guidance Ministry.
1. Recipient of the Rafto Human Rights Foundation prise for human rights activities, Norway 2001.
2. The Nobel Peace Prise, 2003.

Contributions towards Promotion of Peace

0. Leading several research projects for the UNICEF office in Tehran.
1. Co-founder of the Association for Support of Children's Rights, 1995. She was the association's president until 2000, and has continued to assist them as legal adviser. Currently the association has over 500 active members.
2. Providing various stages of free tuition in children's rights and human rights.
3. Co-founder of the Human Rights Defence Centre with four defence lawyers, 2001. She is the centre's president.
4. Delivering over 30 lectures to university and academic conferences and seminars on human rights. The lectures have been delivered in Iran, France, Belgium, Sweden, Switzerland, Britain and America.
5. Representing families of serial murder victims (the Foruhar family).
6. Proposing to the Islamic Consultative Assembly (Majlis) to ratify a law on prohibiting all forms of violence against children; as a result the law was promptly ratified in the Summer of 2002.
7. Works with women in Society for Defence of Children's Rights. In 1997 challenges the law denying child custody rights to women. Writes several books, one entitled "The Rights of a Child."

Challenges concerning promotion of peace

0. Arrested and jailed in June 2000. Investigating cases involving the deaths of Iranian intellectuals and reformers in 2000, Ebadi obtained evidence that some religious leaders and conservative politicians had been behind the murders. She was subsequently arrested and imprisoned for more than three weeks, held in solitary confinement.

1. She has been attacked in Iranian newspapers and labelled a traitor. She was forced by protestors to stop giving a speech at Al-Zahra women's university in December of 2003.
2. She has been criticised by some Religious Muslims in Iran for not wearing the *hijab,* the traditional Muslim headscarf, when she travels abroad and for shaking hands with men during such travels.

In spite of the international attention she gained after receiving the Nobel Prise, Ebadi confessed in an article in London's *Sunday Times* that she still feared for her own safety: "Anyone who fights for human rights in Iran lives in fear. But I have learnt to overcome my fear. In Iran anything could happen to anyone. My fight is to make sure that only good things happen to my people".

Conclusion

This study begins with identifying the women's involved in promoting peace, as the list is too broad we have shortened the list to the Nobel Prise winners and focused on the achievement and contributions of them towards the promotion of peace. After a depth study of their journey with the peace we found that, their journey was not so easy but still due to commitment and zeal to work for society, humanity, environment, and misery they all have given us a path to follow and stand tall in promoting the peace as effectively as compared to the other agents of promoting peace. What did all these women peace Laureates have in common? They were all women of high ideals, prepared to work and sacrifice to bring something better into being, and they laboured in the certainty that their objectives would eventually be realised.

They all carried immense will power and commitment towards their work which inspired them to struggle against odds, to withstand disappointments and defeats, to resolve never to give up. They shared a faith in humanity, whether born of religious conviction or humanism. Most displayed remarkable courage. In the good fight for peace and reconciliation, we are dependent on persons who set examples, persons who can symbolise what we are seeking and mobilise the best in us." That all the women Laureates hand faith in the power of good".

The best feminine qualities which will help us to develop peace on earth". Above all, however, what these Nobel Women have shown us is the potential of the human spirit.

Women's contribution to peace building and reconciliation is still hampered by constraints such as subject.

0. Poverty, gender based violence, poor organisational capacity among women, limited motivation.
1. Facilitation of women initiatives. Peace and reconciliation programmes remain largely centralised and not adequately coordinated.

References

- NCERT (2006). Position Paper National focus group on Education for peace, New Delhi.
- Nanda B.R. Mahatma Gandhi-A Biography, OXFORD University Press, Calcutta, Chennai, Mumbai.
- http://www.biographyonline.net/
- www.nobelprise.org
- Ministry of women and child development government of India, Report of theworking group on empowerment of women for the xi plan.
- http://www.notablebiographies.com/news/Ca-Ge/Ebadi-Shirin.html#ixzz3HoXBFYB6

27

Psychological Perceptions of Gender Based Violence

Dr Sudarsan Raju Chandolu
Principal, College of Education
Andhra University
Narikeli Pramod Kumar
Asst. professor Mizoram University

Abstract

Gender based violence is silent enemy in the global society and a never ending phenomenon. Gender-based violence includes psychological, sexual, and physical violence such as domestic violence; rape and sexual abuse of children by family members; forced pregnancy; sexual slavery; traditional practices harmful to women, such as dowry-related violence; burning or acid throwing, honor killings, female genital mutilation, dating violence in mid-adolescence, violence in operational conflict, emotional abuse, compulsion and abusive language. Forced marriages, trafficking of women and girls for prostitution, sexual harassment and threats are additional examples of violence against women. Gender-based- violence is not exclusively a woman's concern. It is both a cause and consequence of gender perceptions. The use of the term 'gender-based violence' provides a new context in which to examine and understand the never ending phenomenon of violence against women. It shifts the focus from women as victims to gender and the unequal power relationships between women and men created and maintained by gender stereotypes as the basic underlying cause of violence against women. Present paper focus on important contributions, psychological perspectives and approaches of gender based violence.

Keywords: *Gender, Violence, Women, Psychological, Society and Global.*

Introduction

Gender-based violence, recently emerging as a persistent global issue, significantly contributes to preventable mortality and morbidity for women across diverse cultures. The term "gender-based-violence" refers to violence that targets individuals or groups on the basis of their gender. The United Nations Human Right Committee on the Elimination of Discrimination against women defines it as "Violence that is directed against women because she is a woman or that affects women disproportionately". This includes psychological, physical, sexual harm, suffering, and the threat of such acts, compulsion and other deprivation of freedom. Together with "sexual violence" and "violence against women", "gender-based-violence" is used interchangeably. This does not mean that all acts against a woman are gender based violence.

A new lexicon, prompted by the expansion of human rights analysis, describes particular threats including dowry deaths, honour murder, sati, and disproportional exposure to HIV/AIDS as well as globally generic threats including marital rape, abuse, battering and murder. Stress related syndromes, depression, chemical dependency, substance abuse, and suicide are consequences observed in the context of violence in women's lives. Emerging psychological, social, legal, medical, and educational strategies promote social change beginning with raising the status of women. The gravity and variability of gender based violence across cultures compel to promote the recognition, intervention and prevention of gender-based violence that are both locally specific and internationally instructive. The causes of gender-based violence were the attitudes to women, girls and children in general, which are linked to the social construction of female and male. Poverty and some cultural practices.

Gender-based violence is physical, psychological, or sexual violence perpetrated against an individual or group on the basis of gender or gender norms. The majority of victims of Gender-based violence are women, but many victims of Gender-based violence are male. Gay, bisexual, and transgendered individuals are often targeted due to their perceived failure to conform to societal gender norms (Stemple, 2009). Forms of Gender-based violence include, sexual abuse, sexual assault, rape, economic violence, intimate partner violence, violence arising from traditional practices such as dowries and female genital mutilation, honour killings, trafficking in human beings for purposes of sexual harassment and intimidation, forced prostitution, sexual exploitation, and bullying based on failure to conform to perceived gender roles.

Defining the Scope of the Problem

Gender-based violence occurs in every corner of the world. Its manifestations and prevalence rates vary, and robust statistics are scarce. For example, the UN Secretary General's report (2006) cites in-country studies estimating that from 10 to 70 per cent of women have experienced violence.

Gender-based violence targeting gay, lesbian, transgendered and bisexual people is also endemic. Approximately 80 countries criminalise consensual homosexual acts and multiple countries fail to prosecute crimes against those who identify as gay, lesbian, or transgendered. Unable to cover each type of Gender-based violence comprehensively, we focus on the social psychological context of Gender-based violence and interventions that are informed by and seek to change this context. We connect social psychological perspectives and existing evidence regarding the impact of reduction and mitigation strategies in order to contribute to the broader conversation about reducing all forms of Gender-based violence.

Types of Gender-based-Violence

Types of gender-based violence are as follows:

0. Physical Violence – beating, punching, kicking, biting, burning, killing, selling and trading in human beings for forced sexual abtivitier, forced labour, slavery and removal of organs.
1. Sexual Violence – robbing the dignity of woman that includes rape and marital rape, child sexual abuse, forced prostitution, sexual harassment, forced sodomy or anal rape and sexual exploitation.
2. Verbal Violence – use of abusive and filthy language against a woman or her near and dear ones.
3. Emotional Violence – leading to internal deprivation of love and affection, depriving her custody of children, concern, compassion and care.
4. Psychological Violence – non-sexual verbal abuse that is insulting, degrading, demeaning; humiliating acts, denying basic expenses for family survival, isolating a person from family and friends, restricting movements, deprivation of liberty, deprivation of liberty and free movement.
5. Intellectual Violence – denial of rights to take part in decision making and discussion for pressing issues.
6. Harmful Traditional Practices – female genital mutilation, early marriage, forced marriage, honor killing and maiming, killing, withholding food for female children.
7. Social Violence – discrimination or denial of opportunities and services, demeaning, disparaging and humiliating a woman or her parental relatives and friends.
8. Financial Violence – depriving financial means and bare of daily life necessities, it also includes taking away, misuse and donating the assets which a woman possesses or earns.

9. Other forms of Violence – denial of education, access to health facilities and treatment, reproductive rights, etc.

Psychological perception of Gender based Violence around the World

0. Gender based violence is quite common in almost all the developing countries. The phenomenon of violence against women within the family in India is complex and extremely embedded. Gender-based violence is not just a 'women's issue', but an issue that concerns all men and not just individual perpetrators. Gender based violence is the most pervasive of all types of violence in the world is multidimensional,multisectoral, multidisciplinary and holistic. It provides a complete structure, which includes psychological factors, not enough concentration has been given to psychological perspectives.Psychologists around the world have made contributions in research, clinical assessment and intervention for prevention of gender-based violence.

Although each country has unique factors that determine the services and resources available to battered women and children's are exposed to domestic violence and abusive partners, it is the interaction among gender, religious beliefs, political structure, attitudes toward violence in general and violence toward women, such as civil conflicts and wars, state-sponsored violence and the migration between countries that ultimately determine women's vulnerability and safety.

Psychological Perspectives on the Elimination and Prevention of all forms of Violence.

The Psychology Coalition at the United Nations (UN) is to advocate for UN agencies, Governments, civil society organisations, all other stakeholders, and the Special Rapporteur on Violence Against Women, to take into account important contributions that psychological perspectives and approaches can make to treating, eliminating and preventing violence against women and girls (VAWG) worldwide.

Since the 1993 Human Rights Conference in Vienna officially recognised violence against women as a human rights violation, increased awareness of the forms and levels of violence against women and girls, which include: rape in armed conflicts, domestic violence, genital mutilation or cutting, sexual exploitation in trafficking, and forced prostitution. However, in spite of Government commitments, United Nations policies, programmes and advocacy of civil society association, violence against women and girls continues to be a human rights abuse in all countries and across all sectors of society.

Significance of Psychological Perspectives Gender based Violence:

0. Implement the UN Secretary-General's Campaign "Unite to End

Violence against Women and Girls" and publicise support for human rights and social justice for all.

1. Provide human resources, policies, programmes, facilities, and services to promote the mental health and psychosocial recovery and well being for women and girls who have experienced physical, sexual or psychological violence, including services delivered by qualified psychologists themselves or other trained mental health providers.
2. Establish programmes to promote the education of men and boys in human rights and to promote and mobilise males as partners in the elimination of violence against women and girls.
3. Provide programmes to promote the psychosocial empowerment of women and girls who have suffered violence, so that they are less vulnerable to future instances of violence and better equipped to cope with violent situations if these should arise.
4. Promote access to effective responses and practice by psychologists and mental health workers by facilitating communication at a global level through the use of technology, including cell phones and other devices.

Consequences of Gender Based Violence

The consequences of gender-based violence are many and they include poor health, depression and death in some situations. Violence also breeds violence so that children living and growing up in a violent home are likely to be violent and so the cycle of violence is sustained.Violence also really creates psychological and emotional problems for the survivors of it. While the violence may be an incident in the life of the perpetrator, it has life long consequences for the survivors.

Contributing Factors of Gender-Based Violence

Research has identified factors associated with Gender-based violence at the individual, situational, and societal levels. Various academic disciplines and practitioners weight each level differently in their theories and the design of interventions. For example, clinical psychologists and legal scholars have often focused on the individual level, specifically on the pathological personality traits of Gender-based violence perpetrators as a means to identify, counsel, or prosecute potential or previous perpetrators (Fischel, 2010). Sociological and feminist scholarly perspectives traditionally focus on situational and societal levels, such as gendered power asymmetries in a society or an organisation (Brownmiller, 1975; Tangri, Burt, & Johnson, 1982). A social psychological perspective on factors contributing to Gender-based violence focuses on the interaction between individual characteristics and the immediate situation in which Gender-based violence occurs (Anderson & Anderson, 2008).

The social psychological perspective posits that Gender-based violence occurs as a result of the interaction of individual, situational, and societal factors (Anderson & Carnagey, 2004; Malamuth, 2003). Within a given society, many individuals' exhibit personality traits or are exposed to norms that promote or condone Gender-based violence.

Cause and Effects:

Societal and situational causes of gender-based violence:

From a social psychological perspective, societal factors will be most predictive of a GBV event when they are salient in the immediate situation. Such societal factors include power asymmetries, gender norms, roles, scripts, societal representations of women, and armed conflict or other crises, among others. These factors can become salient when physical or social arrangements create the expectation of such a factor (e.g., the asymmetrical representation of men at a meeting promotes the idea of male dominance at the organisation), when implicit rules that stem from these factors are violated (e.g., a man's behaviour that appears to violate a gendered norm causes him stress), or when they are raised in social interactions or media communications (e.g., representations of violence against women are primed by pornography playing on a nearby computer screen).

Individual Causes of Gender-based Violence:

Societal and situational factors alone cannot explain GBV; they likely combine with individual stressors and attributes to fuel GBV. We explore these interactions in this section, beginning with a dircussion of the literature's shift from focusing on a pathological model of GBV perpetrators to a non-pathological model. We then focus on qualities deemed to be non-pathological predictors of GBV perpetration, such as low self esteem, impulsivity, and sexism, among others. Both the pathological and non-pathological literatures are plagued by the methodological problem that GBV prevalence is often measured through self-report or biased samples of convicted perpetrators of GBV (excluding those who evade conviction or treatment).

Effects of Gender-based Violence:

Effects of gender based violence are categorised as physical, psychological, and socio-economic effects. The effects are:

- *Physical:* Sexual and Reproductive health problems, Injury, Chronic health problems, Disability and Death.
- *Psychological:* Effects can be both Direct/Indirect. Anxiety, depression, fear, inability to concentrate, mistrust of others, loneliness, post-traumatic stress disorder, suicide, etc., are direct effects and indirect effects are psychosomatic illnesses, withdrawal, alcohol or drug use etc.

- *Socio-economic:*Rejection, ostracism and social stigma at community level; Reduced ability to participate in social and economic activities; Acute fear of future violence, which extends beyond the individual survivors to other members in community; Damage to women's confidence resulting in fear of venturing into public spaces (this can often curtail women's education, which in turn can limit their income-generating opportunities); Increased vulnerability to other types of gender-based violence; Job loss due to absenteeism as a result of violence; Negative impact on women's income generating power.

Interventions

Though many interventions have been designed to combat and reduce GBV, we focus on programmes whose methodology is clearly described and which have been empirically evaluated. The set of inadequately detailed evaluations of interventions is large, leaving methodological and theoretical gaps. To compensate for the empirical shortcnminfs, we rely on psychological models of behaviour change to hypothesise potential mechanisms through which interventions may be effective.

Primary Interventions

0. Educational interventions
1. Preventing dating violence
2. Interventions Outside of School for Adolescents and Young Adults
3. Programmes Directed towards Likely Targets of GBV
4. Anti-trafficking interventions
5. Rape and assault prevention interventions

Secondary Interventions

- Media campaigns targeting individuals suffering GBV
- Group interventions to change violent behaviour or reduce repeat violence
- Psycho educational model
- Cognitive behavioural model
- Gender-based cognitive behavioral approaches
- Individual Interventions to Reduce Gender-Based Violence
- Legal Responses to Gender-Based Violence

Conclusion

The root cause of gender-based violence lied in unequal power relations between women and men. However, a variety of factors on the society level, community level, family level and the level of individual, often combine to raise the probability of violence occurring. The effects of gender-based violence are far-reaching and extend beyond the individual survivor, to the family and society as a whole. Potential social responses to gender-based violence are most effective when there is a common understanding of the nature and causes of gender-based violence and it is addressed from all angles, through the participation of multiple sector and entire communities.

Various theories of gender-based violence, and thus theories of how to reduce gender-based violence, place different weights on individual, situational, and societal factors that drive gender-based violence. By placing interventions in the context of social psychological theory and evidence, identify the driving factors of gender-based violence and the most useful ways to measure intervention outcomes. Psychological approach by targeting perceived social norms about domestic violence with media and makes available information to ameliorate or address violence. Gender-based violence reduction programs are conscidentiourly develop a theory of the specific form of violence they aim to reduce and intervene by examining the individual, situational, and societal factors that support the most frequent instances of that violence. The vast literature regarding gender-based violence is demonstrative of many of the successes of prior decades of interventions and studies that increased understanding of gender-based violence and reduced its incidence and severity.

References

- Krug E et al., eds. (2002).*World Report on Violence and Health.* Geneva, World Health Organisation.
- Manjoo, R. (March 2012). Statement of the Special Rapporteur on Violence against Women, Its Causes and Consequences to the Commission on the Status of Women.
- Pickup, F., Williams, S., Sweetman, C. *Ending Violence against Women: A Challenge for Development and Humanitarian Work*, Oxfam GB 2001.
- UNHCR (2003) "Sexual and Gender-Based Violence against refugees, returnees and internally displaced persons. May 2003.
- United Nations (2002). Women, Peace and Security, Study submitted by the Secretary-General pursuant to Security Council resolution 1325 (2000), United Nations, New York.
- Walker, Lenore E. (1999). Psychology and domestic violence around the world. American Psychologist, Vol 54(1), 21-29.
- Website: UN Millennium Goals: www.un.org/millenniumgoals/
- World Health Organisation (2012). Mental health and psychosocial

support for conflict-related sexual violence: principles and interventions. Access at: http://www.unicef.org/protection/files/Summary_EN_.pdf

- World Health Organisation. (November 2012). Violence Against Women: Intimate partner and sexual violence against women. Fact Sheet No. 239. http://www.who.int/mediacentre/
- World Health Organisation: www.who.int/gender/violence

28

The Different Faces of Gender Equality

Dr Anu Rahi
Thakurdwara, Moradabad

Introduction

During the early years of this country women were not entitled to the same right and privileges as men women were not allowed to vote and were usually required to surrender control of their property to their husband upon marriage moreover their educational and occupational opportunities were severely limited. It was commonly believed that a woman's place was in the home; raising children and tending to domestic affairs.

The first efforts to achieve equality for women occurred in the 1800s during the early part of that century, coeducational studies at the university level were offered for the first time. State laws were passed which allowed women to retain their property after marriage. Also, the first women's rights became active in the abolitionist movement during the civil war era. Some become well know public orators, an uncommon occupation for women at the time.

Women were long considered naturally weaker then men, squeamish, and unable to perform work requiring muscular or intellectual development. In most pre-industrial societies, for example, domestic chores were relegated to women, leaving "heavier" labour such as hunting and plowing to men. This ignored the fact that caring for children and doing such tasks as milking cows and washing clothes also required heavy, sustained labour. But physiological tests now suggest that women have a greater tolerance for pain, and statistics reveal that women live longer and more resistant to many diseases. The resulting stereotype that "a woman's place is in the home", has largely determined the ways in which women have expressed themselves.

Despite their increased presence in the workforce, most women still have primary responsibility for house work and family care.

Difference between Gender Equality and Gender Equity

"Gender equality requires equal enjoyment by women and men of socially valued goods opportunities, resources and rewards".

In other words, gender equality refers to equal access to social goods, services and resources and equal opportunities in all spheres of life for both men and women. When there is gender inequality, it is women that there are more likely to be disadvantaged and marginalised; but we should not ignore the negative impact that gender inequality can have on men as well. There fore gender equality is the concern of all and changes must be brought about for both men and women. However, this is not to say that men and women are equally affected by gender inequality. It remains true that women have the greater share of disadvantages. Another incident of the work place that demonstrates the inequality in the treatment of men and women is sexual harassment.

Sexual Harassment

Sexual Harassment refers to "Unwanted sexual advances, whether touches, looks, pressures to have sex, or even jokes." (Hnslin & Nelson, 1996, p. 300). It can be two forms.

The first one known as *quid pro quo* harassment occurs when the harassment is linked to the granting of a benefit; for example, a women is pressured to have sex with her employer in order to get a promotion.

The second type refers to sexual harassment that is not linked to any privilege but that results in unfriendly environment. Over the years as women come to realise that offensive behaviour of a sexual nature at the workplace need not to be accepted as a normal and invitable part of job. Anybody can be a victim of sexual harassment be it a men or woman.

Sexual harassment is not an issue to be taken lightly. It can have ruinous results on the victim's physical as well as mental health and it certainly adversely affects the productivity of the worker who stands as victim there is still the unfortunate tendency to consider male norms as a measure for women's position. Providing women and men with the same opportunities is the first step; but for true gender equality to be achieved there is a need for gender equity.

Gender Equity

"Gender equity is the process of being fair to women and men". (UNFPA) Gender equity implies fairness in the way women and men are treated. The different life experiences and needs of men and women are taken into consideration and compensation is made for women's historical and social disadvantages. Gender equity thus serves to level the Playing field and empower women. Therefore, we can say that fair dealing is essential to achieve true equality.

Position of Women in India

Where we worship goddess luxmi, Durga, Gauri there are most Indian communities have what we call a "son preference", and this is something that is widespread throughout the country. Cultural beliefs have made people to submit to the notion that having sons is one way to go to haven after death and guaranteed financial security. Therefore, it is clear that these culture work to devalue the role of women in these societies, they strive to achieve equality with men, making gender equality in India an issue.

Gender discrimination continues to be an enormous problem with in Indian society. Traditional patriarchal norms have relegated women to secondary status with in the hourehold and workplace. This strongly affects women's health, financial status, education and political involvement. Women are commonly married young, quickly become mothers, and are then burdened by stringent domestic and financial responsibilities They are frequently malnourished since women typically are the last member of a household to eat and the last to receive medical attention. Only 54 per cent of Indian women are literats as compared to 75 per cent of men, women receive little schooling, and suffer from unfair and biased inheritance and divorce laws. These laws prevent women from accumulating substantial financial assets making it difficult for women to establish their own security and autonomy.

In 2009 the passing of the compulsory education Act was a historical moment for the children of India that clearly indicated the commitment of the state to providing educational opportunities for all children. The act reinforced faith in school education as being in the best interest of children as well as society. The Act makes available to the girl child in a very real sense all that is overdue to her.

Domestic Violence

Globally one out of every three women faces violence at the hands of their husbands, fathers, or brothers and uncles in their homes, Domestic violence can be described as when one adult in a relationship misuses Power to control another through violence and other forms of abuse psychological violence includes verbal abuse.

Such violence may also include rape and sexual abuse psychological violence includes verbal abuse. Harassment, confinement and deprivation of physical, financial and personal resources for some women emotional abuse may be more painful than physical attacks because they effectively undermine women's security and self-confidence.

Working women i.e., those who are in paid employment, face problems at the workplace just by virtue of their being women social attitude to the role of women lags much behind the law. The attitude which considers women fit for certain jobs and not others.

Problems at Workplace

Sexual harassment at the workplace is a universal problem even through the occurance of sexual harassment at the workplace is widespread in India and elsewhere. This is the first time it has been recognised as an infringement of the fundamental rights of a woman under Article 19(1) (g) of the constitution of India "to practice any profession or to carry out any occupation, trade or business". In India, Articles 14,15 and 21 of the Indian constitution provide safeguards against all forms of discrimination.

In any civilised society. It is the fundamental right of people to able to lead their lives with dignity, free from mental or physical torture to ensure these transgressors must pay for their unsolicited sexual advances. At the same time organisations such as men against violence and abuse that conduct gender sensitisation programmes and self defence classes to combat sexual harassment at the workplace, must be encouraged.

Importance of Self Defence Training for Women

In today's world women are independent and go out for work. In the same time they also face the problems of stalking molesting, harassment etc., to deal with such problem it is necessary that woman should be trained in self defence. The girls should know how to fight handle them selves without any dependent on others. She should know her strength and learn to fight against 'he'. In today's world many girls and women face harassment molesting and stalking problems why? Just because every one think that she do not have any strength to fight and they start harassing her. There should be a self defence training in every school in the country to protect themselves. The primary level students can start their training in order to protect themselves. When these children grow up their confident level would be high and would be a better fighter than men. Men are considerd to be stronger than women. But do not think that woman can not fight. Many girls are shy and uncomfortable but this should no longer be there. Girls should know how to fight back if some one tries to do something wrong with her.

Findings

India is rapidly advancing in its developmental goals and more and more women are joining the workforce. It is the duty of the state to provide for the wellbeing and respect of its citisens to prevent frustration low self esteem, insecurity and emotional disturbance, which in turn could affect business efficacy; leading to loss of production and loss of reputation for the organisation or the employer. In fact the recognition of the right to protect against sexual harassment is an intrinsic component of the protection of women's human rights. It is also a step towards providing women independence, equality of opportunity and the right to work with dignity. The government has also drawn up a draft National policy for the empowerment of women which is a policy statement, outlining the state's response to problems of gender discrimination. As persistent gender inequalities continue, we need to rethink Concepts and strategies for promoting women's dignity and rights.

References

- D'Souza, V (1975). Family status and male work participation In: V.D'Souza (ed.), women in contemporary India. India, Monohar; en.m.wikipedia.org/wiki/women-in-india/the free encyclopedia.
- en.m.wikipedia.org/.....violence-againstwomen-wikipedia.org
- Gupta Manisha and Renu Khanna (2002), Process Documentation of Gender Training of Dilaasa, Mumbai.
- Importance of self Defence for women study. Mode com. Retrieved 06, 2013 from
- http://www.Studymode.com/essay/Importanceofself-Defence-for women-
- 178957.html.
- ncw.nic.in/frmLLawsRelatedwomen.as
- WWW.women empowermentiniindia.com/

29

Schooling and Skill Development: Enroute to Gender Equality and Inclusive Development

Anand Valmiki

Asst. Professor Regional Institute of Education

Bhopal (NCERT) Valmiki2009@gmail.com

Abstract

1. We must equip and nurture our youth with the right kind of education, skill-set and opportunity to reap this demographic dividend (Address of President of India to the Parliament on 09.06.2014). Skills and knowledge are the driving forces of economic growth and social development for any country. As India moves progressively towards becoming a 'knowledge economy' it becomes increasingly important that the nation must focus on advancement of skills and these skills have to be relevant to the emerging economic environment with the twin targets of achieving the economic growth and inclusive development. The present paper attempts to explore the inter-linkages between schools, skill development and gender equality in twenty-first century by highlighting the prominence of 'capabilities approach'. Thus, the paper revolves around the central theme of promoting gender equity through skill development in schools to achieve the goal of inclusive development. Various sections of this paper deliberate the concept of gender equality in brief; conceptual understanding of skills; and the rationale behind the skill development to attain gender equality to sustain inclusive development.

Keywords: Gender Equality, Skill, Capabilities Approach, Inclusive Development

Introduction

In the pre-independence era skill was usually transferred from father to son. This informal method of skill acquisition continted for centuries. With the advent of industrialisation the need for more skilled workforce became enormous in ninteenth and twentieth century. Independent India during Nehruvian era underwent rapid industrialisation process that demanded more and more skillful workforce. Was this demand for skilled workforce undermined in policy making and practice? Did schooling in Independent India ever imparted "skills" to the children that enabled them to make their 'career choices' as well as facilitate 'vertical mobility' in higher education? Have we ever attempted to impart "skills" to our children that would empower them to be 'employable' in the market in their future? Are educators aware of the fact that "skills" are gateway to, social inclusion' and 'employment' that eventually carve a path to 'equality' and 'inclusive development'? This chapter conceives the answer to the above questions as big YES. After independence, as a matter of policy, a number of committees and commissions recommended the vocational education system inextricably interlinked with common school curriculum. National Policy of Education (1968), Kothari Commission (1964) and Central Advisory Board of Education in 1975 emphasised the need for (pre)vocational skills in schools and diversified vocational training at secondary schools. The focus of such initiatives was to build a sustainable skill based education system. The Kothari Commission on Educational Reforms, 1966 had visualised that 25 per cent of the students at the secondary stage would go for the vocational stream. Scholars and educators of Nehruvian era predicted that 'skill development' in the nation will have to be in consonance with the wheels of modernisation that are rolling through the industry, agriculture and tertiary sector. Nevertheless, current scenario in India is that only 5 per cent of the population of 19–24 age group has acquired some sort of skills through vocational education, while the corresponding figure for Korea is as high as 96 per cent. Experts estimate that 32 per cent of its current population is under the age of 15. India with more than 1.2 billion citisens has the second largest education system in the world (after China). However, the National Knowledge Commission and the Planning Commission reiterate lack of skill to be a major hurdle in nation's inclusive development.

In such a context of inclusive development, this chapter takes a position that socialising school children into skills and facilitating them to acquire skills becomes central to schooling. Furthermore, in order to achieve the goal of inclusive development, this chapter perceives that skills have to be imparted in schools so as to empower both girl students and boy students to achieve the immaculate goal of gender equality and eliminate the remnants of historical marginalisation, social exclusion and oppression of one the sub-categories of gender, i.e., women. The subsequent sections deliberate the concept of gender equality in brief; and the rationale behind the skill development to attain gender equality and sustain inclusive development. It also highlights the contextualisation of capabilities approach to attain gender equality through skill development in schools. The perspective that this chapters adheres is to permeate vocational training in schools as a part and parcel of integral/common curriculum for schools.

Gender Equality via Right to/within/through Education

> The term gender equality is reflected in one of the six Education For All (EFA) goals elucidated in the Dakar Framework for Action [2000] which envisages 'eliminating gender disparities in primary and secondary education by 2005, and achieving gender equality in education by 2015, with a focus on ensuring girls' full and equal access to and achievement in basic education of 'good quality'. Goal 3 of the Millennium Development Goals i.e., *Promote Gender Equality and empower women* is incorporated as major socio-political agenda of the state in India.

Gender equality refers to the equal rights, responsibilities and opportunities of women, men, girls and boys. Gender equality is achieved when the different behaviours, aspirations and needs of women and men are equally valued and favoured and do not give rise to different consequences that reinforce inequalities. As such, gender inequalities arise from the unequal power relations between women and men. For women in particular, equality means the realisation of rights that have been denied as a result of cultural, institutional, behavioural and attitudinal discrimination. Equality is both a goal and a means whereby individuals are accorded equal treatment under the law and equal opportunities to enjoy their rights and to develop their potential talents and *skills* so that they can participate in national political, economic, social and cultural development and can benefit from its results. Consequently, a need is felt to develop workers into knowledge workers who will be more flexible, analytical, and adaptable as well as multi skilled. In the new knowledge economy (of twenty-first century) the skill sets will include professional, managerial, operational, and behavioural, inter personal and inter functional skills. For this purpose, this chapter draws on Duncan Wilson's (2003) three-fold characterisation of 'rights in education' and adapts the characterisation of rights in the context of skills and gender equality. The three-fold characteristics of 'rights in education' are:

0. Right to Education
1. Right within Education
2. Right through Education

The Right of children for Free and Compulsory Education Act, 2009 (Act No.35 of 2009) is already in vogue as a state agenda for universalisation of school education between age of six to fourteen years. However, the standpoint of this paper moves beyond the concept of free and compulsory education and advocates 'Rights with in Education' which means every child will have to be endowed with the right to get imparted with the skills that are required for her/him to function successfully in twenty-first century. Furthermore, Right to Education will also have to ensure 'Rights through Education' whereby a child is instilled with skills that are necessary to legitimise and institutionalise equality, more specifically gender equality. Thus, skill becomes central to achieve gender equality which is quite substantive and perpetuates and reinforces inclusive development. The sections below will deliberate on skills; skill development and twenty-first century skill for gender equality.

Skills: What Body of Literature/Research Says?

As the concept of "skill" is gaining its prominence tremendously due to various forces such as globalisation of 'Market Economy', inclusion, equality and development, it is pertinent to overview the literature pertaining to skill to develop a conceptual understanding of skills. Skill may be defined as "the ability to do something well". I has various synonyms such as "expertise, skillfulness, expertness, adeptness, adroitness, deftness, dexterity, ability, prowess, mastery, competency, capability, efficiency, aptitude, artistry, art, fitness, flair, virtuosity, experience, professionalism, talent, cleverness, smartness, ingenuity, versatility, knack, readiness, handiness".

For some, the ability to use one's knowledge effectively and readily in execution or performance dexterity or coordination especially in the execution of learned physical tasks a learned power of doing something competently. Skill is "an ability and capacity acquired through deliberate, systematic, and sustained effort to smoothly and adaptively carryout complex activities or job functions involving ideas (cognitive skills), things (technical skills), and/or people (interpersonal skills)". This section briefly reviews the historical genesis of the skill; its contextual usage in scholarly/ research works.

Skill was characterised by Pear (1927) as being concerned with the quantity and quality of motor output: 'skill is the integration of well-adjusted muscular performances' (Pear, 1948, p. 92). While for Pear the emphasis was on manual, motor skills, his contemporary Hans Reynold in 1928 defined skill as 'any combination, useful to industry, of mental and physical pualhties which require considerable training to acquire' (More, 1980, p. 15). While Reynold was therefore introducing a cognitive dimension alongside the manual, his emphasis on training ignores the fact the skills may equally be acquired through practice, without training. Usually the term skill is used to refer to a level of performance, in the sense of accuracy and speed in performing particular tasks (skilled performance). Skilled performance has long been a subject of psychological enquiry and is of obvious interest to employers. In Cox's (1934) study of manual skill, which was not defined but involved both physical psychomotor abilities and mental cognitive abilities, performance in terms of speed and accuracy was measured in experiments with repetitive assembly operations. Hence, the concept of skill acquired enormous significance with industrialisation process across the globe in nenteenth and twentieth centuries.

Another strand of skills research has concerned transfer of training, particularly the extent to which proficiency and experience in one task helps performance in another. In general, transfer of motor skills has only been found to occur where the tasks have particular elements in common, undermining the argument for developing general abilities that will improve performance in various activities (Adams, 1987; Gagné, Foster and Crowley, 1948). This observation has been shown to apply equally to the transfer of cognitive skill (Singley and Anderson, 1989). One conclusion of Cox's studies was that 'skill developed by the mere repetition of one manual operation confers little advantage in the performance of other operations that may be subsequently undertaken' (Cox, 1934, p. 176).

Welford (1968, pp. 12-13), who defined skill as a combination of factors resulting in 'competent, expert, rapid and accurate performance', regarded this as equally applicable to manual operations and mental activities. Welford's (1968; 1976) work focused on perceptual-motor performance, as has much of skills research since the two are intimately linked in practice (Fuchs, 1962; Lintern and Gopher, 1978). Welford's work shows how actions are selected and coordinated at different levels of skilled performance and the conditions of practice and training that promote the acquisition and transfer of skill.

More recently, research into skilled performance has increasingly taken into account broader cognitive skills such as problem solving and decision making. This demonstrates the difficulty in regarding such cognitive competences as knowledge rather than skill. Indeed, there is substantial evidence that acquiring skill and demonstrating skilled performance involve a combination of underlying perceptual, cognitive and motor skills (Carlson and Yaure, 1990; Salthouse, 1986). Also, retaining even relatively simple motor skills appears to depend upon understanding of results (Lavery, 1962) and verbalised knowledge (Berry and Broadbent, 1984), or knowledge that is articulated in the course of developing such skills.) Moreover, knowledge and working memory play a major role in acquiring skills (Chase and Ericsson, 1982) including procedural skills (Carlson, Sullivan and Schneider, 1989), problem-solving skills (Carlson et al., 1990) and complex cognitive skills (Logie et al., 1989; McKeithen et al., 1981).

Fitts and colleagues (Fitts et al., 1961; Fitts and Posner, 1967) developed a three stage framework for skill acquisition: (i) the cognitive phase of understanding the nature of the task how it should be performed involves conscious cognitive processes; (ii) the associative phase involves inputs linked more directly to appropriate actions and reduced interference from outside demands and finally and (iii) the autonomous phase occurs when actions are automatic requiring no conscious control.

Proctor and Dutta (1995, p. 18) in what is arguably the most authoritative text on skill acquisition and performance, define skill as 'goal-directed, well-organised behaviour that ir acquired through practice and performed with economy of effort'. Each eldment of this definition is important: first, skill develops over time, with practice; second, it is goal-directed in response to some demand in the external environment; third, it is acquired when components of behaviour are structured into coherent patterns; and finally, cognitive demands are reduced as skill develops. In further articulating their conception of skill, Proctor and Dutta (1995) distinguish perceptual skills, response selection skills, motor skills and problem-solving skills. Perceptual skills are concerned with the ability to make distinctions and judgements; more complex situations require attentional control for processing but many tasks that initially require attention become automatised. Skill in selecting the appropriate response can be developed with practice; reaction time is affected by the number of alternatives and can be accelerated by providing advance information, thereby reducing the alternatives. Motor skills are the manual aspects of performance such as speed and accuracy of physical movements or dexterity. Problem-solving skills, while dependent upon intellect and mental models, can be acquired and developed through practice.

Skill Development and Schooling: Capabilities Approach

The 11th Five Year Plan (2007-12) has recognised India's massive need to skill millions of formal and informal workers in the next ten years. In response, the government developed an ambitious scheme of increasing the proportion of formal and informal skilled workers in its total workforce from a mere 2 per cent now to 50 per cent by 2022, thus creating a 500 million strong resource pool. Improved training and skill development is critical for providing decent employment opportunities to the growing youth population and necessary to sustain the high growth momentum. The 12th Five Year Plan (2012-17) envisages that "while skill formation has to be mainstreamed in the formal education system right from class X onwards, skill creation outside the formal education needs coordinated action and innovative approach". Planning Commission (2011) opines that children acquire skills faster if taught earlier. It goes on to say that it is important to offer pre-vocational courses in classes IX and X either as an add-on or as an alternative to work education or third language, where applicable. Furthermore, students opting for such pre-vocational courses could be encouraged and facilitated to take up advanced vocational subjects at the higher secondary level. Providing vertical mobility options for students opting for vocational courses, to pursue undergraduate and postgraduate level, if they so desire, appears imminent, failing which the vocational courses at the school-level may not pick up. For a high quality vocational education at school level to evolve and grow in the country, there is a need to train and equip our teachers on a continuous basis with latest skills and the vocational pedagogy itself.

Gender and Economic Policy Discussion Forum which deliberated on Empowering Women through Skill Development - Challenges and Opportunities identifies that low social value is attached to girl´s education, and as they are considered secondary income earners, lower importance is given to training of girls for employment. It also goes on to say that much focus has to be given on improvements in access to education and training for girls, including the provision of services, such as transport, hostels, scholarships, and other incentives to encourage women to enrol for education and training. It is in such a context, this chapter argues that skill development programmes have to be initiated in schools with an emphasis on skilling girl children for more employability in the market with in a broad framework of *capabilities approach*. Elaine Unterhalter (2003) interprets that "the key idea of the capability approach is that social arrangements should aim to expand people's capabilities – their freedom to promote or achieve 'functionings' which are important to them". According to Sen (1992) the foundational idea is that what matters to people is that they are able to achieve actual functionings that is 'the actual living that people manage to achieve'. Walking is a functioning, so are eating, reading, writing and talking. The concept of functionings reflects the various things a person may value doing or being varying from the basic (being adequately nourished) to the very complex (being able to take part in the life of the community). Sen argues that when we make interpersonal comparisons of wellbeing we should find a measure which incorporates references to functioning's, that is what has been achieved, but also reflects the intuition that what matters is not merely achieving the functioning but being free to achieve it. So we should look at 'the freedom to achieve actual livings that one can have a reason to value' (Sen, 1999, 18) or, to put it another way, 'substantive freedoms' or 'the capabilities' to choose a life one has reason to value (Sen, 1992, 40). A person's capability refers to the alternative combinations of functionings that are feasible for her to achieve". The Capability Approach considers development through education to be understood not only as increasing income or better access to resources, but as the enhancement of people's freedoms to do and be what they have reason to value (McCowan 2011, p. 285). This capabilities approach goes beyond economic development and rights and broadens the perspective of enabling people's freedom and choices to function in the society. In the light of the above discussion, this chapter argues that skills are such capabilities that can be nurtured through schooling where the future citisens 'freedoms to do and be' are enhanced.

NCERT's position paper on 'Gender Issues in Education' by National Focus Group acknowledges that substantive gender equality in education is a more complex notion that relates to the nature and quality of education, and has to focus on how education can enables girls to exercise their choice and claim their rights. Hence, it is argued in this paper that skills will enable girls to exercise their choice in market spaces as well as private spheres. The following section explicates the skills that are required for young generation to exercise their choices and rights, specifically girl-students in the twenty-first century.

Gender and twenty-first Century Skills

With the realisation that school education is increasingly becoming academic-oriented; the government has decided to revive skill development programmes in schools to ensure 'all-round development' of students. We must equip and nurture our youth with the right kind of education, skill-set and opportunity to reap this demographic dividend. A well educated population, adequately equipped with knowledge and skill is not only essential to support economic growth, but is also a precondition for growth to be inclusive since it is the educated and skilled person who can stand to benefit most from the employment opportunities which growth will provide. It is by providing skill training in schools, a strong foundation can be built for students which can later be put to use for entrepreneurship and also in their everyday life. Besides the demographic dividend, another factor that adds to the urgency for improved skill development is the increasing number of newly educated youth, especially women, who are willing to seek employment in the service sector. School curriculum and schooling become active instruments of cultural reproduction and social control without seeking to alter the informal and the formal processes of socialisation. This chapter argues that education and skill development sector has to adequately respond to this emerging need, making it imperative to provide skill development and training in marketable skills and services.

The most recent developments in the knowledge society and the subsequent changes in the world of work at the global level are raising skill/qualification requirements for job entry and subsequently demand for a more knowledgeable and skilled workforce. In this context, this chapter explicates that there is a dire and urgent need for a paradigm shift in the skill development sector, in favour of innovations, improvements and high quality training. Furthermore, the chapter expounds that it is very pertinent that the concept of training and skill development will have to move beyond the conventional goal of imparting technical and managerial competencies, to playing a broader role of even including basic literacy, numeracy, critical social and political awareness, awareness about gender, and enhancing life skills. Such interventions by their nature will encourage higher self-esteem among girl children and overall personality development. This chapter is in consonance with the exposition that for skill development to be more effective, training needs to bend towards developing the kind of skills women and men already knows and move towards the skills unknown to boys and girls previously. This chapter broadly categorises the skills that are required for gender equality to become more inclusive in twenty-first century and these skills can be incorporated under an umbrella term known as twenty-first century skills. The term twenty-first century skills refers to a broad set of knowledge, skills, work habits, and character traits that are believed—by educators, school reformers, employers, and others—to be critically important for success in today's world, particularly in contemporary careers and workplaces. Generally speaking, twenty-first century skills can be applied in all academic subject areas, and in all educational, career, and civic settings throughout a student's life. It should be noted that the "twenty-first century skills" concept encompasses a wide-ranging and amorphous body of knowledge and skills that is not easy to define and that has not been officially codified or categorised. While the term is widely used in education, it is not always defined consistently, which can lead to confusion and divergent interpretations. In addition, a number of related terms—including applied skills, cross-curricular skills, cross-disciplinary skills, transversal skills, non-cognitive skills and soft skills that are widely used in reference to the general forms of knowledge and skill commonly associated with "twenty-first century skills." While these different terms may not be strictly synonymous, and they may have divergent or specialised meanings in certain technical contexts, these diverse sets of skills are being addressed in this one entry for the purposes of practicality and usefulness.

Generally speaking, the twenty-first century skills concept is articulated, in this chapter, by the belief that teaching students the most relevant, useful, in-demand, and universally applicable skills must be prioritised in today's schools and by the related belief that many schools may not sufficiently prioritise such skills or effectively teach them to students. The basic idea is that students, who will come of age in the twenty-first century, need to be taught different skills than those learned by students in the twentieth century discussed in earlier sections on this chapter, and that the skills they learn must reflect the specific demands that will placed upon them in a complex, competitive, knowledge-based, information-age, technology-driven economy and society. While the specific skills deemed to be "twenty-first century skills" may be defined, categorised, and determined differently from person to person, place to place, or school to school the term does reflect a general—if somewhat loose and shifting—consensus. The following list provides a brief illustrative overview of the knowledge, skills, work habits, and character traits commonly associated with twenty-first century skills:

Types of Skills:

0. *Technical/ Work-specific skills* (Vocational Skills) are specific to a job and are not easily applied in other environments or situations. These skills tend to be technical and specialised.These skills can be imparted/ acquired through vocational training. Vocational training is about imparting of specialised skills and knowledge, instilling social and

political attitudes and behaviour patterns for successful economic activities by people engaged in dependent employment, self-employment in both Formal as well as Non-formal trainings. Integration of vocational education at the school level is the only practical way of imparting basic technical skills to a large number of new entrants to the labour force. Planning Commission Task Force on skill development further goes on to recommend that "Vocational Education can be provided in schools either by 'weaving' the subjects into the curriculum or by providing separate 'optionals' at the School and College level. The Planning Commission affirms that software aspect can be looked at by the National Council of Education Research & Training (NCERT) and the *extent* to which these subjects can be covered should be largely left to the Secondary School Boards and Universities (2007, p.i). Highlighting the role of NCERT The following recommendations are made by the Task Force of the Planning Commission (2007) to integrate technical skills in schools :

0. Flexibility should be provided in the school curriculum to give weightage to vocational subjects during the examinations and for the grant of credits.
1. VT and VE programmes can be made available to students after Class VIII at any time and after Class V for those over 15 years of age in order to cater to dropouts from the formal education system. As regards 'streaming' of students into VT, this could begin after class X, given the Government of India's mandate to universalise elementary education and expand opportunities for secondary education.
2. The Pundit Sunder Lal Sharma Central Institute of Vocational Education (PSSCIVE) should become the coordinating agency for VE and promote the interface between education and industry. It can be designated as the National Institute for Vocational Education Planning and Development.

This chapter advocates close linkages between various institutes such as Institute for Applied Manpower & Research (IAMR), The National Council of Vocational Training (NCVT), Industrial Training Institutes (ITIs), NCERT, PSSIVE and evolve strategies to integrate Vocational Education and Training at school level for the purpose of providing exposure to school students about various skills and train them in one or two skills of their choice, propensities, proclivities and inclinations. Furthermore, Polytechnics should only be opened in those areas where there is a public demand and a likelihood of employment. National Mission on Skill Development, Skill Development Council and Skill Development Centre's need to provide incessant inputs to schools and the Polytechnics. Keeping in view importance of skill development in *agriculture* and its vast potential, this chapter is of the view that agriculture training institutes have to be set up all over the country, to empower persons dependent on agriculture.

Following are the technical/work-specific skills suitable for twenty-first century:

0. Commerce Based
1. Office Secretaryship
2. Accounting and Auditing
3. Marketing and Salesmanship
4. Banking
5. Retail
6. Financial Management
7. Business Administration

1. Engineering Based

0. Electrical Technology
1. Automobile Technology
2. Civil Engineering
3. Air Conditioning and Refrigeration Technology
4. Electronics Technology
5. Geospatial Technology
6. Foundry
7. IT Application

2. Health and Paramedical Based

0. Ophthalmic Technique
1. Medical Laboratory Techniques
2. Auxiliary Nursing and Midwifery
3. X-ray Technician
4. Healthcare Science
5. Health and Beauty Studies
6. Medical Diagnostics

3. Home Science Based

0. Fashion Design and Clothing Construction
1. Textile Design
2. Design Fundamental

3. Music Technical Production
4. Beauty Services

4. Agriculture Based

0. Poultry and Farming
1. Horticulture
2. Dairying Science and Technology

5. Hospitality and Tourism Based

0. Food Production
1. Food and Beverage Services
2. Mass media Studies and Media Production
3. Bakery and Confectionaries
4. Front Office
5. Travel and Tourism

6. Others

0. Tr'nsportation System and Logistic Maintenance
1. Life Insurance and related Sector
2. Library and Information Sciences

1. *Life skills/Functional/transferable skills/Self-management skills* can be applied in most environments and situations. "Life skills" are defined as psychosocial abilities for adaptive and positive behaviour that enable individuals to deal effectively with the demands and challenges of everyday life. There are many different understandings of life skills but no definition is universally accepted. Different organisations attach different meanings to the term. The International Bureau of Education (IBE) derives its understanding from the Delores four pillars of learning - learning to know, learning to do, learning to be and learning to live together - and defines life skills as personal management and social skills which are necessary for adequate functioning on an independent basis. For instance, meaningful targets for an overall goal aimed at "improving all aspects of the quality of education and ensuring excellence of all so that recognised and measurable learning outcomes are achieved by all, especially in literacy, numeracy and essential life skills" (EFA Goal 6). Additionally, it is essential to ask how life skills are defined in particular life situations and throughout life (Ouane 2002; Goody 2001). It is believed that life skills are developed as a result of a constructive processing of information, impressions, encounters and experiences, - both individual and social - that are a *part of one's daily life and work* and the rapid changes that occur *in the course of one's life.* The social dimensions are particularly important as they condition life itself and compel individuals to purposefully acquire skills, develop attitudes and values in order to face and master real life situations (Ouane 2002).

Life skills can be loosely grouped into three broad categories of skills: cognitive skills for analysing and using information, personal skills for developing personal agency and managing oneself, and inter-personal skills for communicating and interacting effectively with others. Essentially, there are three kinds of skills—-

"thinking skills"- those related to thinking and these skill relate to reflection at personal level,

"social skills"- skills related to dealing with others and include interpersonal skills,

> *"emotional skills"* can be perceived as a skill not only in making rational decisions but also in being able to make others agree to one's point of view. Elaborate list of life skills are presented below that are essential in twenty-first century to ensure gender equality:
>
> "Decision-making and problem-solving; creative thinking and critical thinking; communication and interpersonal skills; self-awareness and empathy; coping with emotions and coping with stress; Perseverance, self-direction, planning, self-discipline, adaptability, initiative; leadership, teamwork, collaboration, cooperation Civic, ethical, and social-justice literacy; economic and financial literacy, entrepreneurialism dealing with conflict that cannot be resolved, dealing with authority, solving problems, making and keeping friends/relationships, cooperation, self-awareness, creative thinking, decision-making, critical thinking, dealing with stress, negotiation, clarification of values, resisting pressure, coping with disappointment, planning ahead, empathy, dealing with emotions, assertiveness, active listening, respect, tolerance, trust, sharing, sympathy, compassion, sociability, self-esteem; critical thinking, reasoning, analysis, interpretation, synthesising information; personal expression; public speaking and presenting, listening; health and wellness literacy, including nutrition, diet, exercise, and public health and safety; environmental and conservation literacy, ecosystems understanding".

This chapter maintains that an eclectic approach is required to evolve school programmes that integrate vocational and life skills with the core curriculum. This paper emphasises that NCERT, NCTE and CBSE will have to advance a liaison with Skill Developlent Council and evolve curriculum on skills for various stages of schooling which is intricately integrated with the core curriculum of schools.

Conclusion: Gender, Skills and Inclusive Development

Skills, knowledge and innovation are driving forces of economic growth and social development in any country of the world. Countries with higher levels of education and highly skilled citisens are not only more competitive in the global economy, but can also quickly respond to challenges and seise opportunities.There is a dual rationale for promoting gender equality. Firstly, that equality between women and men - equal rights, opportunities and responsibilities – is a matter of human rights and social justice. And secondly, that greater equality between women and men is also a precondition for (and effective indicator of) sustainable people-centred development. The perceptions, interests, needs and priorities of both women and men must be taken into consideration not only as a matter of social justice but because they are necessary to enrich development processes. All in all, this chapter foresees the synergy between schools and skill development to promote gender equality from the perspective of inclusive development.

References

- Adams, J.A. (1987). Historical review and appraisal of research on the learning, retention and transfer of human motor skills. Psychological Bulletin, Vol. 101, p. 41-74.
- Chenoy, D (2012), "Empowering Women through Skill Development : Challenges and Opportunities", Power Point Presentation at the GEPD forum II, Institute of Social Studies Trust and Heinrich Boll Foundation, at the India Habitat Centre, 24 April 2012.
- Government of India (2011). Faster, Sustainable and More Inclusive Growth: An Approach to the 12th Five Year Plan, Planning Commission. Retrieved from www.planningcommission.nic.in
- King, K (2012), "The Geopolitics and Meanings of India's Massive Skills Development Ambitions", in International Journal of Educational Development, 32 , 2012, pp 665–673.
- Faster, Sustainable and More Inclusive Growth: An Approach to Twelfth Five Year Plan. Planning Commission, Government of India, 2011.
- Berry, D.C.; Broadbent, D.E. (1984). On the relationship between task-performance and associated verbalised knowledge. Quarterly Journal of Experimental Psychology, Vol. 36a, p. 209-231.
- Chase, W.G.; Ericsson, K.A. (1982). Skill and working memory. In Bower, G.H. (ed.). The psychology of learning and motivation. New York: Academic Press, p. 1-58.
- Carlson, R.A., Sullivan, M.A.; Schneider, W. (1989). Practice and working memory effects in building procedural skill. Journal of

Experimental Psychology: Learning, Memory and Cognition, Vol. 15, p. 517-526.

- Carlson, R.A., Khoo, B.H., Yaure, R.G.; Schneider, W. (1990). Acquisition of a problem-solving skill: levels of organisation and use of working memory. Journal of Experimental Psychology: General, Vol. 119, p. 193-214.
- Carlson, R.A.; Yaure, R.G. (1990). Practice schedules and the use of component skills in problem solving. Journal of Experimental Psychology: Learning, Memory and Cognition, Vol. 16, pp. 484-496.
- Cox, J.W. (1934). Manual skill: its organisation and development. Cambridge: Cambridge University Press.
- Empowering Women through Skill Development-Challenges and Opportunities. Forum II, Briefing Note 2, April, 2012. Retrieved from http://in.boell.org/sites/default/files/downloads/Briefing_note_2.pdf
- Fitts, P.M.; Bahrick, H.P.; Noble, M.E.; Briggs, G.E. (1961). Skilled performance. New York: John Wiley.
- Fitts, P.M.; Posner, M.I. (1967). Human Performance. Belmont, CA: Brooks/Cole.
- Fuchs, A.H. (1962). The progression-regression hypothesis in perceptual-motor skill learning. Journal of Experimental Psychology, Vol. 63, p. 177-182.
- Gagné, R.M.; Foster, H.; Crowley, M.E. (1948). Measurement of transfer of training. Psychological Bulletin, Vol. 45, pp. 97-130. Gender and Economic Policy Discussion Forum
- Goel P. Vijay technical and vocational education and training (tvet) system\ in india for sustainable development. Retrieved from http://www.unevoc.unesco.org/up/India_Cnuntry_ P'per.pdf, Ministry of Human Resource Development, Government of India
- Goody, J. (2001) *Competencies and Education: Contextual Diversity*. In: Rychen, D.S, Salganik L.H. (eds.) (2001) *Defining and Selecting Key Competencies*, Göttingen, Hogrefe and Huber Publications.
- Lavery, J.J. (1962). Retention of simple motor skills as a function of type of knowledge of results. Canadian Journal of Psychology, Vol. 16, pp. 300-311.
- Lintern, G.; Gopher, D. (1978). Adaptive training of perceptual-motor skills: issues, results and future directions. International Journal of Man-Machine Studies, Vol. 10, pp. 521-551.
- Logie, R. et al. (1989). Working memory in the acquisition of complex cognitive skills. Acta Psychologica, Vol. 71, pp. 53-87.
- McCowan, T. (2011), Human rights, capabilities and the normative

basis of 'Education for All'. Theory and Research in Education. Vol. 9, No. 3, pp. 283-298.

- McKeithen, K.B. (1981). Knowledge organisation and skill differences in computer programmers. Cognitive Psychology, Vol. 13, pp. 307-325.
- More, C. (1980). Skill and the English working class, 1870-1914. London: Croom Helm.
- OSAGI (2001)."Important concepts underlying gender mainstreaming", factsheet by the
- Office of the Special Adviser on Gender Issues and the Advancement of Women.
- Available online: http://www.un.org/womenwatch/osagi/pdf/factsheet2.pdf
- Ouane, A (2002) Key competencies In Lifelong Learning. *Institutionalising lifelong learning: Creating Conducive Environments for Adult Learning in the Asian Context*, UNESCO Institute for Education, Hamburg
- Pear, T.H. (1927). Skill. Journal of Personnel Research, Vol. 5, pp. 478-489.
- Pear, T.H. (1948). Professor Bartlett on skill. Occupational Psychology, Vol. 22, pp. 92-93.
- Position paper -national focus group on gender issues in education. Retrievdd fromhttp://www.ncert.nic.in/rightside/links/pdf/focus_group/gender_issues_in_education.pdf
- Report of the Task Force on Skill Development, Planning Commission Government of India New Delhi May, 2007.
- Salthouse, T.A. (1986). Perceptual, cognitive and motoric aspects of transcription typing. Psychological Bulletin, Vol. 99, pp. 303-319.
- Sen, A. (2001), Development as freedom. Oxford: University Press.
- Sen, A. (2005), Human Rights and Capabilities. Journal of Human Development. Vol. 6, No. 2, July 2005, pp. 151-166.
- Singley, M.K.; Anderson, J.R. (1989). The transfer of cognitive skill. Cambridge, MA: Harvard University Press.
- Targeting Development: Critical Perspectives on the Millennium Development Goals [London: Routledge].
- Wilson, D [2003] Human Rights: Promoting gender equality in and through education. Background paper for EFA GMR 2003/4 Welford, A.T. (1968). Fundamentals of skill. London: Methuen.

30

Role of Gender in Problems and Educational Aspirations of the Out of School Slum Children

Dr Ali Mohammad
Associate Professor, I.A.S.E., Faculty of Education
Jamia Millia Islamia
Nida Khan
Research Scholar, I.A.S.E., Faculty of Education
Jamia Millia Islamia, New Delhi-25

Abstract

Gender affects every aspect of our life, from how we think to how we need. The development of a nation depends largely on the educational attainment of its masses (both boys and girls), so our first and foremost task is to identify masses that are unable to get the benefit of education. Every child either boy or girl, has its own way of thinking and learning. It is in this context the researcher examined the role of gender in problems and aspirations of the out of schools children living in the slums of Delhi. The present research was of descriptive survey type. The survey studied gender variation in the problems of the out of school slum children relating to school, family, personal, studies, teachers and classmates and the educational aspirations of the out of school slum children related to family support, pupils views, pupils efforts and reality of aspired goals. The sample comprised of 400 out of school slum children enrolled in the centre schools run by the different NGO's in Delhi. The study revealed that the girls of out of school slum children had greater problems and educational aspirations as compared to boys of out of school slum children.

Keywords: *Gender, Problems, Educational Aspirations and Out of school Children*

Introduction

Education has both conservative and progressive functions. As Godfrey Thomson points out, educational system has the responsibility to pass on social heritage of the human race. This does not mean that education should ignore its progressive function. Progressivism is welcome, but it should not inculcate contempt for the past traditions. While striking a balance between the two functions, he suggests that, "the aim of education should be to preserve order without hindering change", and H.G. Wells wants 'to lift the minds out of blind alleys' through education. One of the greatest tasks of education today is to strike a balance between these two opposite functions of education. The other serious problem is to make education relevant to the needs of today and aspirations of tomorrow.

Every society in the world aims to give efficient education, to present educational facilities based on equality and justice and to prepare people efficiently for their future lives. India too provides equal educational opportunities for all its citisens.

But in spite all efforts of the government there is still a population which lacks all educational facilities due to several reasons. This population mainly consist the children of the urban slum areas.Thus especially those who living in the slums of metropolises is doomed to suffer inequality because of the rapid growth of population due to urbanisation. People migrate from rural areas and settle down in slums of urban area in search of employment. The variety of factors such as economic, demographic and socio-cultural is responsible for pushing the rural population to the urban areas. A variety of such phenomenon has resulted in the formation of the urban slums.

Slum is a commonly used term for thickly populated urban areas with dilapidated and substandard housing. The Census of India (2001) has defined slum as "a compact area of at least 300 populations or about 60-70 households of poorly built congested tenements, in unhygienic environment usually with inadequate infrastructure and lacking in proper sanitary and drinking water facilities". The children living in these slums called by different names such as street children, high risk children, abandoned children etc. The UNICEF has called them "children in difficult circumstances". They work on the street either under the supervision of employers inside or outside their family or are in business for themselves. They return to their families in the night. They are out of their homes forced by poverty, violence, drink and sexual abuse. A classification scheme outlined by United Nations International Children Emergency Fund (UNICEF) is commonly used in international literature to differentiate homeless children. These categories are:

1. Children on the street- These are children with continuous family contact. Refer to children who engage in street based activities.

2. Children of the street- These are the children who have weaker ties to their families or occasional family contact, and
3. Abandoned children- These are abandoned and neglected children who have no connection to family at all.

Need for the Study

People living in the slum are found in all the major cities of the developing countries and play a prominent role in urban scenario. They survive by doing mobile street work such as washing, parking, begging, cleaning gutters, pickling rags and so on (Swart Kruger & Richter,1997). Due to low occupational and economic level the slum children possess very low or no formal education. They do not place much importance to education, as it does not fetch them immediate benefits. These slums children do not have any access to basic amenities of health, sanitation as well as education. In spite of the various efforts made by the government and some of the non government organisations, the pace of progress is not very satisfactory.

In spite of Common school system for all, pupils living in the slum not get this opportunity. People living in slum areas of cities and towns play a key role in urban life. They do every odd work beginning from rag picking to construction of houses. Labour needed in every aspect of urban life is supplied by slum areas. But they lead an insecure life with many fears and threats. So their prime concern is to earn money to struggle for their existence. Children of the families in slum areas are thus brainwashed to join economic venture of the families and in many cases the means of earning money may not be the just ways. Lack of economic and social security's pushes these children to dishonest means of livelihood.

A large number of projects and programmes were launched to reduce the gender and regional disparities but the problems faced by slum children were by and large ignored. Various measures were suggested in different policies and five year plans for the development of rural and backward areas but no concrete strategies were evolved to look into the educational problems of urban deprived. The average socio-economic indicators like *per capita income*, infant mortality rate, literacy level, and enrolment of school going children are much better in urban areas as national average, but the same is not true of the slum areas. The situation in some urban areas is even worse than many rural areas. It is only recently the government has woken up to the reality and started thinking about the educational needs of this segment of population, which remained neglected for decades.

Many children from slum areas do not have access to schools with adequate facilities and teachers who are tuned for teaching the underprivileged. If the remote and backward areas have natural geographical barriers like hills, mountains and adverse weather conditions, children of slums areas have hindrances like busy road, railway track and temporary obstructions. In reality, the supply side constraints in urban settings cannot be removed by considering the physical distance norms. It is the settlement structure, social stratification and population density that play critical role in the demand for amenities and facilities.

Educational facilities made available to the slum children of urban areas through schools run by different NGO's can do a lot for educating them and uplifting their condition. Thd slum children have their own educational aspirations of life, which they fail to fulfill due to lack of facilities and home support. Moreover, they might be facing a lot of problems in availing and utilising educational facilities whatever is made available to them. The proposed study intends to study the role of gender in their educational aspirations and problems of these out of school slum children.

Statement of the Problem

Keeping this in view the following study is proposed:

"Role of gender in problems and educational aspirations of the out of school slum children"

Operational definitions of the terms

The following terms are defined to clarify their use in the context of this study:

Gender: Means those characteristics which explain their behavioral characteristics with reference to sex.

Problem: Means hurdle or barrier that obstructs an individual to reach his goal or an objective. It is mainly related to school, classmates, studies, teachers, personal and family. It is the context of education only.

Educational aspiration: Expectation framed by individual to achieve education in terms of their abilities, past academic performance, ambitions and family situations.

Out of school children: It refers to the children of school going between 6-14 years of age and regularly not attending the any school providing formal education.

Objectives of the Study

The following were the specific objectives of the study:

- To study the problems of the out of school slum children with reference to gender.
- To study the level of educational aspirations of the out of school slum children with reference to gender.

Review of Literature

Panda (2000):- *Studied the education of urban poor. In his study he undergoes a pilot study of slum dwellers of Delhi. He examined the educational facilities in terms of school, non-formal centres as well as various etc available in the slums. He conducts a door-to-door survey in the slums. Overall 68 hourehold*s *survey was done. The study revealed that the slum under study had electricity and drinking water facilities, majority of slum dwellers 76.5 had single room accommodation. The boys and girls attend the school but not very regularly. Particularly in case of girls, their parents fear that once their daughters become literate, it will be difficult to get them married.*

Chugh (2003):- *Studied the learning achievement of slum children in 16 Government schools of Delhi. Overall 372 children from grade 5th and 56 teachers were involved in the study. The study revealed that the mathematics competencies were better as compared to the language competencies although they were very much below the target of 80 per cent as suggested by the minimum level of learning. The data also revealed that one fourth students are under performers. Even for language the situation was not better. She also concluded that the children being from the same socio-economic background, the school levels factors are also responsible for the variations in the achievement test.*

Tsujita (2009):- *Studied the educational status of slum children between 5 and 14 years old. He concluded that the attendance ratio of slum children is much more than that of children in Delhi as a whole. Parental perception of education and financing education are the major constraints. Even if children are attending schools majority of them are over aged. There are both demand and supply side reasons for discouraging slum children from attending schooling. Moreover, the existing various Government programmes can be improved to reach slum households.*

Rathore (2012):-*Studied the reasons and remedies of school dropouts at the primary level. The researcher selected four talukas on the basis of random sampling. He used lottery system to select these talukas. The total dropouts in these schools were 30. The study revealed that the main reason of the dropout of the school is poverty (96.66 per cent—-parents and teachers). Mostly dropouts are of farm labour and their monthly income is below Rs 2000. Reasons of dropping out are work at home, not interested in studies and parents illiteracy.*

Jennifer Sheridan (2001): Studied the effects of parent's unrealised educational aspirations on children's educational outcome. The result indicates that parents who planned to attend college have significantly higher odds of completing high school, attending college and graduating college for every level of parent's education. Furthermore this relationship differs by the gender of both parent and offspring.

Yisak Tafere (2010): Studied changing educational aspiration of children living in poverty in Ethopia. The results suggest that children had high aspirations at an earlier age but that these changed later, with poverty rarely influencing their earlier aspirations but having a strong impact later on. Children with high educational achievement, mostly urban children and some rural girls, maintained their high ambitions. Education policy imposed constraints and provided varied opportunities for rural and urban children that affected their educational achievement and aspiration.

Alessandra Minello & Nicola Barban (2011): The general aim of this paper is to investigate the educational aspirations of the children of immigrants living in Italy and attending the last year of primary school (8th grade). They consider both secondary school track and university aspirations as indicators of educational preferences in the short and long run. The hypothesis, confirmed both for short and long aspirations, is that attending a school where most of the Italian pupils have high educational aspirations may lead children of immigrants to enhance their own aspirations.

Loic Menzies (2013): studied how educational aspirations of English schools work with parents to keep them on track. The study revealed that pupils aspire to something that is unfamiliar to parents; schools should help parents understand what their children's aspirations involve. It is more useful to help parents understand what is involved in studying at University than simply promoting it as an aspiration. Schools should therefore talk to parents about the role of independent research and reading around a subject at university so that they can encourage their children to begin doing so at home.

Design of the Study

Method

For the present research the descriptive survey method was adopted.

Population and Sample

All the out of school children of slums of Delhi constitutes the target population. Out of the total population only 400 randomly selected students from the conveniently selected 20 centre schools/ slum schools run by different NGO's of Delhi taken as the sample of the study.

Tool

Problem checklist (PC)*:* A checklist was developed to find out the problem of the out of school slum children by the investigator. This tool is the adaptation of Problem Checklist by Nirmal Bhagia. The purpose of the tool was to find out the different problems faced by the out of school children in the urban slums. Since problems are many and can be categorised under many headings. But in this study the problem are categorised under following heads namely: Family, school, teachers, personal, friends, and studies. The tool is in the form of checklist containing 84 questions. Test retest method was used to calculate the reliability of the tool and reliability of whole measure was calculated which was found as 0.76.

Level of Educational Aspiration Test (LEAT): The investigator used Level of Educational Aspiration Test by Yashmin Ghani Khan, which consists of 30 questions related to family support, pupils views, pupils efforts and reality of aspired goals. Test retest method was used to calculate the reliability of the tool and reliability of whole measure was calculated which was found as 0.81 after an interval of a month.

Statistical Techniques Used

After the collection of data statistical technique of percentage was applied and results were interpreted.

Analysis of the Data

Table 1.1-Problems: Gender-wise

Problems	Total	Boys	Girls
Classmates	42(10.50)	23(5.75)	19(4.75)
Teacher18(4.50)	10(2.50)	8(2.00)	
Study	134(33.50)	80(20.00)	54(13.50)
Schonl	224(56.00)	111(27.75)	113(28.25)
Personal	175(43.75)	83(20.75)	92(23.00)
Family	89(22.25)	42(10.50)	47(11.75)

The problems faced by the out of school slum children are divided in six broad areas and the distribution of the problems faced by boys and girls is shown in above table 1.1. It is found from the study that out of school children boys had more problems as compared to girls. Among all areas boys had higher problems with classmates, teacher and studies. Girls had higher problems with school, family and personal.

Table 1.2-Educational aspirations: Gender-wise

	Total	Boys	Girls
Highly Realistic	44(11.00)	20(5.00)	24(6.00)
Realistic &Normal	125(31.25)	49(12.25)	76(19.00)
Unrealistic	231(57.75)	107(26.75)	124(31.00)

It is found from the study that girls had are more realistic as compared to boys in their educational aspirations. Out of the total out of school slum children only 11 per cent had realistic educational aspirations in which girl's contribution is 6 per cent and boys is 5 per cent. Among all 19 per cent girls had realistic and normal educational aspirations as compared to boys (12.25 per cent). It is also found that most of the out of school children are unrealistic in their educational aspirations in which 31 per cent were girls and 26.75 per cent were boys.

Conclusion

The present study on out of school slum children highlights diversity of their problems and reality of their educational aspirations. Even if the non-formal centre run by different NGO's have taken up the task of educating them and ultimately lodge them in the mainstream of formal education, the facilities provided by them are insufficient. So, Government and Non-Government organisations needs a systematic approach for planning, organisation and effective implementation of their programmes in the light of social, economic and cultural context of particular slum area. Thus the study demands effective educational planning to realise the universal primary education a major component of "education to all".

References

0. Alessandra Minello & Nicola Barban - The educational aspirations of the children of immigrants living in Italy, DONDENA Working paper No-46, May 2011.
1. Best, J.W: Research in Education, Prentice Hall Publication, 1982.
2. Garrett, H: Statistics in Psychology and Education, Vakils, Feffer and Simons Ltd., Tenth Indian Reprint, 1981.
3. Gokce, F- Discrimination in Primary Education in the Slums of Turkey: Problems about Equity of education, International Journal of Human and Social Sciences, Feb 2009.
4. Hunt, F-Dropping out from School: A Cross Country Review of literature, Research Monograph No-16, May 2008.
5. Kopoka- The problem of street children in Africa: An ignored Tragedy, Paper presented at International Conference on Street Children and Street children's Health in East Africa, Tanzania, April 19-21, 2000.
6. Komal, L: Methodology of Educational Research, Second Revised Edition, Vikas Publishing House Private Ltd., New Delhi, 1993.
7. Loic Menzies (2013)-Educational aspirations of English schools work with parents to keep them on track, JRF, January 2013.
8. Mohanty: Education for all, Deep and Deep Publication, New Delhi, 1994.

9. Mufane- Debt relief initiatives and poverty alleviations: lessons from America, 2000.
10. Mukherjee, D- Reducing Out of School Children in India- lessons from a micro study, MPRA, Paper No- 35047, November 2011.
11. Nanda- Working Street Children's Perceptions of their Wealth, Illness and Health- seeking Behavior- A qualitative study in New Delhi, Master's thesis, Department of International Health, KIT, Amsterdem.
12. Shrestha, P- Street Children's Access to Education in Dar-es-salam, paper presented at the International Conference on Reaching the Marginalised- How to approach Inclusive Education, 10-11 Sept 2009
13. Sheridon, Jennifer -The effects of parent's unrealised educational aspirations on chhldren's educational outcome, CDE Working paper No-99-33, March 2001.
14. Payne, R- Voices from the Street: Street Girl life in Accra , Ghana, CEDAR, Research Paper No- 40, Jan 2004.Trujita- Depriviation of education in urban areas: A basic profile of slum children in Delhi- IDE, Disscussion paper no-199, Mar-2009.
15. Yisak Tafere - Changing educational aspiration of children living in poverty in Ethopia, Working paper No-56, Young lives, June 2010.

31

Gender Equality: A Developmental Strategy

DrAnuradha Aggarwal
Lecturer, Shambhu Dayal (P.G.) College, Ghaziabad
Dr Kanak Rani
HOD, Modern College of Professional Studies Ghaziabad

There are a number of issues relating to livelihood and social security that has an effect on women's lives that have come to for in context of globalisation and liberalisation of the Indian economy. At the same time, the discourse on women's empowerment has increase rapidly in number, both in the state and in the civil society, even though with multiple meanings and approaches to it. Climate change is foreseen to increase women's vulnerabilities on account of livelihood, women's employment and food insecurities. Rights-based development has come to the fore in the context of impact of ICTs on women globalisation and neo-liberalism. There is a need of evolving multiple securities, including social security, for women in the informal sector. An inclusive approach that involves women in participatory development and decentralised democratic governance will strengthen women's empowerment. Certain insights and strategies are also suggested for grassroots women's activism.

The disparity between women and men can take many different forms. Indeed, gender disparity is not one homogeneous phenomenon, but a collection of disparate and interlinked problems. In some regions in the world, disparity between women and men directly involves matters of life and death, and takes the brutal form of unusually high mortality rates of women and a consequent preponderance of men in the total population, opposed to the preponderance of women found in societies with little or no gender bias in health care and nutrition.

Sex differentials have been observed extensively high in North Africa and in Asia, including China and South Asia. Gender bias can manifest itself in the form of the parents wanting the newborn to be a boy rather than a girl. It is particularly prevalent in East Asia, in China and South Korea in particular, but also in Singapore and Taiwan, and it is beginning to emerge as a statistically significant phenomenon in India and South Asia as well. Even when demographic characteristics do not show much or any male bias, there are other ways in which women can have less than a square deal. Girls have far less opportunity of schooling than boys do. There are other deficiencies in basic facilities available to women, varying from encouragement to cultivate one's natural talents to fair participation in rewarding social functions of the community. Even when there is relatively little difference in basic facilities including schooling, the opportunities of higher education may be far fewer for young women than for young men. Indeed, gender bias in higher education and professional training can be observed even in some of the richest countries in the world, in Europe and North America. In terms of employment as well as promotion in work and occupation, women often face greater handicap than men.

In many societies the ownership of property can also be very unequal. Even basic assets such as homes and land may be very asymmetrically shared. The absence of claims to property can not only reduce the voice of women, but also make it harder for women to enter and flourish in commercial, economic and even some social activities. There are often enough, basic inequalities in gender relations within the family or the household, which can take man Gender issues in population, health and development in India different forms.

Even in cases in which there are no overt signs of male bias in, say, survival or son preference or education, or even in promotion to higher executive positions, the family arrangements can be quite unequal in terms of sharing the burden of housework and child care.

Basic concepts of gender inequality in India are:

0. Imbalance in sex ratio
1. Son preference
2. Domestic and sexual violence
3. Unequal education access
4. Bias work opportunities
5. Maternal mortality
6. Maternal unhealthy
7. Improper family planning
8. Policies for women empowerment

Eliminate discrimination against women

The term discrimination against women shall mean any distinction, exclusion, or restriction made on the basis of sex which has the effect or purpose of impairing or nullifying the recognition, enjoyment or exercise by women, irrespective of their marital status, on a basis of equality of men and women, of human rights and fundamental freedoms to the political, economic, social, cultural, civil or any other field. Appropriate measures should be taken in all fields, in particular in the political, social, economic and cultural fields, including legislation to ensure the full development and advancement of women, for the purpose of guaranteeing them the exercise and enjoyment of human rights and fundamental freedoms on a basis of equality with men.

Adoption of temporary special measures aimed at accelerating equality between men and women shall not be considered as goal but these measures shall be continued when the objectives of equality of opportunity and treatment have been achieved.

Some areas in which elimination of discrimination required are:

0. Family matter
1. Representations in national constitutions
2. Against women in rural areas
3. The field of education
4. The field of employment
5. On the grounds of marriage or maternity
6. In the political and public life of the country
7. Economic and social life
8. Against the Girl Child
9. Violence against women

Eliminate discrimination in family matters

All appropriate measures to eliminate discrimination against women in all matters relating to marriage and family relations and in particular shall ensure, on a basis of equality of men and women;

(a) The same right to enter into marriage.

(b) The same right freely to choose a spouse and to enter into marriage only with their free and full consent.

(c) The same rights and responsibilities during marriage and at its dissolution.

(d) The same rights and responsibilities as parents, irrespective of their marital status, in matters relating *to their children,* in all cases the interests of the children shall be paramount.

(e) The same rights to decide freely and responsibly on the number and spacing of their children and to have access to the information, education and means to enable them to exercise these rights.

(f) The same rights and responsibilities with regard to guardianship, wardship, trusteeship and adoption of children, or similar institutions where these concepts exist *in national legislation*; in all caser thd interests of the children shall be paramount.

(f) The same personal rights as husband and wife, including the right to choose a family name, a profession and an occupation.

(g) The same rights for both spouses in respect of the ownership, acquisition, management, administration, enjoyment and disposition of property, whether free of charge or for a valuable consideration.

Equality of men and women in their national constitutions

Discrimination against women should be condemned in all its forms, agree to pursue by all appropriate means and without delay a policy of eliminating discrimination against women and to this end, undertake:

(a) To embody the principle of the equality of men and women in their national constitutions or other appropriate legislation if not yet incorporated herein and to ensure through laws and other appropriate means, the practical realisation of this principle;

(b) To embody the principle of the equality of men and women in their national constitutions or other appropriate legislation if not yet incorporated herein and to ensure through laws and other appropriate means, the practical realisation of this principle;

(c) To establish legal protection of the rights of women on an equal basis with men and to ensure through competent national tribunals and other public institutions the effective protection of women against any act of discrimination;

(d) To refrain from engaging in any act or practice of discrimination against women and to ensure that public authorities and institutions shall act in conformity with this obligation.

(e) To take all appropriate measures to eliminate discrimination against women by any person, organisation or enterprise;

(f) To take all appropriate measures, including legislation, to modify or abolish existing laws, regulations, customs and practices which constitute discrimination against women.

(g) To repeal all national penal provisions which constitute disbrimination against women.

Eliminate discrimination against women in rural areas

The particular problems faced by rural women and the significant roles which rural women play in the economic survival of their families, including their work in the non-monetised sectors of the economy should be taken care and shall take all appropriate measures to ensure the application of the provisions of this convention to women in rural areas. Appropriate measures to eliminate discrimination against women in rural areas in order to ensure, on a basis of equality of men and women that they participate in and benefit from rural development and, in particular, shall ensure to such women the right:

(a) To participate in the elaboration and implementation of development planning at all levels.

(b) To have access to adequate health care facilities, including information, counseling and services in family planning.

(c) To benefit directly from social security programmes.

(d) To obtain all types of training and education, formal and non-formal, including that relating to functional literacy, as well as, inter-alia, the benefit of all community and extension services, in order to increase their technical proficiency.

(e) To organise self-help groups and cooperatives in order to obtain equal access to economic opportunities through employment or self-employment.

(f) To participate in all community activities.

(g) To have access to agricultural credit and loans, marketing facilities, appropriate technology and equal treatment in land and agrarian reform as well as in land resettlement schemes.

Eliminate discrimination in the field of education

All appropriate measures to eliminate discrimination against women in order to ensure to them equal rights with men in the field of education should be taken to ensure, on a basis of equality of men and women.

(a) The same conditions for career and vocational guidance for access to studies and for the achievement of diplomas in educational establishments of all categories in rural as well as in urban areas; this equality shall be ensure in pre-schnol, general, technical, professional and higher technical education, as well as in all types of vocational training;

(b) Access to the same curricula, the same examinations, teaching staff with qualifications of the same standard and school premises and equipment of the same quality;

(c) The elimination of any stereotyped concept of the roles of men and women at all levels and in all forms of education by encouraging coeducation and other types of education which will help to achieve this aim and, in particular, by the revision of text books and school programmes and adaptation of teaching methods.

(d) The same opportunities to benefit from scholarships and other study grants.

(e) The same opportunities for access to programmes of continuing education, including adult and functional literacy programmes, particularly those aimed at reducing at the earliest possible time, any gap in education existing between men and women

(f) The reduction of female student drop-out rates and the organisation of programmes for girls and women who have left school prematurely.

(g) The same opportunities to participate actively in sports and physical education.

(h) Access to specific educational information to help to ensure the health and well being of families, including information and advice on family planning.

Eliminate discrimination against women in the field of employment

All appropriate measures should to be eliminate discrimination against women in the field of employment in order to ensure, on a basis of equality of men and women.

(a) The right to work as an inalienable right of all human beings;

(b) The right to the same employment opportunities, including the application of the same criteria for selection in matters of employment;

(c) The right to free choice of profession and employment, the right to promotion, job security and all benefits and conditions of service and the right to receive vocational training and retraining, including apprenticeships, advanced vocational training and recurrent training;

(d) The right to equal remuneration, including benefits, and to equal treatment in respect of work of equal value, as well as equality of treatment in the evaluation of the quality of work;

(e) The right to social security, particularly in cases of retirement, unemployment, sickness, invalidity and old age and other incapacity to work, as well as the right to paid leave; and

(f) The right to protection of health and to safety in working conditions, including the safeguarding of the function of reproduction;

Eliminate discrimination on the grounds of marriage or maternity

In order to prevent discrimination against women on the grounds of marriage or maternity and to ensure their effective right to work, States Parties shall take appropriate measures;

(a) To prohibit, subject to the imposition of sanctions, dismissal on the grounds of marriage or of maternity leave and discriminate in dismissals on the basis of marital status;

(b) To introduce maternity leave with pay or with comparable social benefits without loss of former employment, seniority or social allowance;

(c) To encourage the provision of the necessary supporting social services to enable parents to combine family obligations with work responsibilities and participation in public life, in particular through promoting the establishment and development of a network of child care facilities; and

(d) To provide special protection to women during pregnancy in types of work proved to be harmful to them.

Eliminate discrimination in the political and in the political and public life

All appropriate measures to eliminate discrimination against women in the political and in the political and of the country should be taken to ensure to women on equal terms with men, the right to-

(a) Vote in all elections and public referenda and to be eligible for election to all publicly elected bodies;

(b) Participate in the formulation of government policy and the implementation there of and to hold public office and perform all public functions at all levels of government;

(c) Participate in non-governmental organisations and associations concerned with the public and political life of the country.

Eliminate discrimination against women economic and social life

All appropriate measure to eliminate discrimination against women in other areas of economic and social life should be taken in order to ensure on a basis of equality of men and women. It means women should have the same rights particularly in:

a) Family benefits

b) Bank loans, mortgages and other forms of financial credit

c) The right to participate in recreational activities, sports and cultural life

Eliminate discrimination against the Girl Child

All forms of discrimination against the girl child and violation of her rights shall be eliminated by undertaking strong measures both preventive and punitive within and outside the family. These would relate specifically to strict enforcement of laws against prenatal sex selection and the practices of female-foeticide, female infanticide, child marriage, child abuse and child prostitution etc. Removal of discrimination in the treatment of the girl child within the family and outside and projection of a positive image of the girl child will be actively fostered. There will be special emphasis on the needs of the girl child and earmarking of substantial investments in the areas relating to food and nutrition, health and education, and in vocational education. In implementing programmes for eliminating child labour, there will be a special focus on girl child.

Elimination of Violence against Women

All forms of violence against women, physical and mental, whether at domestic or societal levels, including those arising from customs, traditions or accepted practices shall be dealt with effectively with a view to eliminate its incidence. Institutions and schemes for assistance will be created and strengthened for prevention of such violence, including sexual harassment at work place and customs like dowry; for the rehabilitation of the victims of violence and for taking effective action against the perpetrators of such violence. A special emphasis will also be laid on programmes and measures to deal with trafficking in women and girls.

Women Development and its Approaches

The flourishing movements of various forms of feminism have been taken place; however, the nexus between economic development and women was not clearly articulated until now. Women first came into focus in development as objects of welfare policies, including birth control, nutrition, pregnancy, and so forth. "In 1962 the UN General Assembly asked the Commission on Women's Status to prepare a report on the role of women in development. Ester Boserup's path breaking study on *Women's Role in Economic Development* was published in 1970". These events marked monumental moments in developing liberal paradigm of women in development, and the welfare approach still remains dominant in development practices today. These are approaches in gender and developments are as follows:

Early Approaches

- Women in development
- Women and development
- Gender and development

Neoliberal Frameworks

- *Gender and Neoliberal Development Institutions*
- *Smart Economics*

Alternative Approaches

- *Marxism and Neo-Marxism*
- *Dependency Theory*
- *Basic Needs Approach, Capability Approach, and Ecofeminism*

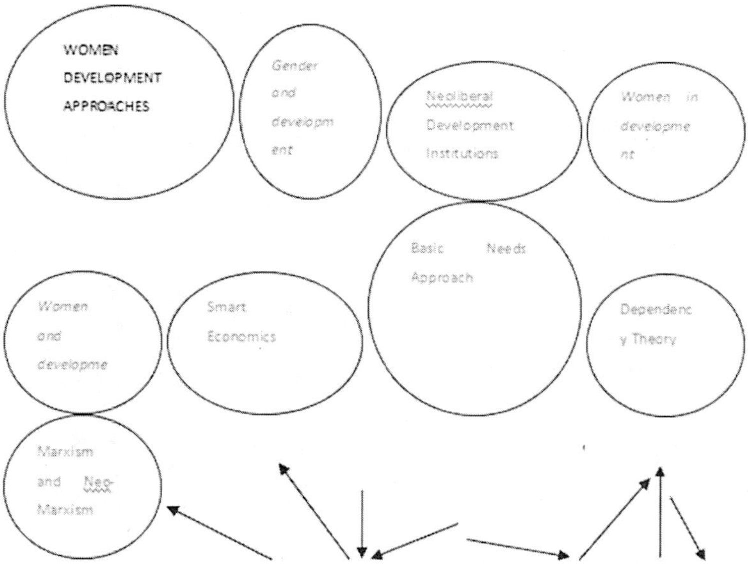

Early Approaches

Women in Development

The term "women and development" was originally coined by a Washington-based network of female development professionals in the early 1970s who sought to put in question the trickle down theories of development by contesting that modernisation had identical impact on men and women. The Women in Development movement (WID) gained momentum in the 1970s, driven by the resurgence of women's movement in northern countries, whereby liberal feminists were striving for equal rights and labour opportunities in the United States. Liberal feminism, postulating that women's disadvantages in society may be eliminated by breaking down stereotyped customary expectations of women by offering better education to women and introducing equal opportunity programmes, had a notable influence on the formulation of the WID approaches, whereby little attention was given to men and to power relations between genders.

The translation of the 1970s feminist movements and their repeated calls for employment opportunities in the development agenda meant that particular attention was given to the productive labour of women, leaving aside reproductive concerns and social welfare. Yet this focus was part of the approach pushed forward by advocates of the WID movement, reacting to the general policy environment maintained by early colonial authorities and post-war development authorities, wherein inadequate reference to the work undertook by women as producers was made, as they were almost solely identified as their roles as wives and mothers. The WID's opposition to this "welfare approach" was in part motivated by the work of Danish economist Ester Boserup in the early 1970s, who challenged the assumptions of the said approach and highlighted the role women by women in the agricultural production and economy.

A dominant strand of thinking within WID sought to link women's issues with development, highlighting how such issues acted as impediments to economic growth; this "relevance" approach stemmed from the experience of WID advocates which illustrated that it was more effective if demands of equity and social justice for women were strategically linked to mainstream development concerns, in an attempt to have WID policy goals taken up by development agencies. The Women in Development approach was the first contemporary movement to specifically integrate women in the broader development agenda and acted as the precursor to later movements such as the Women and Development, and ultimately, the Gender and Development approach, departing from some of the criticised aspects imputed to the WID.

Women and Development

Women and Development (WAD) is a theoretical and practical approach to development. It was introduced into gender studies scholarship in the second half of the 1970s, following its origins, which can be traced to the First World Conference on Women in Mexico City in 1975, organised by the UN. It is a departure from the previously predominant theory, Women in Development and is often mistaken for WID, but has many distinct characteristics.

WAD arose out of a shift in thinking about women's role in development, and concerns about the explanatory limitations of modernisation theory. While previous thinking held that development was a vehicle to advance women, new ideas suggested that development was only made possible by the involvement of women, and rather than being simply passive recipients of development aid, they should be actively involved in development projects. WAD took this thinking a step further and suggested that women have always been an integral part of development, and did not suddenly appear in the 1970s as a result of exogenous development efforts. The WAD approach suggests that there be women-only development projects that were theorised to remove women from the patriarchal hegemony that would exist if women participated in development alongside men in a patriarchal culture, though this concept has been heavily debated by theorists in the field. In this sense, WAD is differentiated from WID by way of the theoretical framework upon which it was built. Rather than focus specifically on women's relationship to development, WAD focuses on the relationship between patriarchy and capitalism. This theory seeks to understand women's issues from the perspectives of neo-Marxism and dependency theory, though much of the theorising about WAD remains undocumented due to the persistent and pressing nature of development work in which many WAD theorists engage.

The WAD paradigm stresses the relationship between women, and the work that they perform in their societies as economic agents in both the public and domestic spheres. It also emphasises the distinctive nature of the roles women play in the maintenance and development of their societies, with the understanding that purely the integration of women into development efforts would serve to reinforce the existing structures of inequality present in societies overrun by patriarchal interests. In general, WAD is thought to offer a more critical conceptualisation of women's position that does WID.

The WAD approach emphasises the distinctive nature of women's knowledge, work, goals, and responsibilities, as well as advocating for the recognition of their distinctiveness. This fact, combined with a recognised tendency for development agencids to be dominated by patriarchal interests, is at the root of the women-only initiatives introduced bx WAD subscribers.

Gender and Development

Gender and Development approach focus on the socially constructed basis of differences between men and women and the need to challenge existing gender roles and relations. This approach was majorly influenced by writing of academic scholars such as Oakley (1972) and Rubin (1975) which emphasise the social relationship between men and women. These relationships they argue have systematically subordinated women. This departs from WID which perceived women's problem in terms of their biological differences rather than gender. Influenced by this work, by the late 1970s, some practitioners working in the development field stated questioning the adequacy of focusing on women in isolation. GAD challenged the WID focus on women as important 'target group' and 'untapped resources' for development. GAD marked a shift in thinking about the need to understand how women and men are socially constructed and how 'those constructions are powerfully reinforced by the social activities that both define and are defined by them.' GAD focus primarily on gender division of labour and gender as a relation of power embedded in institutions. Consequently, two major frameworks 'Gender roles' and 'social relations analysis' are used in this approach. Gender role focus on social construction of identities within the household, it also reveals the expectations from 'maleness and femaleness' in their relative access to resources. Social relations analysis exposes the social dimensions of hierarchical power relations imbedded in social institutions; also its determining influence on 'the relative position of men and women in society'. This relative position tends to discriminate against women.

Unlike WID, the GAD approach is not concerned specifically with women, but with the way in which a society assigns roles, responsibilities and expectations to both women and men. GAD applies gender analysis to uncover the ways in which men and women work together, presenting results in neutral terms of economics and efficiency. In an attempt to create gender equality, denoting women having same opportunities as men, including ability to participate in the public sphere; GAD policies aims to redefine traditional gender role expectations. Women are expected to fulfill household management tasks, home based production as well as bearing and raising children and caring for family members. The role of a wife is largely interpreted as 'the responsibilities of motherhood'. Men however, are expected to be breadwinners whom are associated with paid work, and market production. In the labour market, women's overall financial related payment tends to be lower usually earning less. For instance, 'a study by the Equality and Human Rights Commission found massive pay inequities in some United Kingdom's top finance companies, women received around 80 per cent less performance-related pay than their male colleagues.' In reaction to inequalities between gender, Beijing Platform for Action established gender mainstreaming in 1995 as a strategy across all policy areas at all levels of governance for achieving gender equality.

Caroline Moser developed the Moser Gender Planning Framework for GAD-oriented development planning in the 1980s while working at the Development Planning Unit of the University of London. Working with Caren Levy, she expanded it into a lethodology for gender policy and planning. The Moser framework follows the Gender and Development approach in emphasising the importance of gender relations. As with the WID-based Harvard Analytical Framework, it includes collection of quantitative empirical facts. Going further, it investigates the reasons and processes that lead to conventions of access and control. The Moser Framework includes gender roles identification, gender needs assessment, disaggregating control of resources and decision making within the household, planning for balancing the triple role, distinguishing between different aims in interventions and involving women and gender-aware organisations in planning.

Neoliberal Approaches

Gender and Neoliberal Development Institutions

Among development institutions, gender issues have increasingly become part of economic development agendas, as the examples of the World Bank shows. Awareness by international organisations of the need to address gender issues evolved over the past decades. The World Bank, for example, started focusing on gender in 1977 with the appointment of first Women as Development Adviser. In 1984 the bank mandated that its programs consider women's issues. In 1994 the bank issued a policy paper on Gender and Development, reflecting current thinking on the subject. This policy aims to address policy and institutional constraints that maintain disparities between the genders and thus limit the effectiveness of development programmes. Thirty years after the appointment of a first Women in Development Adviser, a so-called Gender Action Plan was launched to underline the importance of the topic within development strategies and to introduce the new Smart Economics strategy. In 2012, the World Development Report was the first report of the series examining Gender Equality and Development.

Women have been identified by some development institutions as a key to successful development, for example through financial inclusion. One example is the Women's Development Business (WDB) in South Africa, a Grameen Bank microfinance replicator. The goal is to ensure that rural women are given the tools to free themselves from the chains of poverty through allocation of financial resources directly to women including enterprise development programmes. The idea is to use microfinance as a market-oriented tool to ensure access to financial services for disadvantaged and low-income people and therefore fostering economic development through financial inclusion.

As a reaction, a current topic in the feminist literature on economic development is the 'gendering' of microfinance, as women have increasingly become the target borrowers for rural microcredit lending. This, in turn, creates the assumption of a "rational economic woman" which can exacerbate existing social hierarchies). Therefore, the critique is that the assumption of economic development through microfinance does not take into account all possible outcomes, especially the ones affecting women.

The impact of programmes of the Bretton Woods Institutions and other similar organisations on gender are being monitored by Gender Action, a watchdog group founded in 2002 by Eliane Zuckerman who is a former World Bank economist.

Gender, Financial Crises and Neoliberal Economic Policy

The global financial crisis and the following politics of austerity have opened up a wide range of gender and feminist debates on neoliberalism and the impact of the crisis on women. One view is that the crisis has affected women disproportionately and that there is a need for alternative economic structures in which investment in social reproduction needs to be given more weight. The International Labour Organisation (ILO) assessed the impact of the global financial crisis on workers and concluded that while the crisis initially affected industries that were dominated by male workers (such as finance, construction and manufacturing) it then spread over to sectors in which female workers are predominantly active. Examples for these sectors are the service sector or wholesale retail trade.

There are different views among feminists on whether neoliberal economic policies have more positive or negative impacts on women. In the post-war era, feminist scholars such as Elisabeth Wilson criticised state capitalism and the welfare state as a tool to oppress women. Therefore, neoliberal economic policies featuring privatisation and deregulation, hence a reduction of the influence of the state and more indhvidual freedom was argued to improve conditions for women. This anti-welfare state thinking arguably led to feminist support for neoliberal ideas embarking on a macroeconomic policy level deregulation and a reduced role of the state. Therefore, some scholars in the field argue that feminism, especially during its second wave, has contributed key ideas to Neoliberalism that, according to these authors, creates new forms of inequality and exploitation.

As a reaction to the phenomenon that some forms of feminism are increasingly interwoven with capitalism, many suggestions on how to name these movements have emerged in the feminist literature.

Smart Economics

Advocated chiefly by the World Bank, smart economics is an approach to define gender equality as an integral part of economic development and it aims to spur development through investing more efficiently in women and girls. It stresses that the gap between men and women in human capital, economic opportunities, and voice/agency is a chief obstacle in achieving more efficient development. As an approach, it is a direct descendant of the efficiency approach taken by WID which rationalises investing in women and girls for more effective development outcomes. As articulated in the section of WID, the efficiency approach to women in development was chiefly articulated by Caroline Moser in the late 1980s. Continuing the stream of WID, smart economics' key unit of analysis is women as individual and it particularly focuses on measures that promote to narrow down the gender gap. Its approach identifies women are relatively underinvested source of development and it defines gender equality an opportunity of higher return investment. Gender equality itself is here depicted as smart economics, in that it enables women to contribute their utmost skills and energies to the project of world economic development. In this term, smart economics champions neoliberal perspective in seeing business as a vital vehicle for change and it takes a stance of liberal feminism.

The thinking behind smart economics dates back, at least, to the lost decade of the Structural Adjustment Policies (SAPs) in the 1980s.In 1995, World Bank issued its flagship publication on gender matters of the year Enhancing Women's Participation in Economic Development (World Bank 1995). This report marked a critical foundation to the naissance of Smart Economics; in a chapter entitled 'The Pay-offs to Investing in Women', the Bank proclaimed that investing in women "speeds economic development by raising productivity and promoting the more efficient use of resources; it produces significant social returns, improving child survival and reducing fertility, and it has considerable intergenerational pay-offs". The Bank also emphasised its associated social benefits generated by investing in women. For example, the Bank turned to researches of Whitehead that evidenced a greater female-control of household income is associated with better outcomes for children's welfare and Jeffery and Jeffery who analysed the positive correlation between female education and lower fertility rates. In the 2000s, the approach of smart economics came to be further crystallised through various frameworks and initiatives. A first step was World Bank's Gender Action Plan (GAP) 2007-/2010, followed by the "Three Year Road Map for Gender Mainstreaming 2010-13". The 2010-13 framework responded to criticisms for its precursor and incorporated some shifts in thematic priorities. Lastly but not least, the decisive turning point was 2012 marked by its publication of "World Development Report 2012: Gender Equality and Development". This Bank's first comprehensive focus on the gender issues was welcomed by various scholars and practitioners, as an indicator of its seriousness. Other international organisations, particular UN families, have so far endorsed the approach of smart economics. Examining the relationship between child well-being and gender equality, for example, UNICEF also referred to the "Double Dividend of Gender Equality". Its explicit link to a wider framework of the Millennium Development Goals (where the Goal 3 is Promoting Gender Equality and Women's Empowerment) claimed a wider legitimacy beyond economic efficiency. In 2007, the Bank proclaimed that "The business case for investing in MDG 3 is strong; it is nothing more than smart economics". In addition, "Development organisations and governments have been joined in this focus on the 'business case' for gender equality and the empowerment of women, by businesses and enterprises which are interested in contributing to social good"[42]. A good example is "Girl Effect initiative" taken by Nike Foundation.[53] Its claim for economic imperative and a broader socio-economic impact also let a strategic need of NGOs and community organisations that seeks justification for their program funding[42]. Thus, some NGOs, for example Plan International, captured this trend to further their programme. The then-president of the World

Bank Robert B. Zoellick was quoted by Plan International in stating "Investing in adolescent girls is precisely the catalyst poor countries need to break intergenerational poverty and to create a better distribution of income. Investing in them is not only fair, it is a smart economic move". The global financial meltdown and austerity measures taken by major donor countries further supported this approach, since international financial institutions (IFIs) s and international NGOs received a greater pressure from donors and from global public to design and implement maximally cost-effective programmes.

Smart economics subordination of women under the justification of development invited fierce criticisms. Chant expresses her grave concern that "Smart economics is concerned with building women's capacities in the interests of development rather than promoting women's rights for their own sake". She disagrees that investment in women should be promoted by its instrumental utility: "it is imperative to ask whether the goal of female investment is primarily to promote gender equality and women's 'empowerment', or to facilitate development 'on the cheap', or to promote further economic liberalisation". Although smart economics outlines that gender equality has intrinsic value (realising gender quality is an end htself) and instrumental value (realising gender equality is a means to a more efficient development), many points out that the Bank pays almost exclusive attentions to the latter in defining its framework and strategy. Zuckerman also echoed this pint by stating "business case ignores the moral imperative of empowering women to achieve women's human rights and full equal rights with men." In short, Chant casts a doubt that if it is not "possible to promote rights through utilitarianism."

A wide range of scholars and practitioners has criticised that smart economics rather endorse the current *status-quo* of gender inequality and keep silence for the demand of institutional reform. Its approach "does not involves public action to transform the laws, policies, and practices which constrain personal and group agency". Naila Kabeer also posits that "attention to collective action to enable women to challenge structural discrimination has been downplayed". Simply, smart economics assumes that women are entirely capable of increasingly contributing for economic growth amid the ongoing structural barriers to realise their capabilities.

Sylvia Chant (2008) discredited its approach as 'feminisation of responsibility and/or obligation' where the smart economics intends to spur growth simply by demanding more from women in terms of time, labour, energy, and other resources. She also agrees that "Smart economics seeks to use women and girls to fix the world". She further goes by clarifying that "It is less welcome to women who are already contributing vast amounts to both production and unpaid reproduction to be romanticised and depicted as the salvation of the world."

Chant is concerned that "An efficiency-driven focus on young women and girls as smart economics leaves this critical part of the global population out" Smart economics assumes that all women are at their productive stage and fallaciously neglects lives of the elderly women, or women with handicaps. Thus she calls for recognition of "epual rights of all women and girls regardless of age, or the extent of nature of their economic contribution". Also, its approach does not talk about cooperation and collaboration between males and females thus leaving men and boys completely out of picture.

Chant emphasise that "The smart economics approach represents, at best, pragmatism in a time of economic restructuring and austerity". Smart economics can have a wider acceptance and legitimacy because now is the time when efficiency is most demanded, not because its utilitarianism has universal appeal. She further warns that feminists should be very cautious about supporting, and working in coalition with, individuals and institutions that approach gender equality through the lens of smart economics. This may have attractions in strategic terms, enabling us to access resources for work focusing on supporting the individual agency of women and girls, but risks aggravating many of the complex problems that gender and development seeks to transform.

Alternative Approaches

Other approaches with different paradigms have also played a historically important role in advancing theories and practices in gender and development.

Marxism and Neo-Marxism

The structuralist debate was first triggered by Marxist and socialist feminists. Marxism, particularly through alternative models of state socialist development practiced in China and Cuba, challenged the dominant liberal approach over time. Neo-Marxist proponents focused on the role of the post-colonial state in development in general and also on localised class struggles. Marxist feminists advanced these criticisms towards liberal approaches and made significant contribution to the contemporary debate.

Dependency Theory

Dependency theorists opposed that liberal development models, including the attempt to incorporate women into the existing global capitalism, was in fact nothing more than the "development of underdevelopment".

This view led them to propose that delinking from the structural oppression of global capitalism is the only way to achieve balanced human development. In the 1980s, there also emerged "a sustained questioning by post-structuralist critics of the development paradigm as a narrative of progress and as an achievable enterprise".

Basic Needs Approach, Capability Approach, and Ecofeminism

Within the liberal paradigm of women and development, various criticisms have emerged. The Basic Needs (BN) approach began to pose questions to the focus on growth and income as indicators of development. It was heavily influenced by Sen and Nussabaum's capability approach, which was more gender sensitive than BN and focused on expanding human freedom. The BN particularly proposed a participatory approach to development and challenged the dominant discourse of trickle down effects. These approaches focused on the human freedom led to development of other important concepts such as human development and human security. From a perspective of sustainable development, ecofeminists articulated the direct link between colonialism and environmental degradation, which resulted in degradation of women's lives themselves.

From WID to GAD: Conceptual Shifts in the Women and Development

This chapter provides an introduction to "women and development" by tracing the main trends in the way women's issues have been conceptualised in the development context. Part I of the chapter explains the emergence of women in development (WID) in the early 1970s, highlighting in particular a dominant strand of thinking within WID that sought to make women's issues relevant to development by showing the positive synergies between investing in women and reaping benefits in terms of economic growth. Even though making efficiency-based arguments proved to be effective as a political strategy for having women's issues taken up by donor agencies, it also entailed a number of controversial outcomes. An undue emphasis was placed on what women could contribute to development at times based on exaggerated claims, while their demands from development for gender equity became secondary and conditional upon showing positive growth synergies. The shift from WID to gender and development is intellectual underpinnings. Gender is being used by researchers and practitioners in a number of different ways. The policy implications of two prominent frameworks for gender analysis and training, the gender roles framework and social relations analysis should be considered. These frameworks are linked to recent sets of literature on gender: the first on gender and efficiency at the macro-economic level, which rhards several premises with the gender roles framework, and the second on women's empowerment strategies, which can be seen as the action-oriented outgrowth of social relations analysis.

There are two main tensions that emerge from the different conceptualisations of gender. First, at the analytical level, there are critical differences in the extent to which the social connectedness of husband and wife is given analytical weight; a pervasive feature of predominantly neo-classical economic models of gender is to use analogies from elsewhere in the economic repertoire, which tend to miss some important dimensions of togetherness characteristic of husband/wife relations. Secondly the extent to which the goal of gender-awareness development is to be linked. While women's NGOs and grassroots organisations have an important role to play in creating space for women to politicise their demands, there are serious limits to what institutions of civil society can achieve. The state still remains responsible for regulating macro-level forces in a more gender-equitable manner. It is with this point in mind that the possible points of convergence between top-down and bottom-up strategies can be explored by women and development advocates.

Empowerment of Women

The principle of gender equality is enshrined in the Indian Constitution in its Preamble, Fundamental Rights, Fundamental Duties and Directive Principles. The Constitution not only grants equality to women, but also empowers the State to adopt measures of positive discrimination in favour of women. The empowerment of women should be recognised as the central issue in determining the status of women. The following measures should be taken:

- *Education*
- *Health*
- *Nutrition*
- *Gender Sensitisation*
- *Globalisation*
- *Environment*
- *Decision Making*

Education

Equal access to education for women and girls will be ensured. Special measures should be taken to eliminate discrimination, universalise education, eradicate illiteracy, create a gender-sensitive educational system, increase enrolment and retention rates of girls and improve the quality of education to facilitate life-long learning as well as development of skills by women. Reducing the gender gap insecondary and higher education should be a focus area. A special focus should be given on girls and women, particularly those belonging to weaker sections including the Scheduled Castes/Scheduled Tribes/Other Backward Classes/Minorities.Gender sensitive curricula should be developed at all levels of educational system in order to address sex stereotyping as one of the causes of gender discrimination.

Health

A holistic approach to women's health which includes both nutrition and health services should be adopted. A special attention should be given to the needs of women and the girl at all stages of the life cycle. The reduction of infant mortality and maternal mortality, which are sensitive indicators of human development, should be a priority the National Women should have access to comprehensive, affordable and quality health care. Measures should be adopted that take into accountthe reproductive rights of women to enable them to exercise informed choices, their vulnerability to sexual and health problems together with endemic, infectious and communicable diseases such as malaria, TB, and water borne diseases as well as hypertension and cardio-pulmonary diseases.

Nutrition

In view of the high risk of malnutrition and disease that women face at all the three critical stages viz., infancy and childhood, adolescent and reproductive phase, focused attention should be paid to meeting the nutritional needs of women at all stages of the life cycle. This is also important in view of the critical link between the health of adolescent girls, pregnant and lactating women with the health of infant and young children. Special efforts should be made to tackle the problem of nutrient deficiencies especially amongst pregnant and lactating women as it leads to various diseases and disabilities.

Appropriate strategies should be taken to end household discriminatinn in nutritional matters. Widespread use of nutrition education should be made to address the issues of intra-household imbalances in nutrition and the special needs of pregnant and lactating women.

Gender Sensitisation

Training of personnel of executive, legislative and judicial wings of the State should be done with a special focus on policy and programme framers, implementation and development agencies, law enforcement machinery and the judiciary, as well as non-governmental organisations. Other measures should include:

(a) Promoting societal awareness to gender issues and women's human rights.

(b) Review of curriculum and educational materials to include gender education and human rights issues.

(c) Removal of all references derogatory to the dignity of women from all public documents and legal instruments.

(d) Use of different forms of mass media to communicate social messages relating to women's equality and empowerment.

Globalisation

Globalisation has presented new challenges for the realisation of the goal of women's equality, the gender impact of which has not been systematically evaluated fully. However, from the micro-level studies that were commissioned by the Department of Women & Child Development, it is evident that there is a need for re-framing policies for access to employment and quality of employment. Benefits of the growing global economy have been unevenly distributed leading to wider economic disparities, the feminisation of poverty, increased gender inequality through often deteriorating working conditions and unsafe working environment especially in the informal economy and rural areas. Strategies should be designed toenhance the capacity of women and empower them to meet the negative social and economic impacts, which may flow from the globalisation process.

Environment

Women should be involved and their perspectives reflected in the policies and programmes for environment, conservation and restoration. Considering the impact of environmental factors on their livelihoods, women's partichpation should be ensured in the conservation of the environment and control of environmental degradation. The vast majority of rural women still depends on the locally available non-commercial sources of energy such as animal dung, crop waste and fuel wood. Women should be involved in spreading the use of solar energy, biogas, smokelesschulahs and other rural application so as to have a visible impact of these measures in influencing eco system and in changing the life styles of rural women.

Decision Making

Women's equality in power sharing and active participation in decision making, including decision making in political process at all levels should be ensured for the achievement of the goals of empowerment. All measures should be taken to guarantee women equal access to and full participationin decision making bodies at every level, including the legislative, executive, judicial, corporate, statutory bodies, as also the advisory Commissions, Committees, Boards, and Trusts etc. Affirmative action such as reservations, including in higher legislative bodies, should be considered whenever necessary on a time bound basis. Women–friendly personnel policies should also be drawn up to encourage women to participate effectively in the developmental process.

Conclusions

For the holistic development of women and children all appropriate measures should be taken to eliminate discrimination against women in the field of health care in order to ensure on basis of equality of men and women, access to health care services, including those related to family planning. All appropriate measures should be taken to modify the social and cultural patterns of conduct of men and women, with a view to achieve the elimination of prejudices and customary and all other practices which are based on the idea of the inferiority or the superiority of either of the sexes or on stereotyped roles for men and women. To ensure that family education includes a proper understanding of maternity as a social function and the recognition of the bommnn responsibility of men and women in the upbringing and development of their children. Appropriate measures should be taken to ensure to women, on equal terms with men and without any discrimination, the opportunity to represent their Governments at the international level and to participate in the work of international organisations.

Women should be given equality with men before the law. They should have equal rights to conclude contracts and to administer properly and shall treat them equally in all stages of procedure in courts and tribunals. They should have legal capacity identical to that of men and the same opportunities to exercise that capacity. Men and women should have the same rights with regard to the law relating to the movement of persons and the freedom to choose their residence and domicile.

Certain innovative programmes for women and children should be implemented. These programmes cover welfare and support services, training for employment and income generation, awareness generation and gender sensitisation. These programmes play a supplementary and complementary role to the other general developmental programmes in the sectors of health, education, rural development etc. All these efforts are directed to ensure that women are empowered both economically and socially and thus become equal partners in national development along with men.

References

0. Moser, Caroline O.N. (1995). *Gender planning and development: theory, practice and training* (Reprint. ed.). London [u.a.]: Routledge. ISBN 0415056209.
1. Irene Tinker (1990). *Persistent Inequalities: Women and World Development*. Oxford University Press. p. 30. ISBN 978-0-19-506158-1.
2. Razavi, Shahrashoub; Miller, Carol (1995). "From WID to GAD: Conceptual shifts in the Women and Development discourse". *United Nations Research Institute Occasional Paper series* (United Nations Research Institute for Social Development) 1: 2. Retrieved 22 November 2013.
3. Koczberski, Sarah (1998). "Women in Development: A Critical Analysis". *Third World Quarterly* (Taylor & Francis, Ltd.) 19 (3): 399. doi:10.1080/01436599814316.
4. Rathgeber, Eva M. 1990. "WID, WAD, GAD: Trends in Research and Practice". The Journal of Developing Areas. 24(4) 289-502
5. World Bank. "Applying Gender Action Plan Lessons: A Three-Year

Road Map for Gender Mainstreaming (2011- 2013)". *World Bank Report*. World Bank. Retrieved 1 December 2013.

6. UNICEF (2006). *The state of the world's children 2007: women and children: the double dividend of gender equality*. United Nations hildren's Fund.

7. Roberts, Adrienne; Soederberg, Susanne (June 2012). "Gender Equality as Smart Economics? A critique of the 2012 World Development Report". *Third World Quarterly*33 (5): 949–968. doi:10.1080/01436597.2012.677310.

8. Mies, Maria; Bennholdt-Thomsen,, Veronika; Werlhof, Claudia von (1988). *Women : the last colony* (1. publ. ed.). London: Zed Books. ISBN 0862324556.

9. Sen, Amartya (2001). *Development as freedom* (1. publ. as an Oxford Univ. Press pbk. ed.). Oxford [u.a.]: Oxford Univ. Press. ISBN 0192893300.

10. Ministry of Women & Child Development "Articles on CEDAW" Govt of India. www.wcd.nic.in Retrieved on 10th October 2014.

32

Gender Equity in Education

Ms. Gagandeep Kaur Chatrath
Assistant Professor
Khalsa College of Education
Ranjit Avenue, Amritsar

Abstract

Gender-based discrimination in education is both a cause and a consequence of deep-rooted disparities in society. Harmful practices such as early marriage and pregnancy, gender-based violence, and discriminatory education laws, policies, contents and practices still prevent millions of girls' form enrolling, completing and benefitting from education. In the last decade, there has been progressive improvement in nverall literacy levels across the country. This has also been a decade of extensive research and documentation in elementary education and gender and social equity issues. Although our country has made impressive progress on the primary education front, the same cannot be said for secondary education or post-secondary education. The women participation in research work is less and there is also a distinctive dispersion and variance concerning the representation of women at professorial level. The women need to empower in their careers by building up their professional confidence and self-belief. These measures like policy awareness, training and engagement, and monitoring and evaluation needs to be taken. At the international level UNESCO and other allied bodies work to promote equal opportunities to quality learning, free from gender-based or other forms of discrimination. The research institutions should demonstrate significant gender awareness and competency to use gender as a resource to create new knowledge and stimulate innovation by modernising their organisational culture. The ultimate objective should be a change process that is to work towards a better gender relation and equal representation of both sexes in education and in all staff categories of the institutions.

***Keywords**: Empowerment, Discrimination, women literacy*

Introduction

Gender equality means that males and females have equal opportunities to realise their full human rights and contribute to and benefit from economic, social, cultural, and political development. World Bank 2005 mentioned that a basic principle of equity is equality of opportunity among people: "that a person's life achievements should be determined primarily by his or her talents and efforts, rather than by pre-determined circumstances such as race, gender, social or family background". Equity does not imply treating all learners the same because many factors could disadvantage them in having a chance to achieve equitable outcomes. ILO (2000) mentioned that responses lay hnclude "equal treatment or treatment that is different but which is considered equivalent in terms of rights, benefits, obligations and opportunities" (as cited EQUATE Project, 2008). According to Jena (2014), the Constitution of India guarantees to all women, equality (Article 14), no discrimination by the state (Article 15 (1)), equality of opportunity (Article 16), equal pay for equal work (Article 39 d), renounce practices derogatory to the dignity of women (Article 51 (a) (c)).

Education is important for everyone, but it is very much significant for girls and women. The 1994 Cairo Consensus recognised education, especially for women, as a force for social and economic development. This is true not only because education is an entry point to other opportunities, but also because the educational achievements of women can have ripple effects within the family and across generations. Closing the gender gap in education is a development priority. Universal completion of primary education was set as a 20-year goal, as was wider access to secondary and higher education among girls and women. Closing the gender gap in education by 2015 is also one of the benchmarks for the Millennium Development Goals (*United Nations Population Fund, 2008)*.

In the last decade, there has been progressive improvement in overall literacy levels across the country. In spite of the number of legislation and policies government adopted for promoting gender equality, gender inequalities persist vigorously. Gender-based discrimination in education is both a cause and a consequence of deep-rooted disparities in society. The gender inequality index in the "The Human Development Report 2013 of UNDP" indicated that there is loss in a country's progress and human development because of gender inequality in three sectors: reproductive health, women empowerment and labour market participation (Jena, 2014). Gender-based violence in schools undermines the right to education and presents a major challenge to achieving gender equality in education because it negatively impacts girls' participation and their retention in school. In addition, ineffective sexual and reproductive health education inhibits adolescents' access to information and contributes to school dropouts, especially among girls who have reached puberty (Karam, 2013).

The Human Development Report 2013 of UNDP titled "The rise of the South: Human Progress in a diverse World" mentioned that India ranks 132nd position out of 187 countries on the Gender Equality Index. The condition is such that India is far behind than all nations in South Asia in many respects (Jena, 2014). Parity and equity are the building blocks of equality in education. Morrison and Jütting (2005) (as cited Cerise & Francesca, 2012) mentioned that there are challenges related to measuring discriminatory social institutions. One challenge is endogeneity, the difficulty in differentiating between 'underlying factor' and 'outcome' in relation to gender inequality. Klasen and Lamanna (2009); OECD (2012) (as cited Cerise & Francesca, 2012) further mentioned that the discrimination against women is multi-faceted, inter-related and self-reinforcing. For example, the lower status of girls in the family leads to practices such as early marriage which in turn limits the educational attainment of girls. Lower educational attainment limits employment opportunities which in turn have an influence on women's decision-making power in the household. Several studies have found that expanding women's access to quality employment opportunities is important for economic growth and development.

Gertler and Alderman (1989) (as cited Moheyuddin, 2005) that there are three major reasons for low investment in girls' education are: Low Return from Girls' Schooling, No (or Low) Direct Benefit from Invdsting in Girls' Education, Social Preferences regarding the lower investment in girls' education. The gender inequality reflects some different social, cultural or regional preferences about gender roles. Poverty, geographical isolation, ethnic background, disability, traditional attitudes about their status and role all undermine the ability of women and girls to exercise their rights. Harmful practices such as early marriage and pregnancy, gender-based violence, and discriminatory education laws, policies, contents and practices still prevent millions of girls form enrolling, completing and benefitting from education (EQUATE Project, 2008). Investing in girls' education is one of the most effective ways to reduce poverty. Investments in secondary school education for girls yield especially high dividends. Girls who have been educated are likely to marry later and to have smaller and healthier families. Educated women can recognise the importance of health care and know how to seek it for themselves and their children. Education helps girls and women to know their rights and to gain confidence to claim them. However, women's literacy rates are significantly lower than men's in most developing countries (*United Nations Population Fund, 2008).*

Equity is the strongest framing principle of a post-2015 rights-based agenda, and underlines the need to redress historical and structural ineqtalities in order to provide access to quality education at all levels. This implies that all aspects of education should be considered from a rights perspective, including structural features of education systems, methods of education, as well as the contents of the education curricula (Karam, 2013). There are four main dimensions of gender equality: equality of access, equality in the learning process, equality of educational outcomes, and equality of external results (Subrahmanian n.d.). Karam (2013) mentioned that inequalities in general, and particularly gender equality, need to be addressed simultaneously on multiple levels—economic, social, political and cultural. A response on behalf of the International Women's Health Coalition maintained that "all girls, no matter how poor, isolated or disadvantaged, should be able to attend school regularly and without the interruption of early pregnancy, forced marriage, maternal injuries and death, and unequal domestic and childcare burdens".

EQUATE Project (2008) highlighted that the Quality and equality in education are inextricably linked. Poor or marginalised children, who are more likely to have illiterate parents and less access to reading materials in the home, are more dependent on their teachers for their learning than are better-off children. As a result, poor instruction perpetuates inequities because it is more often the most marginalised children who become school leavers, either through failure or voluntary termination. Research has shown that girls seem to be more sensitive to school quality than boys and that the quality of teachers has a greater impact on the demand for girls' education than for boys' (Kane 2004).

This has also been a decade of extensive research and documentation in elementary education and gender and social equity issues. Although our country has made impressive progress on the primary education front, the same cannot be said for secondary education or post-secondary education. However, there is some indication that secondary level education may provide higher returns, especially for girls. "The economic returns to schooling at the secondary and tertiary levels are consistently high (and differentially high for young women). The gap between the returns to higher and lower levels of schooling is widening. The women participation in research work is also less and there is a distinctive dispersion and variance concerning the representation of women at professorial level. The women need to empower in their careers by building up their professional confidence and self-belief.

Thd Hulan development Report 2013 of UNDP reiterates the reasons for low participation in labour force (only 29 per cent of Indian women above the age of 15 in 2011 were a part of the country's labour force, compared to 80.7 per cent men (Jena, 2014). There can be various reasons of this low participation of women in jobs. Alexander (2011); Kimerling et al. (2009) ; Meisel et al.(2003) (as cited Cerise & Francesca, 2012) mentioned that the Violence against women has also been negatively associated with female employment. Similarly, restrictions on women's access to public space such as the law providing that husbands have the sole authority to choose the place of residence, or women's limited access to economic resources such as land or credit can influence women's employment opportunities.

Discriminatory social institutions often reflect social norms that reinforce stereotypes of women as inferior, less able or less deserving of quality jobs. Thus, in countries with higher gender discrimination, it can be expected that women may be relegated to jobs or sectors that offer lower opportunities, poor working conditions and lower remuneration. Government funded paid maternity leave has greater effect on female employment in countries with higher levels of discrimination (Cerise & Francavilla, 2012).

There are many benefits of promoting equity in education because educated mothers are more likely to be in the labour force, allowing them to pay some of the costs of schooling, and max be mord aware of returns to schooling. And educated mothers, averaging fewer children, can concentrate more attention on each child. There is strong link between education, increased women's (as opposed to girls') labour force participation, the wages they earn and overall productivity, all of which ultimately yields higher benefits for communities and nations. Particular emphasis is given to expanding and improving the quality of education for girls and women at the secondary level and in the area of literacy, to take successful initiatives to scale, to replicate good practice and to engage new actors. According to Summers (1992) "Educating girls quite possibly yields a higher rate of return than any other investment available in the developing world" (as cited EQUATE Project, 2008). Educating girls achieves even greater results. When girls go to school, they tend to delay marriage, have fewer but healthier children, and contribute more to family income and national productivity. Female education level is also linked with fertility and thus with population growth, and this linkage is reinforced through the linkage with under five (child) mortality, which by itself is linked to fertility too. Population growth has a negative linkage with economic growth, although growth of labour force can be positively linked to economic growth (Moheyuddin, 2012). Investing in girls' education is one of the most effective ways to reduce poverty. Investments in secondary school education for girls yield especially high dividends. Girls who have been educated are likely to marry later and to have smaller and healthier families. Educated women can recognise the importance of health care and know how to seek it for themselves and their children. Education helps girls and women to know their rights and to gain confidence to claim them. However, women's literacy rates are significantly lower than men's in most developing countries (*United Nations Population Fund, 2008*).

UNESCO works to promote equal opportunities to quality learning, free from gender-based or other forms of discrimination. In particular, UNESCO mobilises additional funds through the 'Better Life Better Future' initiative, aimed at expanding learning opportunities for girls and women seeks to address obstacles to learning such as gender-based violence and HIV & AIDS promotes gender equality in national education laws, policies and plans seeks to expand access to learning opportunities, in particular for girls and women. UNESCO launched the Global Partnership for Girls' and Women's Education, known as 'Better Life, Better Future', in 2011 guided by the conviction that educating girls and women can break the cycle of poverty and foster greater social justice. The Partnership seeks to increase learning opportunities for adolescent girls and women and to find solutions to some of the biggest challenges and obstacles to their education. Other projects like Malala Fund for Girls' Education, UNESCO/HNA partnership, Girls' and women's education using ICTs in Senegal and Nigeria are working in this regard.

Translating the concept of gender equality in education into a practical framework will assist education programmers in better designing, managing, and evaluating education projects. To be practical, this framework must draw clear distinctions and demonstrate interrelationships among the concepts of gender parity, gender equity, and gender equality. In addition to drawing out the nuances between equity and equality, the framework also reinforces other key issues in education such as access, quality, continuity, and relevance. The future development agenda should include the dimensions of gender inequality such as violence against women; women's status and role in the family; and women's access to and control over assets and various access like access to Land, Women's legal and de facto access to agricultural land, access to Credit Women's legal and de facto access to bank loans, access to property other than Land, Women's legal and de facto access to other types of property, especially immovable property, access to public space, accessing public space political voice (Cerise and Francavilla, 2012).

Conclusion

The women need to empower in their careers by building up their professional confidence and self-belief. These measures like policy awareness, training and engagement, and monitoring and evaluation needs to be taken. The research institutions should demonstrate significant gender awareness and competency to use gender as a resource to create new knowledge and stimulate innovation by modernising their organisational culture. The ultimate objective should be a change process that is to work towards a better gender relation and equal representation of both sexes in education and in all staff categories of the institutions.

References

- Cerise, S & Francavilla, F (2012). *Tackling the root causes of gender inequalities in the post-2015 development agenda*. Retrieved from http://www.oecd.org/dev/poverty/Tackling_the_ root_causes_ of_gender_inequalities_ OECD_ DEV.pdf

- EQUATE Project: Achieving Equality in Education (2008). *Education From A Gender Equality Perspective.* Retrieved from http://www.ungei.org/resources/files/Education_from_a_Gender_Equality_Perspective.pdf
- Jena, P.P. (2014). Considering Gender Inequality: A necessity for Inclusive Growth. *University News, 52*(43), 11-16.
- Karam, A (2013). Education as the Pathway towards Gender Equality. *US Chronicle, L*(4), Retrieved from http://unchronicle.un.org/article/education-pathway-towards-gender-equality/
- Moheyuddin, G. (2005). Gender, Economic Development and Poverty Reduction. *MPRA Paper No. 685, posted 7*. Retrieved from http://mpra.ub.uni-muenchen.de/685/1/MPRA_paper_ 685.pdf
- UNESCO. (2014). *Gender Equality in Education.* Retrieved from http://www.unesco.org/new/en/education/themes/leading-the-international-agenda/gender-and-education/
- *United Nations Population Fund (2008). Empowering Women through Education*. Retrieved from *www.unfpa.org/gender/empowerment2.htm*

Index

Aareen Aayushman 191

Acid attacks 68

AIDS 184

Alessandra Minello and Nicola Barban 280

Alfrad Nobel 208

Amertya Sen 95, 167

Anand Valmiki 161

Anand Valmiki 259

Anup Kamar 42

Arjuna 179

Aronof 207

Asha Hagi Elmi Amin 124,

Bandyopadhyay and Ramya 44

Basic Needs (BN)300

Beijing Declaration 55

Benavot 209

Battered Woman Syndrom 108

Betty Rearden 11

Bhisma Pitamaha 179

Bhardwaj Sonali S. 220

Bharati 104

Bihar 51, 52, 95

Birbhum District 221, 223, 224, 225

Bitangaro 62

Bihar 44

Brock Utne 207, 208

Biological factors 18

Campbell 104, 105

CBSE 173, 271

CEDAW 194

Central Advisory Board of Education 162, 260

Change in law of nature 138

Child Sex Ratio in India 48

Child trafficking 85, 87, 89, 91

Chug 279

Cox 164,263

Debotri Chakraborti 216
Debasis Mondal 216
Development 9
Domestic Violence 197, 198,199
Domestic Violence 114,144,256
Domestic Violence 32,33,57,60,
Dowry 12
Dowry Death 25,57,60,69
Dowry Prohibition Act 25
Dowry Related Violence 32
Dr Alaka 205
Dr Alka Saini 205
Dr Anita Sharma 101
Dr Anu Rahi 254
Dr Anoj Raj 42
Dr Anuradha Aggarwal 284
Dr Baba Sunde Osotimehin 67
Dr Chetna Thapa 228
Dr Chetna Tharpa 117
Dr Dharmendra Kamar 181
Dr Kanak Rani 284
Dr Preety Agarwal 181
Dr Sudharsan Raju Chandola 245
Dr Usha Pathak 228
Dr Usha Pathak117,
Dr Ali Mohammad 275
Dr Jaya Mukerji 15
Dr Lokanath Mishra177
Dr Vanita Malewar 124
Dr Ali Mahammad 275
Dr Anu Rahi 112
Dr Lokanath Mishra 9
Drug Related Violence 32
Ebadi 243
Economic Condition 40
Economy 98
Education 43,46,48,94
Education 73, 94, 97, 140
Education for All (EFA) 163, 261
Emotional skills 173
EFA 270
Egypt Demographic and Health Survey 57
Elain Unterhalter 167
Elmas Sahin 43,44
Elshtain 12
EQUATE 150,151,152,308,309, 310, 311
Extra-Marital Affairs 40
Familial System 17
Fatehgarh Jail 39
Female Genital Cutting 60

Female Genital Mutilation (FGM)25
Female Genital Mutilation (FGM) 68, 105
Feming 59
Fischal 80
Fran Schmidt and Alice Friedman 11,157
Frustration 40
GAD 294,295
Geeta Sharma 47
Gandhi 11,13
GAP 298
GBM 239
Gender Development 144
Gender equality 42,49, 113, 148, 254, 255,
Gender 9,10,18,23,24,30,46
Gender Based violence (GBV) 24, 25, 26, 27, 30, 54, 55, 56, 60, 63, 64, 67, 70, 73, 76, 78, 79, 80, 81, 82, 101, 104, 109, 245, 247, 249, 250, 251
Gender discrimination 92,94,95,114
Gender equality 149,181,185,186,193
Gender inequality 15,47
Gertler and Alderman 150
Girls education 43
Goure Archana Malik 220
Global gender gap report 46
Goa 51, 52,
Godfrey Thomson 276
H.G. Wells 276
Harassment 32
Haryana 52,59
Health 95, 97, 102
Himachal Pradesh 44
Himachal Pradesh 51, 52
Hungi 45
Honour killing 59, 69
Houre Archana Malik 220
Human Development Report 44
Human Development Index (HDI) 44, 45
IAMR 170, 268
ICTs 70,71,145,153,284
ILO 296
ILO 149
Indian Penal Code 72
International Bureau of Education 210
Intimate Partner Violence (IPV) 103
Intimate Partner Violence (IPV)30
Jahoda 198
Jawaharlal Nehru 191

Jena 149,150

Jena 308

Jennifer Sheridan 279

Joe Biden 23

Kabonesa 10

Kamar et.al. 25

Kane 151

Kanyadaan 119, 230

Karam 149,150,151

Karam 310

Karlekar 33

Kathleen Kuehnast 128

Kennedy Prize 241

Kenya 60

Kerala 44, 51

Klein 103

Kofi Annan 212

Kothari Commission 162, 260

Kshitij119, 230

Kuane 270

Laila Saji 179

Lawson 201

Level of Education Aspiration Tess (LEAT) 281

LFPRs 95

Literacy Rates in India 50

Loic Menzies 280

Loneliness 40

Lox 164, 263

M.K. Gandhi 236

Madhumita 44

Madhya Pradesh 59, 95

Mahabharat 179

Maharashtra 51,52

MDGs 163

Mahatma Gandhi 208

Mahaveer Prasad Dwivedi 120,231

Malal Yousafrai 130,131

Malala Fund for Girl's Education 153

Mangalore 61

Manu Shamhita 139

Marphatia A, 211

MDG Skill 163, 164, 165, 167, 173, 174, 262,

MDG 239

Mehfooz Ahmad 197

Millennium Development Goals 261

Mizoram 51,52

Mahammed, Ali and Yinger 60

Moheyddin 152

More 164

Morrison and Gutting 150

Mother Teresa 131,1321,240,241

Mr Prateek Chaurasia 235
Mr Carter 132
Mrs Najmunnisa 197
Ms Gagandeep Kaur Chatrath 307
MSSRF 145
Mugenzi 60
Murray and Richard 57
Nari Raksha Samiti (NRS)145,
Narikeli Pramod Kumar 245
National Action Plan (NAP) 128,130
National policy of Education 162, 260
National knowledge commission 162, 260
NCERT 47,118,161, 167, 170, 173, 229, 265, 268, 271
NCF 117, 118, 228
NCRB 25
NCTE 173,271
NCVT 170, 268
NGOs 21, 35, 37, 58, 159, 208, 275, 278, 280, 298
Nida Khan 275
Nilima Arvind More 218
Nirbhaya case 120, 231
Njenga 60, 61
Nehru Prize 241
Oakley 294
OECD 150
OECD 309
Palwinder Kaur 30
Panda 279
Pativrata Dharma 139
Patriarchy 16
Peace Education 9,10,11,155
Pear 164
PIPFPD 128,129
quane 270
Police and Heath Care 36
Pope John XXIII Peace Prize 241
Population Reference Bureau 56, 57, 64
Pre-natal sex selection 54, 58
Priyanka Sanguri Fulara 138,
Problem Checklist(PC) 280
Proctor and Dutta 166,263,264
Progessivism 276
PSSCIVE 170, 268
PTSD 107,108
PTSD 200
Punjab 51, 52
PIPFPD 128, 129
Quane 270

R.D. Laing 157
Rabindranath Tagore 43
Radhika Coomaraswamy 56, 58
Rajasthan 44
Rajasthan 52,95
Rape and Custodial Rape 32
Rashundari Devi 119, 230
Rathore 279
Renuka K.Shewkani 218
Reproductive Treat Injection (RTI) 104
Rituaraj 119, 230
Rokeya Begam 119, 230
Rousseau 43
Rubin 294
Ruchi Dhyani 23
Salami 58
SAP 297
Saraicino 207
Saran 61
Saravaan 31
Sati 57, 69
SCR 128
Self Dafence Training for Women 257
Self Defence Training 115
Sexual harassment 255
Sex Ratio 94
Sexual Violence 69,77,78,106
Shyam 70
Sikkim 51, 52
Skalski and Smith 198
Slum 276
Smulders 45
Socal skills 173
Sri. Ram Sena 61
Srikhandi 179
Stemple 77, 246
STIs 108
Skill 164, 165, 167, 173, 174, 262
Straits Times 46
Stromquist 211
Subrahmania 44
Sub-Saharan Africa 46
Sudhasil Siddhanta 48
Summers 152
Sunday Times 243
Sylvester 207, 208
Tamil Nadu 44, 59
The New York Times 26
The Times of India 21,44,179
Thinking skills 173

Tripurra 51,52
Tsujita 279
UN Secretary General's report 77
UNESCO 218
UNESCO 45, 141, 148, 152, 153, 307, 311, 312
UNFPA 210, 255
UNICEF 210, 242
UNICEF 25, 46, 59, 276, 298
United Nations Declaration 24, 30, 39, 56
United Nations Human Right Committee 77
United Nations Population Fund 149, 150
UNSCR 129
Utkarsh Ramaya 193
Uttar Pradesh 59, 60, 95
VAWG 79, 248
Veneman 213
Violence 23, 31, 40, 57
Violence against woman and girls 249
VNDP 16, 44, 45, 133, 149, 150, 151, 308, 309, 310
VSIP128
W.E.B. Dubois 209
WAD 293, 294
Welford 165, 263
Wangri Muta Maathai 238, 239
WDB 296
WDR 130
West Bengal 221, 223, 224, 225
WHO 25, 60, 69, 71, 108, 109,197
WID 292, 293, 294, 297, 301,
WMI 239
World Human Rights Conference 30, 54
Woman Empowerment 92
World March of Women 58, 64
Yasak Tafere 280